PRAISE FOR *THIS IS CHANCE!*

—

"[Jon] Mooallem does a nice job of showing the domino of damage in cinematic slow motion—the crevasses opening in city streets, the land slinking and sliding, the indiscriminate collapse of homes of both the rich and the poor. . . . He also brings to life a half-dozen or so ordinary people who acted in extraordinary ways."

—*The New York Times Book Review*

"You'll feel like you're there as Mr. Mooallem, a veteran journalist and author, describes the surreal sensations of reality coming apart around and underneath you. . . . 'Do any human beings ever realize life while they live it?—every, every minute?' Any human being who reads this powerful, heart-wrenching book, as much art as it is journalism, will ask that same question—and know that once, for three chaotic days in Anchorage, the answer was yes."

—*The Wall Street Journal*

"Mooallem writes about a special person here, a truly empathetic character who has the chance, then and now, to tell us more about ourselves. With finely wrought detail, thanks to Chance's journal entries and broadcast recordings, we can experience the disaster through the same jarring, slowed-down lens that colored her life. . . . Not only is Mooallem an apt writer with this sort of gripping journalistic material . . . but moreover he has an eye for the gaps in our shared reality, for the gaps that emerge between daily life and history."

—*Cleveland Review of Books*

"A great crossover read for teens as well as adults about community, tenacity, and the power of one person to make a difference."

—*Library Journal*

"[Mooallem is] an elegant writer, a fine chronicler of disaster and a smart student of the ironies and contradictions of contemporary culture."

—*The National Book Review*

"A beautifully wrought and profoundly joyful story of compassion and perseverance."

—*BuzzFeed*

"[An] impressively rendered narrative . . . Mooallem seamlessly blends together a character study, an examination of the character of a community, a chronicle of what happened, and an inquiry into the human soul. . . . One finishes this book deeply impressed—with the people of Anchorage, with Genie Chance, and with the author."

—*Kirkus Reviews* (starred review)

"Interweaving accounts of search-and-rescue operations with the story of a local production of *Our Town* staged the weekend after the earthquake, Mooallem delivers a moving tribute to the spirit of community in the face of disaster. This inspiring tale feels bound for the big-screen."

—*Publishers Weekly*

BY JON MOOALLEM

———

This Is Chance!

Wild Ones

American Hippopotamus

THIS IS CHANCE!

THIS IS CHANCE!

THE GREAT ALASKA EARTHQUAKE,
GENIE CHANCE, AND THE
SHATTERED CITY SHE HELD
TOGETHER

JON MOOALLEM

RANDOM HOUSE

NEW YORK

LIBRARY OF CONGRESS CATALOGING-IN-PUBLICATION DATA
Names: Mooallem, Jon, author.
Title: This is Chance!: the shaking of an all-American city,
a voice that held it together / Jon Mooallem.
Description: New York: Random House, 2020 |
Identifiers: LCCN 2019015815 | ISBN 9780525509929 |
ISBN 9780525509936 (ebook)
Subjects: LCSH: Alaska Earthquake, Alaska, 1964. | Chance, Genie,
1927–1998. | Earthquakes—Alaska—Anchorage.
Classification: LCC QE535 .M8255 2020 |
DDC 363.34/95097983509046—dc23
LC record available at https://lccn.loc.gov/2019015815

For Rose

Now there are some things we all know, but we don't take'm out and look at'm very often. We all know that *something* is eternal. And it ain't houses and it ain't names, and it ain't earth, and it ain't even the stars . . . everybody knows in their bones that *something* is eternal, and that something has to do with human beings.

—*Our Town*

CAST OF CHARACTERS

Genie Chance .... part-time news reporter at KENI, wife and mother

Frank Brink .... theater director, community leader

Winston Chance .... Genie's husband

Jan, Albert, and Wins Chance .... Genie's children

Alvin O. Bramstedt ("Bram") .... president and majority owner, KENI

Ty Clark .... news director, KENI

Charlie Gray .... head of engineering, KENI

Bob Fleming .... lead announcer, KENI

Theda Conley .... weather broadcaster and talk show host, KENI

Bill Davis .... psychology professor, mountaineer

Dick Taylor .... Anchorage public works employee

George Sharrock .... mayor of Anchorage

Jim Scott .... veterinarian, mountaineer

Susan Koslosky .... college student, actress

Enrico Quarantelli .... sociologist, cofounder of
the Disaster Research Center

Daniel Yutzy................... graduate student,
Disaster Research Center

ONE MONTH BEFORE

SUNDAY, FEBRUARY 23, 1964

1.

"EVERYTHING MOVES"

———

THE EXPOSITION

THIS BOOK IS CALLED *THIS IS CHANCE!* IT WAS WRITTEN BY Jon Mooallem, published by Random House, edited by Andy Ward.

It tells the story of a single catastrophic weekend in a faraway town, and of the people who lived through it: ordinary women and men who—when the most powerful earthquake ever measured in North America struck, just before sundown on Good Friday, 1964—found themselves thrown into a jumbled and ruthlessly unpredictable world they did not recognize. They would spend the next few days figuring out, together, how to make a home in it again.

The name of the town is Anchorage, Alaska—a blotch of Western civilization in the middle of emptiness. In those days, the state of Alaska was still brand-new and often disregarded as a kind of free-floating addendum to the rest of America. But Anchorage was Alaska's biggest and proudest city, a community whose "essential spirit," one visitor wrote, "reached aggressively and greedily to grasp the future, impatient with any suggestion that such things take time." It was a modern-day frontier town that imagined it was a metropolis, straining to make itself real.

That determination made it difficult for those living in Anchorage to recognize how indifferently the city they were building could be knocked down—to imagine that, early one Friday evening, the very ground beneath them might rear up and shake their town like "a dog shaking an animal he's killed," as one man later described it. Even while the earth was moving, the ferocious strangeness of what was happening to Anchorage was hard for people to internalize or accept. Buildings keeled off their foundations, slumped in on themselves, split in half, or sank. Four-foot-high ground waves rolled through the roads as though the pavement were liquid. A city of infallible right angles buckled and bent.

It wasn't as though, before the quake, people in Anchorage pictured these things happening and dismissed them as impossible; they just never pictured them. They *couldn't*. More to the point: Why would they? Like all of us, they looked around and registered what they saw as stable and permanent: a world that just *was*.

But there are moments when the world we take for granted instantaneously changes; when reality is abruptly upended and the unimaginable overwhelms real life. We don't walk around thinking about that instability, but we know it's always there: at random, and without warning, a kind of terrible magic can switch on and scramble our lives.

As *LIFE* magazine would put it afterward, struggling to explain the hidden volatility that caused the quake, "Somewhere, the earth is quivering all the time."

THIS FIRST CHAPTER OF the book shows an afternoon in town one month before the disaster—by way of introduction. The date was Sunday, February 23, 1964; the time, just before one p.m.

All of Anchorage, it seemed, had gathered on Fourth Avenue for the last day of Fur Rendezvous, a weeklong winter carnival that enveloped downtown. Fur Rendezvous was one of the longest-running traditions in a community that didn't have many traditions yet, something for the burgeoning city to look forward to in the coldest, loneliest stretch of winter. Over the years, the exposition's organizers had kept heaping on more activities and amusements until, by now, Fur Rendezvous had swelled into a kind of ramshackle Mardi Gras of the North. There were auctions, craft markets, concerts, carnival rides, pony rides, go-kart races, ski races, a beard-growing contest, and a homemade fur hat competition. There were beauty pageants and dances, and appearances by out-of-town celebrities like "television's first flying cowboy," the "King of Organ Sounds," and a dog purported to be the actual Lassie, who had jetted into Anchorage in her own first-class seat. The Girl Scouts were selling cotton candy. The Boy Scouts were selling hot dogs. The Mormon Church was also selling hot dogs. And this year, Fur Rendezvous was proud to present its first-ever judo tournament.

That Sunday afternoon, everyone had come out for the races. The deciding heat of the World Championship Sled Dog Races was about to start, the finale of each year's Fur Rendezvous week.

Dog mushers would dart along a twenty-five-mile trail through the streets of Anchorage, then east into the foothills of the Chugach Mountains and back again—starting and finishing right here, on Fourth Avenue, in the heart of downtown.

After a week of excitement, the orderliness and decorum of the crowd was beginning to fray. Spectators spilled far beyond the bleachers set up on either side of the road. Kids clambered up a sprawling mountain ash tree to get a better view, moving rambunctiously, snapping off limbs. At one point, a chagrined city employee counted eighty adults standing on the roof of the log cabin in front of city hall. "They have estimated the crowd at twelve thousand people," announced a debonair man named Ty Clark, covering the races for local radio station KENI. "Twelve *thousand* people!" Clark sounded astonished—but more than astonished, pleased. All afternoon, in fact, he would have an almost superstitious tic of emphasizing for listeners how very *big* this event in Anchorage was, and the formidable bigness of Anchorage in general. "This is the one time of year—the *only* time of the year," he noted, "that we ever get that many people into the business district of Alaska's largest city."

KENI's live coverage of the sled-dog races had become its own big and freewheeling tradition, stretching far beyond what seemed possible for a small-market AM station in the middle of Alaska at the time. The station had virtually its entire staff—thirty-two people—working that Sunday and was broadcasting from nine different locations along the route, as well as from its helicopter, the KENI Kopter, circling overhead. They'd also deployed a couple of television cameras to simulcast on KENI-TV, Anchorage channel 2. And for the first time, KENI was relaying its coverage of the races to the small town of Cordova, 150 miles away. "It gets bigger and better every year!" Ty said.

Ty was anchoring the broadcast from the starting line on Fourth Avenue alongside his boss, Alvin O. Bramstedt, who had helped launch KENI in 1948, then taken over the station and aggressively built it up. KENI was now the flagship of Alaska's largest radio network, Midnight Sun Broadcasters Incorporated, which included sister stations in Fairbanks, Ketchikan, and Juneau. Bramstedt, the network's president and majority owner, had become one of Anchorage's most prominent businessmen. Around town, everyone knew him as "Bram."

He was a tall and polished-looking man, despite the rheumatoid arthritis that had been breaking down his body since his twenties. At forty-six, his hands were craggy and stiff. He hobbled instead of walked; his legs were like lumber. Still, he never complained. He seemed to move through the city in a vapor of his own cheerfulness and sincerity, verging on sappiness. His faith in Alaska's future was unconditional; his love of America, and belief that it must beat back the threat of communism, was absolute. (Bram was convinced that at least one or two of his staff at KENI were Soviet spies; it wasn't that anyone seemed particularly suspicious, but he took for granted that the Russians were infiltrating American media, and these were just the odds.) And though Bram reveled in competition—for years, he'd been paying his young son fifty cents an hour to watch Anchorage's only other television channel and make a list of every commercial, so that KENI might poach its advertisers—his main rival had also been the best man at his wedding and remained one of his closest friends.

Bram had always considered broadcasting more of a public

service than a business. It was the cornerstone of any decent democracy, with a responsibility to educate the public and the capacity to bind a community together. KENI reflected those ideals. It was arguably the most successful of Anchorage's five commercial radio stations and clearly the one most enmeshed with civic life. Its headquarters were a city landmark, housed inside the grand Fourth Avenue Theatre building in the center of downtown, with the KENI television tower shooting skyward from the roof and visible for blocks. The station's newscasters were well-known personalities and zipped through town to run down breaking news in the KENI Kamper, a squat camping trailer retrofitted into a mobile studio.

They were covering a city still in the process of inventing itself. Anchorage had been established only fifty years earlier, in 1915, when a couple thousand workers arriving to build the Alaska railroad pitched a huddle of tents on the shores of Ship Creek. The population had exploded at the start of the Cold War, sparked by military buildup at the army and air force bases north of town, but it wasn't until 1959, when the territory of Alaska became America's forty-ninth state, that the society Alaskans were building started to feel more secure. Before long, Anchorage was being described as the fastest-growing city in America, possibly in the world.

By early 1964, the population in and around the city had grown to nearly a hundred thousand people—almost half of Alaska's total. There were two daily newspapers, a couple of movie houses, and, mixed among the seedy bars and motels on Fourth Avenue, a few genuinely upscale restaurants and businesses, including the fourteen-story Westward Hotel. Even as some people still lived in crude, homemade shacks or surplus military Quonset huts, an impressive ridgetop enclave of stylish, upper-middle-class homes had recently risen on the city's western edge: a bona fide suburban-feeling neighborhood called Turnagain by the Sea. Still, it was becoming obvious the economic boom that had started with statehood was petering out, and it was unclear whether anything truly sustainable had taken hold. The state's big oil strikes wouldn't happen for another five years. For the moment, the city's entire economy still seemed to run mostly on optimism and pluck. It was easy to worry that Anchorage was a bubble that could pop, if it wasn't already silently deflating.

A mix of aspiration and insecurity had started to color everything happening in Anchorage. Each new construction or business opening came to feel monumental—a bit more proof to people that their community was real. The new J. C. Penney building downtown, completed one year earlier, felt like an especially dignified arrival. It was one of the first major chain retailers to believe in Alaska enough to build in the state, and nothing, apparently, signaled a sophisticated civilization rising out of the wilderness like a five-story department store full of undergarments and blenders. "There is no doubt that civilization is rapidly enveloping Anchorage," Bram insisted in a recent on-air editorial, as though saying so frequently enough ensured it stayed true. "A tent city in the Ship Creek flats a few short years ago is now a sprawling metropolis."

Bram often delivered a kind of fireside chat for the community, called "News in Depth," to open or close the evening news. In the run-up to this year's Fur Rendezvous, he had used one of those segments to take stock of the astonishing evolution he'd witnessed in Alaska since broadcasting his first sled-dog race twenty-four years earlier. He summarized the role of sled dogs in the settling of the territory—how they carried mail and information across the vacant landscape, like living precursors of KENI's radio waves—and paid florid tribute to them as "aristocrats of the unbroken trail." Bram found, in both the sled dogs and the men who mushed them, a metaphor for life in Alaska, even in these modern times—for the spirit of cooperation and persistence that living there still required, for the "courage and stouthearted stamina" that drove Alaskans forward. Alaskans understood, Bram argued, that they were "all in the same harness," pulling together.

Now, with eight minutes to go before race time downtown, Ty Clark reminded KENI listeners that Bram would be giving an encore reading of that editorial at the annual Mushers Banquet that evening. "And let's be truthful about it," Ty told his boss. "You received a lot of requests for copies of that, did you not?"

"That's true," Bram said bashfully. "No copyright, either. I just give it away to all my friends!"

The two men had an easy rapport. Bram was the folksy and nostalgic one; Ty was looser, a decade younger, and probably the most bacchanalian member of KENI's close-knit fraternal order. One weekend, after the station's staff packed onto a small plane to cover a sporting event in another town, they spent the flight home drinking champagne and singing "Tiny Bubbles," and it was Ty who led the choir, staggering up the aisle to refill everyone's cups. At the sled-dog races, Bram teased him on-air for being KENI's "playboy." "He really doesn't work for a living," Bram said. "He just sort of hangs around."

Still, Bram liked Ty. He respected him. And this would make it difficult, a few years later, when Ty's drinking finally got to be too much and Bram had to fire him. Bram was no teetotaler. And after Bram let him go, no one else in Anchorage seemed eager to hire him, either.

Bram died first, in 1991. Ty would pass away two years later, at age sixty-six, after a diagnosis of liver cancer. "I wasn't surprised, really," he confessed, shortly before his death.

He had resurrected his radio career in a small community on Alaska's Kenai Peninsula, where he hosted a call-in show called *Sound Off* for twenty years. His cancer was inoperable—it ate into his lungs, gallbladder, kidneys, and abdomen, too—and he refused chemotherapy. He had no inclination to travel anywhere, or see anything new. "I just want to do the things that Ty Clark has always done," Ty said.

He kept doing *Sound Off* every morning until, one morning, he didn't.

"OK, THERE WE GO!" Ty hollered gleefully. "It's one o'clock—dog-mushing time!"

A countdown blared over the public-address system, riling the dogs. Then the pistol fired and the mushers, released in staggered starts, went streaking down the center of Fourth Avenue behind a noisy blur of fur and legs. Anyone who'd managed to find a place to sit on the roadside stood up. Then, one by one, the dog teams turned right on Cordova Street and sprinted out of view.

From there, the race wound through the city's eastern neighborhoods and skirted the campus of Alaska Methodist University. The new liberal arts school was not yet four years old and preparing to graduate its first full senior class: fifty-one students.

The university's founders imagined their new institution, without irony, as a "Harvard of the North," a cultural hub that would enrich the entire city by forwarding the ongoing Alaskan project of opening unexplored frontiers; in Anchorage, they felt, the last remaining frontiers were intellectual and artistic. That February, the city's community theater troupe was rehearsing a production of *Our Town* in a converted lecture hall on campus. A half century later, a woman who'd worked on the crew as a student at the university would lean back in her easy chair, search her imperfect memory, and swear that if you crammed into a particular window near the theater, you could spot the dogsled teams shooting by as they headed into the mountains.

Our Town was being directed by the school's speech and drama professor, Frank Brink. For nearly twenty years, Brink had been the eccentric impresario of Anchorage's bustling community theater scene. One of his actors called him "our Moses of the stage." He was insatiable and prolific, staging everything from Shakespeare to *Fiddler on the Roof,* and managing to produce as many as fifty plays and readings in a single year, all with casts of untrained locals. Every Christmas, Brink also performed his own one-man adaptation of Charles Dickens's *A Christmas Carol,* broadcast live on KENI-TV. It was his gift to Anchorage, he said, and a beloved holiday tradition. He wore a tuxedo and bifocals and played twenty-six different characters by himself.

Our Town was Brink's favorite American play. It was written by Thornton Wilder and follows ordinary life in a small New England town at the turn of the twentieth century. Like this book, it has three acts, set on three different days.

The plot of *Our Town* is slow-moving and sometimes dismissed as hokey—a piece of simpleminded Americana. But those who know the play intimately, like Brink did, understand that there's a chastening edge to Wilder's script—beginning with his invention of the "Stage Manager" character, who speaks directly to the audience throughout the evening, narrating the story.

The Stage Manager is a cryptic creation; the most basic stuff about him can't be immediately discerned. Does he live in the town? Apparently. He knows the other characters onstage and chats with them freely. Yet he also knows that everything that's happening around him is theater. He tells the audience so right away, in the first lines of his opening monologue. Wilder even left blank spaces in the script for the actor to fill in, so that each production of *Our Town* could be personalized for the community performing it. When the play opened in Anchorage, for example, Brink's Stage Manager was supposed to say: "This play is called *Our Town*. It was written by Thornton Wilder; produced by the Alaska Methodist University Theater; directed by Frank Brink."

That Sunday, as the dog teams pounded by, opening night was one month away. Brink would be putting on the play over Easter weekend.

AS THE MUSHERS DOUBLED back from the foothills toward Anchorage again, a part-time reporter for KENI named Genie Chance was parked in her two-door Chevrolet, with a PRESS placard in the windshield, staking out the radio station's checkpoint at the top of Cordova Hill.

She was relieved she'd made it in time. Genie was the only

woman covering the races for KENI and had been given a complicated assignment by her bosses that afternoon. She'd started the day at this same spot. But once the first wave of mushers passed and she'd broadcast her play-by-play, she had to pack up her vehicle and scramble to a checkpoint farther along on the route—threading through the traffic choking several miles of icy roads—before the dog teams plowed by her again. Then, while the mushers traversed the mountain trail and headed back toward the city, Genie had to do it all over again, in reverse, returning to her first checkpoint in time to describe them tearing toward the finish line on Fourth Avenue.

Somehow, she managed it. In fact, she'd made it back with time to spare and was now taking it upon herself to enforce some kind of fuzzy perimeter around the race course. The crowd had parked haphazardly on the shoulder of the road. Kids were milling absentmindedly in the way. "Please, please get off the trail!" Genie pleaded with the crowd. "Keep all children off the trail!"

Genie had moved to Alaska from Texas with her husband and three small children five years earlier—"just to see for ourselves," she would later explain, "if it really was the great land of plenty and opportunity that everybody said it was." She was thirty-seven years old, lithe and bewitchingly beautiful, with short, wavy blond hair and high-cut bangs. Her expression often slipped, reflexively, into a solicitous smile or a sly half smirk, each one carrying its own charisma.

"I'm one of those people with an insatiable curiosity who wants to understand in depth what someone else is doing, thinking, or talking about," Genie wrote. Professionally, she was relentless—a newshound—and, since taking the job at KENI a year and a half earlier, had transformed herself into an industrious roving reporter. She ranged all over the greater Anchorage area, covering crime, courts, and city hall, and ventured farther afield as well. She reported from crab boats, missile sites, military training camps, and Inuit villages; when a party of polar bear hunters went missing or a bush pilot crashed, Genie would embed with the Civil Air Patrol and cover the search. One night, while recovering from pneumonia, she dashed to the scene of a building fire and had to be talked out of climbing one of the fire ladders with her tape recorder. Sometimes, she turned this reporting into copy for one of the station's male announcers to read, but often it was her own voice on the air, relayed live from the VHF radio unit in her car. She was said to be the first female newscaster in the state. In Anchorage, one of her coworkers wrote, everyone knew "that when something happens, their Genie will be right there, on the spot, night or day, telling them all about it." Her voice was part of the fabric of daily life in the city. So was her signature sign-off: "This is Genie Chance, KENI News on the Go!"

She frequently disarmed the people she interviewed, or flat-out intimidated them; she was a woman who bore the conspicuous burden of always being fully and unflaggingly herself. But that unappeasable grit was often mistaken for pushiness or nastiness—a working mother wasn't supposed to be so driven. Many of the men at KENI dismissed her as stuck-up, or dramatic, or incapable of laughing at herself—so they made a pastime of teasing her. "She was kind of obnoxious," one colleague would remember. "Her attitude was, 'Don't bother me.'"

Genie tried to be gracious and stoic, to do what was expected of her without complaint; this, she believed, was the only way to defuse the discomfort of the men around her. At the end of the sled-dog races that afternoon, she would sign off by thanking not only all the KENI listeners and spectators, but Bram and Ty, too, "for allowing this little gal to be a part of the biggest broadcast crew ever assembled for a special events broadcast in Alaska!" She was also sure to thank her husband, Winston—"for his permission."

In retrospect, Genie was snared in a paradox a lot like the one in which the city of Anchorage found itself: insecure enough to feel like she still had something to prove, but also impatient, because she knew she was proving it. Even later, after the earthquake, when she became briefly famous around the world, *The Washington Post* would celebrate her as "an Alaskan housewife and mother of three children who does a man-sized job with a radio microphone."

Eventually, when Genie died, Alaska's governor would order flags in the state to be flown at half-staff. Right now, though, she was merely waiting—parked at the top of Cordova Hill, watching the dogsled trail below for the first flash of action. Finally, the two leading mushers emerged from the woods, neck and neck, and barreled onto the open road below her. Each man leapt off his sled and began sprinting alongside his dogs on foot, to lessen the animals' load as they pushed uphill. The crowd got louder. The KENI Kopter beat overhead. Genie was shouting now—she had to. Her voice was brittle with anticipation, about to break. "Everybody stay back!" she hollered. "Here they come!"

Sometimes the future falls open without warning. The earthquake, when it came, would knock people's lives off-kilter with such brutalizing abruptness that its power seemed to reverberate forever. Some people, like Genie, would find their lives oriented differently in its aftermath. Others would discover their entire worldview had changed. More than half a century later, an attorney in Anchorage would explain, "Even now, I can look at this solid ground out my window and know it's not permanent. It can change anytime. It just *moves*. Everything moves."

Anyway, this is who everyone was, and where everything stood, before what it stood on moved.

ACT ONE

FRIDAY

MARCH 27, 1964

2.

"GOING IN ALL DIRECTIONS AT ONCE CONSTANTLY"

A LONG DAY WINDS DOWN

GENIE CHANCE SAT AT THE TYPEWRITER IN HER BEDROOM, returning a letter from an acquaintance in Juneau. She was stealing some time alone before fixing dinner for her family. It was Good Friday evening, a little before five thirty—the beginning of Easter weekend. Her long day appeared to be winding down.

Genie had set out for Anchorage's Public Safety Building that morning around seven a.m., like she did every morning, to sift through the police department's overnight logs and booking slips, looking for news stories. For all the freedom and conviviality that life at the far edge of the continent fostered, parts of Anchorage still retained an unruly frontier-town atmosphere, and every morning, Genie found herself sorting through fresh reports of assaults and robberies, or flare-ups at the bars on the rougher end of Fourth Avenue, where the city's most troubled and impoverished residents hung out and drank. "We had two murders in one week," Genie had joked in a recent letter to her parents back in Texas. "No armed robberies for some time, though. This town must be getting tame." One recurring phenomenon, she noticed, involved men getting drunk, convincing themselves their wives had cheated on them, and shooting them. "Alaskan divorce," she called it.

The rundown at the police station that morning was relatively un-dramatic. There had been a car accident and a botched liquor store holdup. An ambulance had shuttled a teenager with a broken arm to Presbyterian Hospital. A man named Hans Shade had been taking out the garbage when a larger man, whom he'd tussled with two weeks earlier, stepped out of the shadows, said "Hey fella," and stuck a pocketknife in Shade's side. And a fifty-eight-year-old transient man, looking for a place to spend the night, had walked into the police station and proposed he be booked on a charge of public drunkenness. When the cop working the counter asked if the man had any alcohol on him, he said, "No, but if you'll wait just a minute, I'll take care of that." Then he disappeared and returned swigging a bottle of wine.

Genie scrawled all the details in her notebook and threw together a report. Typically, she'd go outside to the parking lot, patch into KENI from the VHF unit in her car, and summarize the overnight crime for the early morning newscast. Then, around eight o'clock, she'd head to work at the station's studios, six blocks away.

Officially, Genie worked at KENI four hours a day, returning home when her two younger children came back from school for lunch. But as a news reporter, she was constantly on call and was, by now, "accustomed to being in the middle of everything," she wrote. She felt a certain jolt whenever her telephone rang at an odd hour, or a tinny voice called for her on the two-way radio in her car, or her Message Mate, the primitive pager the station's engineers had outfitted her with, began to buzz. Even when there wasn't any breaking news, Genie would often leave her children in the afternoon and go back to KENI anyway, to take on extra projects. Lately, she'd been ghostwriting some of Bram's "News in Depth" commentaries. It was an opportunity for Genie to write more expressively, to research and spotlight causes she believed in or poke fun at the ineptitude of local politicians. Those editorials felt personal to her, even if Bram wound up delivering them on camera, and she could feel her writing getting sharper and more confident as time went on. Bram seemed to be noticing, too. "Jean Chance! Great!" he'd scrawled in a note to her, passing on an appreciative letter from a viewer—which was encouraging, even if Bram had misspelled her name.

Recently, Bram had returned to the KENI studios from a two-week trip to the Lower 48 and asked for a word with Genie. He'd been at a Federal Communications Commission conference in Seattle, he explained, and had hit it off with one of the FCC commissioners. It paid for a station owner like Bram to cozy up to the government regulators, so when the commissioner mentioned he was from Bonham, Texas, Bram leapt at the opportunity to tell him that his newsgirl at KENI, Genie Chance, was from that same small town.

It turned out that the commissioner—his name was Bob Bartley—was a friend of Genie's father, and had impressive things to say about her family. Her father was a judge; they weren't wealthy people, but educated and well regarded in that part of Texas. It seemed clear to Genie, from the way Bram recounted the story, that the respectability of her roots had surprised him; he hadn't necessarily expected Genie to come from people who knew people like FCC commissioners. She also recognized the leverage this connection gave her with her boss, and intuited exactly how she ought to play it. "Oh, I forgot all about Bob being an FCC commissioner," Genie told Bram. She was careful to sound nonchalant, which impressed him even more.

Bram went on. To endear himself to Bartley in Seattle, he'd played up Genie's tremendous talent and importance at KENI, and the respect everyone at the station had for this capable daughter of Bonham. But it was as though Bram had performed some kind of sorcery on himself just by saying that out loud, because he'd apparently returned to Anchorage convinced that Genie *was* tremendously important to KENI, and feeling that he should be capitalizing more on her talent. He explained to Genie that he was planning an expansion of the Midnight Sun network's news-gathering operation and wanted to send her on regular trips down to Juneau to cover state politics and the legislature. He would broadcast her reporting from the capital on all of Midnight Sun's radio stations, across the state.

Genie felt vindicated. Also, annoyed. ("I've been with him two years," she later wrote. "He knew what I could do.") Still, she couldn't possibly travel as much as Bram was proposing. As ambitious as she was, her husband and three children came first. That evening, when she told Winston about the conversation, she was already searching for a diplomatic way to turn the promotion down.

Winston Chance Sr.—Big Winston, as Genie often called him—sold used cars, though not particularly well. He was a brawny and good-looking man, with humongous, meaty bear paws for hands. "They were kind of an odd couple," a friend would remember. "She was so bright and wonderful, and he was . . . just a big, good guy." Few people outside the family knew Winston well, but at home he was affectionate and playful—as long as he wasn't drinking. Genie's sisters told her they wished they'd married a man like Winston: He helped cook. He did laundry. He loved to dance. Sometimes, on school holidays, he'd take the kids with him to the car lot so Genie could work without disruption.

Winston was proud of Genie's career, even as he was starting to find himself in the vulnerable position of being outshone by his own wife. The previous summer, for their sixteenth wedding anniversary, he bought Genie an unconscionably expensive portable tape recorder, hoping it might encourage her to tackle freelance projects that were more ambitious than her daily news reports for KENI. And only a few weeks after Genie started working at the station, when she was invited to fly along with smokejumpers fighting a wildfire and spun into a panic, it was Winston who, in his own bullheaded way, bucked her up and got her out the door. "If you're going to play the game with the big boys, you have to act like one," Winston told her. "Don't complain and don't ask for special treatment. If they can take it, you can too." Ever since then, if Genie felt her courage faltering, she'd repeat those words to herself.

In the end, Winston encouraged Genie to take Bram's promotion, despite the time away from home it would demand. "We'll still be a family," he said, "and we've always managed to stay one somehow." Still, she'd had that conversation with Bram two weeks ago, and they hadn't discussed the new job since. After returning from Seattle, Bram immediately got swept up preparing for another, bigger trip, and Genie, not wanting to force the issue, figured they'd return to it as soon as he got back. Bram was traveling to Japan this time, as part of a goodwill and trade delegation of Alaskan businessmen. They'd departed for Tokyo early that Good Friday morning.

GENIE FED ANOTHER SHEET of letterhead into her typewriter. Once she got writing a letter, it was hard to stop. Her days were harried and split awkwardly between home and work—"I'm sure there must be times that it appears that we are going in all directions at once constantly," she'd written to her sister earlier that week—and hiding out upstairs with her typewriter before dinner, sitting under her hairdryer, felt like an indulgence. Writing letters was as much a way for Genie to collect her thoughts as to share them. Most often, she wrote to her parents in Texas and her two sisters. But even now, typing this letter to a government employee in Juneau, whom she'd only recently befriended while reporting a story, she had shot off on a long, emphatic tangent. Genie was letting loose with inside jokes and mischievous nicknames for the man's coworkers, reeling off homespun aphorisms and paraphrased bits of Shakespeare. She was clacking away, charging onto a fourth page, when her thirteen-year-old son, Winston Jr., appeared at her bedroom door.

Wins had a problem. He had his swimming class the next morning and had forgotten to buy a copy of the Red Cross life-saving manual he was supposed to bring. The bookstore downtown, the Book Cache, didn't close until six o'clock, he told Genie. And it was about five thirty now. They still had time—if she would drive him.

Genie looked up from her typewriter. Wins was a sweet boy, gangly, with thick glasses. He'd spent the previous weekend moping around the house, disgusted with himself because he hadn't made the Junior National Honor Society. He *had* actually made it—the school counselor had just asked Genie to keep it a secret until the day of the induction ceremony—but the episode laid bare the very essence of Wins: he was sensitive, determined, way too hard on himself. And right now, he was most likely reprimanding himself for forgetting to buy the swimming book more effectively than Genie could.

Still, it was maddening: Genie had just been downtown with her daughter. In fact, they'd been two doors away from the Book Cache, at J. C. Penney, browsing the girls' separates department. "Well," Genie told Wins, exasperated, "I'll finish my letter when we get back, and we'll get down there. But please, for heaven's sake, when you have to have something, don't wait till the last minute. You've known for a week you had to have it!" She stood up from her desk and threw on a skirt and sweater, leaving the unfinished letter in her typewriter as she headed downstairs.

Genie's eleven-year-old son, Albert, was watching television in the living room, and preferred not to budge. The science fiction puppet show *Fireball XL5* was just starting. "We shouldn't be gone more than five minutes," Genie told him. Big Winston was still at work, and Genie's youngest, eight-year-old Jan, was at the neighbor's house. "If Jan comes home," Genie instructed Albert, "she's to stay here with you until we get back." Then Genie pulled on her boots and parka and marshaled Wins into the car.

The three kids were accustomed to taking care of themselves, and Genie was impressed by how dependable and grown-up they were becoming. Several months earlier, while Genie slept off the pain of a major dental surgery, she'd been moved to discover a different Chance child at her bedside, peering at her over a book, each time she flitted back into consciousness. The three siblings had decided to take shifts, keeping watch to make sure the ice packs didn't slide off their mother's cheek.

Whatever pride Genie took in their self-sufficiency was also undercut by guilt. She knew her kids were growing independent out of necessity, because she wasn't around as much as other mothers were. Genie had worked other jobs in the years she and Winston had been married, but she'd never given herself over to her work the way she did now at KENI. And while she was growing accustomed to grinding against tradition, she didn't do it cavalierly, or without apprehension. She worried about what kind of mother she was, and what kind of example she was setting—particularly for her little girl, Jan. "I'm out having the time of my life," Genie confessed in a letter to her mother, "but what will it do to her?"

Down in the Lower 48, a swirl of pent-up energy and angst was overtaking American life. The stasis into which the country had settled after World War II seemed to be coming undone, jerked apart by stresses and inequalities that had been building under the surface for years. It was, that Good Friday, only four months since the assassination of John F. Kennedy, and six weeks since The Beatles made their American debut on *The Ed Sullivan Show*. Congress was debating a new civil rights bill. *Dr. Strangelove* was in theaters. *The Feminine Mystique* was on bookstore shelves.

One historian would describe the shifts overtaking American society in 1964 as "seismic." But Anchorage was fifteen hundred miles away from the rest of America; the city was relatively conservative, still intent on proving it was part of the American mainstream, not defying it. Alaskans had a habit of describing national news as happening "Outside," as though the lives they were living in Alaska, and all their struggles, were playing out inside some separate, self-contained enclosure: a fragile snow globe out of which they gazed longingly, perched on America's highest shelf.

And so, though Genie recognized she wasn't necessarily suited to her time, it didn't yet occur to her that she might be ahead of it, either. "Feminism" wasn't a word she used; her ambivalence about work and family seemed to feel like a problem unique to her. Isolated, innocent moments could trigger self-doubt. One afternoon a few weeks earlier, Genie had been upstairs at her desk, typing another letter, when she heard Jan in the kitchen, offering the neighbors' kid, Lee Dresie, some chocolate chips for a snack. Lee was dumbstruck. In the Dresie house, he told Jan, chocolate chips were ingredients for making cookies; you didn't just eat them straight out of the bag. "Well," Genie heard Jan say, "we eat them this way." She was lecturing the boy. "You see, *my* mother is not like yours! She doesn't stay at home and bake cookies. She *works*." Then, Jan added proudly, "She's Genie Chance!" Jan said this as though it really meant something, and Genie seemed both amused and unsettled by whatever, exactly, Jan thought it meant.

The next morning, Jan said it *again,* just as haughtily—only this time, to her father. The family was eating breakfast, watching through the kitchen window as their neighbor scraped the ice off her husband's Cadillac before he left for work. This was the custom among many Anchorage wives, apparently, but in the Chance home, the roles were reversed: Big Winston warmed up the car for Genie.

"Honey," Winston asked her, "if I get you a Cadillac like that, would you scrape the ice off and warm it up yourself?" There must have been a tinge of melancholy or disgruntlement in Winston's voice, because before Genie could answer, Jan interjected to remind her father that he was actually very lucky: "It's not everyone who gets to warm up the car for Genie Chance!"

It was funny, but uncomfortable. And in hindsight, it might feel ominous too, since, after the earthquake, the more successful Genie became, the more Winston seethed. But at the time, Genie put the burden of Jan's precociousness, and Winston's uneasiness, on herself. It felt to her like a confirmation of her own insecurities—evidence that she'd been straying too far from her family. "I guess I better spend a little time being Mrs. Winston Chance, wife and mother, or that little girl won't know what's important in life," she wrote.

The boys, meanwhile, were growing embarrassed by her as they came into their own as young men. During the final stretch of the sled-dog races last month, Genie had lost herself in the excitement and simply started moaning "Oh" and "Yes" into her microphone as the mushers passed—awkwardly enough that another KENI broadcaster appeared to make a sly, off-color crack about her breathlessness on the air. She was relieved her sons had been away on a camping trip and hadn't heard the outburst. "I think Wins is convinced his mother is a nut," Genie confessed. "Albert is not quite sure." But Jan, she added, "Jan is on my side."

3.

"THIS IS AN EARTHQUAKE"

A SAVAGE, GRINDING ROLL

S NOW WAS FALLING AS GENIE TURNED RIGHT ON C STREET and headed downtown to the bookstore with Wins. The city was quiet. Most people had already left work for the start of the holiday weekend. The Salvation Army had just concluded its Good Friday worship. Volunteers at the Third Avenue Elks Club Lodge were coloring Easter eggs for their upcoming hunt. And with a couple of hours until curtain time for Frank Brink's *Our Town*, one young actor was alone in the theater at Alaska Methodist University, tidying the costume closet beside the stage. It was 5:36 p.m. The traffic light turned red as Genie and her son approached the intersection of C Street and Ninth.

The car started bucking as soon as Genie's foot touched the brake. "Oh no," she said, disgusted. She assumed she'd blown a tire. She already resented having to run this errand for Wins, and now she steeled herself for more hassle. Genie gripped the wheel.

Wins held on to his seat beside her. For a moment, they bounced violently, without speaking a word.

The shaking relented. Then, suddenly: a forceful, heaving jolt. It knocked the traffic lights out; power in Anchorage was gone. The motion turned merciless, omnidirectional. The initial shuddering swelled into what one report described as "a savage, grinding roll." The electrical lines overhead started snapping like whips. Wins's eyes went wide. "What is it?" the boy asked. Genie looked over her shoulder, toward the mountains. She tested another theory, less surely this time: "It must be a hard wind," she said.

Genie rolled down her window and heard a cacophony of clanging. She looked across the street. A line of cars parked at the service station were bouncing into one another and separating again. They looked like a grotesque accordion, Genie thought, opening and closing. A man and two women came out of the liquor store to her left. They did not seem to be walking, exactly, but lurching. Then they fell down.

Genie's car was hopping more ferociously now, leaving the ground, edging into the adjacent lane. She tightened her fists around the steering wheel to keep it from jerking. She worried the car might be flipped on its side. Outside, the three pedestrians were back on their feet. The man was trying to protect the two women at a corner of the building out of which they'd just blundered, hugging each one to an adjoining wall and clinging to the brickwork to brace himself. But then the building swayed away from the three of them—the building itself moved! Genie watched it bending left, then right. And as it did, she saw a crack open in the masonry over the man's head, then reclose.

The world and everything in it appeared to be convulsing.

Genie's eyes were seeing it, but her mind couldn't organize all the discordant information into a coherent story. Suddenly, through the windshield, she watched the road roll away from the car. The pavement didn't break apart; it was still solid. But it *rolled,* wavelike, as though some humpbacked shadow creature were surging under its surface, heading for town.

Finally, Genie found a word that could fasten this chaos together in her mind. She said the word aloud: "This is an earthquake."

THE ONSET OF THE QUAKE unfolded like this for many people. Small earthquakes were familiar occurrences in Alaska, yet all around Anchorage, the recognition of this one seemed to flower in people slowly, and meekly, arriving only at the tail end of some stupefied, time-stretching lag.

The earthquake overwhelmed people the way the strongest emotions do. It was pure sensation, coming on faster than the intellect's ability to register it. Big Winston had been kneeling at his used car lot, preparing to push a vehicle that wouldn't start. Mistaking the physical sensation of his body heaving from side to side for dizziness, he deduced that he was having a heart attack. Another woman watched her cast-iron pot of moose stew hop autonomously off the burner, as a neighbor girl outside yelled at a large tree to stop moving. A woman driving on Northern Lights Boulevard tried to puzzle out why "the road wouldn't stay still." So many people's stories described a sluggish process of discovery: you had to *discover* the earthquake, even though it had already been shaking you for what felt like a very long time.

It was amazing what details people noticed—the focal points

their minds chose to lock on to when the moving world went blurry. Across town, the mayor of Anchorage stared at a raven outside his car window, watching it try to land on a thrashing streetlight for several seconds until, finally, the bird gave up and soared off. On Fourth Avenue, a high school track star watched the window of a stationery store rattle and explode, then stood there calmly admiring the perfect hurdling form of the man who came leaping out of it. And at J. C. Penney, a fifteen-year-old in the elevator with some friends watched a book that one of them had dropped suddenly levitate off the floor and hang weightless in midair right in front of him. For a split second, it was like they were in orbit. The elevator was falling.

People discovered it was impossible to walk. The earth rebuked them, splaying their legs, shrugging them off, thrusting their knees to their chins. One man had to run in order to get enough momentum to balance—"like walking on a barrel," he explained. Drivers pulled over, opened their car doors, then fell straight out of them like bundles of newspapers dropped on a street corner. "I had a feeling of being completely defenseless," one man said. An employee at the gas company's headquarters scampered outside only to find himself dodging a driverless two-and-a-half-ton truck. A woman wrapped herself around a parking meter in front of the Federal Building on Fourth Avenue and screamed for all sinners to repent.

Evergreen trees lashed back and forth like stalks of wheat. Muddy water burbled into the street where pipes had split open. On the north side of town, near the railroad, a woman watched as tank cars rolled "fearsomely back and forth on their tracks" and ice floes in Cook Inlet "flung against each other as though a gargantuan hand were splashing in a puddle." The five-story

Hillside Apartments building appeared to shiver. The long, low-slung Ben Franklin variety store moved "up and down in sections, just like a caterpillar," one observer said—flexing, recoiling, but somehow remaining intact—while the Arrow Lumber Company building, at the corner of Fireweed Lane and Barrow, collapsed in a simple, downward rush.

The earth yawned open and swallowed cars. One woman in Turnagain, watching hers vanish, said "good" out loud—she'd never liked that car. But then the ground thrust upward and ejected the vehicle again. Another woman found herself jumping over three-foot-wide crevasses as they split open in front of her, escaping to momentary safety again and again, cradling her baby the whole time. She noticed, fortuitously, that each new rupture was preceded by a warning sound: like "if you dropped a dish and it didn't break, just bounced," she explained.

The sounds of the earthquake were part of the overall dream-like incoherence. Many people mistook the low growl of the churning earth for a nuclear bomb. Alaska, with its strategic location and military bases, had always been a presumptive Soviet target, and many residents now assumed the day had come: warheads were finally being lobbed at them from across the Bering Sea. "I don't know how you'd describe it," one man later said of the earthquake's otherworldly roar. "It's a rumble, and a slithery sound all mixed up—and it's got some crackle to it, too." One woman remembered only absolute quiet, though she conceded that it was possible she had momentarily gone deaf from the shock. A third person reported that he "was not aware of any unusual noise other than people calling for help."

Southeast of Anchorage, a small community called Portage was destroyed when most of its buildings dropped seven feet into the ground and were inundated by the tide. In the town of Valdez, the quake picked up a freighter that had just docked at the port and, as one onlooker put it, "tossed it like I used to toss boats in the bathtub." In Seward, an oil tank farm exploded, and the town's entire industrial waterfront—docks, warehouses, fish-processing plants—crumbled into the water at once. Then later, after the spilled oil and debris ignited into a roaring fire, a tremendous wave barreled in, pushing the entire mess inland to clobber the town. "It was an eerie thing to see," one man said, "a huge tide of fire washing ashore, setting a high-water mark in flame, and then sucking back."

The tsunamis had started. In the town of Kodiak, walls of water triggered by the quake would smash into downtown for several hours that Friday evening, obliterating buildings and hurling fishing boats into the streets. Several small Alaska Native villages were erased. The two hundred people of Old Harbor, on Kodiak Island, survived by clambering to higher ground, en masse, as four separate waves pummeled their village. Kaguyak lost three of its forty-five residents and was washed out completely. Survivors huddled around their children on a hillside to keep them from freezing. They were finally picked up by a crab boat the next morning after fourteen hours in the cold, and had the captain stop so they could gather a few artifacts from their church that they'd spotted floating far offshore. Another village, Chenega, lost twenty-three people—a third of its population—when it was struck by a seventy-foot wave. The following morning, a pilot flying over the area would see hundreds of red snapper—deepwater fish—that had bobbled to the surface, knocked dead by a pressure wave.

The Great Alaska Earthquake, as it would become known,

remains the second most powerful earthquake ever measured, with a magnitude of 9.2. Its epicenter was seventy-five miles east of Anchorage, and shallow: only about fifteen and a half miles underground. For thousands of years, the Pacific Plate had been crunching its way under the opposing edge of the North American Plate—lurching at a low angle, and slowly, about two or two and a half inches every year. Cyclically, over time, an unsustainable amount of pressure would build up, then suddenly release. This was one of those moments; the plates slipped—hard.

One seismologist would later explain that the earthquake was so violent it "made the earth ring like a bell." Its energy seemed to reverberate everywhere, disrupting or reshaping the surface of the planet as it went. An uninhabited island southeast of Anchorage was knocked nearly seventy feet out of its original position. Most of the landmass of North America momentarily jostled upward, in some places by as much as two inches. The quake shook the water in wells around the world, tripping gauges in more than seven hundred far-flung locations, including Puerto Rico, England, Belgium, Libya, and Israel. ("Water levels in wells as far away as South Africa jumped abruptly," a National Academy of Sciences report would note.) In Baton Rouge, a homeowner noticed his swimming pool jiggle.

Twenty-three hundred miles south of Anchorage, in an elegant, modernist ranch home in Pasadena, California, a sixty-three-year-old man and his wife were settling down in their living room with cocktails. The man was an odd duck—a rumpled intellectual and avid nudist who wrote many abjectly bad love poems about women who were not his wife. But he was also an accomplished seismologist—he'd developed the scale on which the magnitude of earthquakes is measured—and was passionate and single-minded enough about his work to have installed a seismograph in his living room. The machine was cumbersome and ugly, mounted on its own cabinet and topped by a large metallic tumbler. He'd wedged the device between a grandfather clock and a stylishly upholstered club chair.

The man's wife hated the seismograph—she initially regarded it as "a rather brutally coarse intrusion among her neat furnishings," he wrote. He insisted that she had come to appreciate having this apparatus in her living room—but, really, who knows: the man was not necessarily someone whose sensitivity to the emotions of others should be trusted.

Now, at 7:42 p.m.—5:42 p.m. Anchorage time—as they sat together, listening to a concert on the radio, the man looked over and saw the seismograph's needle jerking.

"There's a great earthquake recording," Charles Richter remarked to his wife.

"Yes?" Lillian Richter replied sleepily. He was talking over the concert.

4.

"DUMBFOUNDED"

GENIE DASHES AROUND DOWNTOWN

.

GENIE WASN'T AWARE OF ANY OF THIS. AS THE CAR CONTINUED to pitch and roll, she and Wins held on, side by side in the front seat, like sailors riding out a squall. Already, they'd existed inside this augmented reality for close to four minutes. The earthquake would last nearly five, long enough for some people to question if it would ever stop, or even start to give up hope that it would.

Genie stood on the brake, trying to steady the earth. She'd been focusing on a two-story apartment building, a block away, as it swung forward and back—wondering, almost idly, if the scaffolding on the second floor might drop. Now the building seemed to be fixing itself in place again like an animal, startled from a deep sleep, resettling.

The motion let up gradually. Everything became stationary again—even the other drivers around her at the intersection.

Genie looked up and saw the KENI television antenna, still upright on the roof of the Fourth Avenue Theatre building in the distance, and assumed the station would have power back soon and that the six p.m. news broadcast would go on as usual. That meant she had less than twenty minutes to put together a story. She threw her car in gear.

Genie was oblivious to the magnitude of destruction. None of the buildings in her line of sight, or even the utility poles, had toppled, and her mind, still reeling, could only absorb what was visible in front of her. The situation didn't look that bad. Psychologists would come to call this phenomenon "normalcy bias": a tendency of the human imagination to reclose around such disruptions and assume to an implausible degree, even in the midst of catastrophes, that life is still basically normal. Genie sped to the Public Safety Building, three blocks away, to round up some details for a quick news report.

She whirred into the parking lot within sixty seconds of the quake subsiding. Already, firemen were pulling their trucks out of the garage—normal procedure for a power outage, Genie knew; they'd use the radios in their vehicles to communicate until the power was restored inside.

"You wait here," Genie told Wins, stepping out of the car.

"Can I go on to the Book Cache and get my book?" he asked. The bookstore was close, near J. C. Penney. It was closing soon.

"Yes, I shouldn't be here too long," Genie said. She'd drive by in a few minutes and pick him up.

A police captain with a walkie-talkie rushed out of the Public Safety Building, past Genie, as she made her way through the front door. Inside, no one was speaking. Genie recognized the clerk sitting at the police counter and began to ask her, "Say, do you know . . . ?" but the woman was so ashen-faced that Genie's voice fell apart mid-sentence. Genie hadn't noticed until now: the police department's filing cabinets and desks were thrown over; heaps of ceiling plaster littered the floor. This would be her news story, she realized: the shaking had been strong enough to topple furniture in the Public Safety Building—the most damage of any quake she'd experienced in her five years in Alaska. She raced toward the front door to radio KENI's studio from her car.

The building started shaking again. The aftershock was vigorous, but brief—only a few seconds. As it wound down and Genie stepped outside, she found Wins rushing back to the building. Her son looked pale and fearful. She went to put her arm around him. "Come quick!" he told her. "Penney's building is falling down!"

Standing in the doorway of the Public Safety Building, they could see the five-story department store, two blocks away. One high corner of its facade was missing. And now, as Genie and Wins watched through the flurrying snow, the tremendous concrete panel of the exterior next to that opening started to swing away from the building and crash back, as though hinged at the top. Each time the concrete swept outward, it traveled farther. Then, finally, the entire panel dropped into the street with a mounting roar.

"Hop in the car, honey, we're going," Genie told Wins.

"Where?"

"We're going to Penney's."

She wasn't scared. Mostly, she was indignant. The Penney's building was only one year old—Genie had covered the store's opening the previous spring. This was the structure's first real earthquake, and it was failing that test spectacularly. Genie grumbled aloud, cursing the city for allowing such shoddy construction. She assumed the builder had cut corners, was either crooked or incompetent. *This* would be her news story now— the crumbling of Penney's. It still hadn't occurred to her that the earthquake might have torn apart other buildings, too.

Pieces of wall were still falling off the department store when Genie and Wins pulled up. Parts of the building were cleaved open to the cold air, exposed like the chambers of a dollhouse. Genie left the car running, grabbed her camera from the back seat, and told Wins to stay back. As she walked north on D Street, another aftershock struck, and she photographed another concrete panel as it dropped. People poured out of the doorways of Penney's, dusty and in shock. One woman was almost chanting to herself, the words "Oh no, no" dribbling from her mouth. Genie heard a man's voice behind her, saying, "There's no sense trying to lock up. There's no windows left in the building." And when she turned, she saw him, silhouetted in front of his insurance office across the street. The windows behind him were blown out.

Now Genie noticed that *all* the glass was shattered, up and down the block. All at once, she registered the extent of the wreckage surrounding her: the cracks and gashes in other facades, the twisted sign over the Singer Sewing Center, the concrete hunks on the sidewalk and the scatter of stucco and unidentifiable scrap in the street. It was like a camera lens had been suddenly wrenched into focus. A voice said something about people buried in the rubble. Another aftershock struck. A group of men came running down the middle of D Street yelling "Fourth Avenue is gone!" and behind them, one block north, Genie could see the roof of a familiar two-story building resting on the street, jabbed into the pavement at an incomprehensible angle.

This, finally, was the moment of epiphany. It took all this for Genie to feel a certain irrevocable jolt, as you might feel aboard a train that's jumped violently off its track: reality had derailed from her expectations, from her conception of what was even possible, onto some other, unmapped route.

She scrambled back to her car and told Wins to get in. She wanted to drop him at home before she went any farther. "I would more than likely witness enough horror to last two lifetimes," she later wrote, "and I didn't want my son to see it." Even worse: She had no idea what horrors might have already befallen her other little boy and girl at home.

Several fire trucks had arrived at Penney's, blocking Genie's car at the curb. "Get out of my way!" she yelled. "I've got to get out of here!"

THE CHANCE HOME WAS six blocks away. When they got close, Genie exhaled loudly and said, "Thank God."

The stout, wood-shingled duplex was still standing, though the chimney had crumbled. As she pulled up, Jan and Albert shot out of the Dresies' house across the street. Wins leapt out of the car and ran to his sister and brother, and all three kids started talking at the same time, each trying to outtalk his or her siblings. "You just ought to see the inside of our house," Albert kept shouting. "It's a mess!"

Albert had been sitting in his father's rocking chair in the Chances' living room watching television when that first horrible thrust knocked out the electricity and the TV fell off its stand.

Then the heavy bookshelf went down, the sofa started hopping, and Albert retreated to the kitchen, clinging to the twitching furniture and walls as he went. He struggled to pry the back door open—the quake was warping the jamb around it. And as soon as he managed to get out, the door slammed shut behind him, trapping Casey, the family's dog, inside. Albert heaved the door open again and the animal leapt out, straight into his chest, knocking him over, then bolted off into the snow and disappeared. Albert watched the house swing back and forth. Then he staggered across the street to check on his sister at the neighbor's house, losing his balance and buckling to the pavement several times on the way.

Jan had been in an upstairs bedroom at the Dresie home playing board games with their son when the shaking started and the door started slamming open and shut. She heard the Dresies' two-year-old daughter bawling from her crib in an adjacent room and, rushing to her, discovered that all the baby furniture—the crib, the changing table, the bureau—had been built on wheels and was now whipsawing from one side of the room to the other with each swing of the earth. Jan leaned against the crib with all her little body's weight, trying to steady it against the wall, then wedged her free arm through the bars to hold up and comfort the child. Mrs. Dresie tried to reach them from downstairs, but kept being thrown sideways in the narrow stairwell; it was as though she were tossing inside a rotating chute. When, finally, her husband made it up the steps, he found Jan hushing the toddler while the room thumped around them. "It's all right," Jan was saying. "It's just an earthquake." Now, standing outside, Genie asked Jan if she'd been scared, but Jan turned bashful. "Sorta" was all she would say.

Safe and finally reunited with each other and their mother, all three Chance children began to understand, without being told, that Genie would be leaving again. They had a family plan for when their mother was called away to work for breaking news: Wins was in charge. And already he seemed to be taking responsibility for wrangling and comforting his younger brother and sister. Genie took for granted that Big Winston would return home soon, unharmed. His car lot was on the east side of Anchorage, and Genie still didn't consider that the damage might extend beyond the few blocks of downtown she'd seen with her own eyes. Genie called to Mrs. Dresie, standing on her porch, and asked if she'd watch over the children until Big Winston got back. She hugged Albert to her again and asked, "Are you sure you're all right?"

Albert pulled away. "Don't worry about me," he said. "Go on and do your job."

Genie was back at Penney's within minutes.

SHE PARKED ON FIFTH AVENUE, a half block away from the department store, and approached a side of the building she hadn't seen before. Here the roof of Penney's had slumped inward and massive swathes of the five-story exterior had collapsed, spilling high, disordered slopes of plaster, lumber, and concrete up and down the block. The structure looked as though someone had stepped on it and its insides had slopped out.

During the quake, the store's windowless interior had gone dark. The emergency lighting that eventually clicked on was feeble and dim. Wedding crystal and mirrors burst apart. Hangers rattled like a swarm of wasps. Shoppers fell to their knees, praying or wailing the names of their companions over the din, echolocating like bats in the blackness. On the upper floors, you could feel the building swing and extend over the street, its walls unfurling outward somehow, like a snapping flag. When it was finally over, people hustled down the stopped escalators. One woman, who'd been shopping for china on the third floor, worried about being knocked unconscious by falling debris and chose to cover her head with her hands instead of holding on to the railing, She lost her footing and tumbled down the escalator, tearing ligaments in her leg. As parts of the building rained down around her, she realized she'd left her purse upstairs and started to despair. "It wasn't the money," she would explain a few days later. "It was the identification." She worried that the structure would cave in completely and when they finally dug out her body, it would be too mutilated to identify; her family would never know where she died.

Downstairs, the fleeing crowd bottlenecked at one of the exits—the same doorway, on Fifth Avenue, that Genie was now approaching. A man had stood inside, watching as loose chunks of concrete fell from overhead and burst apart on the sidewalk in front of them, waving for people to scamper out safely between each bombardment.

The survivors came out dazed and dirtied, horrified to look back and see what they'd escaped. A college student emerged barefoot, in the cocktail dress she'd only partially zipped herself into in one of the fitting rooms. Two thirteen-year-old twins were wearing new suits. Many of the refugees gathered in a little church nearby, warming up, lighting cigarettes to weather the shock, until the pastor suggested they stop smoking, given the thickening odor of gas in the air.

Genie moved toward the building, snapping photograph after photograph. It was nearly six o'clock, the last half hour of daylight, and she was still intent on collecting material for that evening's television news. Approaching the corner of D Street, Genie stopped short in front of a slab of something in the snow. She stared at it, mesmerized and repulsed, but couldn't place what it was. She remembered, as a girl in Texas, watching her father kill off his few remaining hogs after a snowstorm and hang their hindquarters from the rafters of the barn. This thing in the snow reminded Genie of that somehow. Finally, a man shouted an explanation to her: it was half a woman, he said. He'd seen her get struck by the falling debris.

Genie felt nauseous. She refused to take a picture of it. She refused, even, to admit this object had been a living woman.

Soon, as she got closer to Penney's, she saw that several parked cars had been buried in debris. One Chevy Impala station wagon had been flattened to a height of about two feet; a long hunk of the building's facade, weighing several tons, had landed squarely on its roof. A woman was still alive inside, pinned to the floorboard—Genie could hear her talking. Bystanders had spontaneously gone to work right away, wedging rocks under the concrete to jack it up off the car, or heaving at it hopelessly with their bare hands. Eventually, someone said they knew where a tow truck was and ran off to get it. Now there was a pair of tow trucks on the scene, and each vehicle was being winched to a different end of the slab. The plan was to break the concrete in half, then drag each piece off the vehicle. One man had taken charge, bellowing a signal for the drivers to pull.

"The entire operation in trying to extricate her from that car was volunteers," Genie noticed. She was amazed, particularly by the man who seemed to have taken the initiative to direct the operation—not only by his decisiveness, but by how efficiently everyone else fell in line behind him, following his instructions. All around Penney's, Genie spotted other clusters of ordinary people digging for survivors with little concern for their own safety. She even had to argue with one group to step away when she spotted another exterior panel loosening over their heads, threatening to fall. "We think there's somebody in here!" one of the men yelled at her. "You're going to be in there too, if you don't get out!" she shouted back.

Genie lingered near the crushed station wagon, catching snippets of reports on the radios of a squad car and an ambulance idling nearby. For the first time, she was gaining at least a spotty overview of the havoc around the city, beyond these few blocks. At one point, she recognized the voice of one ordinarily unshakable police officer calling in an apparent landslide in the upscale Turnagain neighborhood across town. "I've never seen anything like this," she heard the cop say. "Surely nobody can be alive. It's nothing but matchsticks." She found herself praying out loud that KENI's engineers would get them back on the air soon, so she could start broadcasting what she knew.

By now, the volunteers with the tow trucks had split the concrete slab just enough for someone else to step in with a cutting torch and open a hole in the station wagon's roof. Soon they were pulling the woman through that opening and fastening her to a stretcher. More than two hundred people had gathered to watch the rescue; the rescuers had to pile through the crowd to load the woman into the ambulance standing by. Her name was Blanche Clark—a fifty-five-year-old film courier who'd just completed her daily run to the Penney's photo counter when the earthquake hit. She was alive, but mangled. Her neck and arm were broken, her legs didn't look right—but she would survive, spending five weeks in traction at Providence Hospital then eventually retiring to California with her husband. As the ambulance carrying her peeled away for the hospital, a savage aftershock hit, and the earth underneath the vehicle bucked again.

Genie moved on quickly. She wanted to investigate the damage she'd heard people yelling about on Fourth Avenue. Turning the corner, she took in the entire impossible panorama at once.

One side of the city's main thoroughfare had simply *dropped*. For two whole blocks, everything was ten or eleven feet lower than it had been, wedged in a ragged chasm that had ripped open under the street. Some of the buildings still appeared to be intact down there. Cars were lined up beside their parking meters. Everything across the street, meanwhile, was seemingly unscathed.

"I was dumbfounded," Genie remembered. The gash deepened as it progressed along those blocks. The D&D Bar, the Sportsman's Club, the Frisco Bar and Café, the pawnshop, the Anchorage Arcade—all the establishments along this seedier end of Fourth Avenue were now underground. In the immediate aftermath, men had emerged from the front doors of those subterranean bars unharmed, many still clutching their drinks, and looked up like stunned miners.

Soon, there was another aftershock. The windows of a bank started popping, spraying glass across the sidewalk ahead of Genie as she headed back to her car. It was snowing harder. Her hands and feet were freezing. She wasn't remotely prepared for whatever work lay ahead of her that night, and resolved to rush home and throw on warmer clothes. At the corner of C Street, she passed under a banner hanging across Fourth Avenue advertising Frank Brink's community theater production that Easter weekend. It floated like a cruel caption over the surreal wreckage behind her as Genie walked away.

In big, hand-painted letters, it read: OUR TOWN.

BIG WINSTON WAS HOME when Genie returned. She told him and the kids to start bringing up the family's emergency supplies from the basement and piling them near the back door: sleeping bags, flashlights, jars of water, cans of food. She wanted to be ready to evacuate if a second big one struck.

Genie's family must have seemed innocent to her. They hadn't seen what she'd seen, the relentless stream of "sights my mind could not have stood under other circumstances," as she'd describe it. She couldn't bring herself to share that knowledge with them, not even with Winston. She pushed those images down, barricading them somewhere in the pit of her stomach or the back of her mind, preparing herself for when she eventually got on the air. She felt obligated to shield KENI's listeners from that horror as well. The citizens of Anchorage were scattered around the city, without power, without phones. Genie intuited that if she described that woman trapped in the flattened station wagon, or that body in the snow, each person listening would rush to assume it was their missing mother, wife, sister, or daughter. "Each person had lived through his own hell during those terrifying minutes," Genie would later explain. "To add to it with a description of blood and gore could cause panic. We could not have panic."

She was steeling herself, making subconscious calculations

about who could be trusted with the truth and who had to carry the burden of it. Her reasoning reflected her understanding of how society worked, especially in a crisis: a belief that ordinary people relied on the maturity, proficiency, and good judgment of extraordinary leaders to protect them. That assumption was reinforced endlessly during the Cold War. Planning for a potential nuclear attack, the government presumed that a panicked and helpless public would need crisp, foolproof protocols to follow. So the government prescribed regular duck-and-cover drills, practiced large-scale evacuations of city neighborhoods around the country, and encouraged homeowners to build fallout shelters in their yards. A year and a half earlier, at the height of the Cuban Missile Crisis, Alaska's governor had given a statewide radio address instructing every Alaskan to assemble a two-week supply of food and water, clothing, blankets, and lanterns. Genie had obediently stashed away those supplies; this was the stockpile Winston was now hauling upstairs from the basement.

There were times when Genie felt her job, as a reporter, was to be skeptical of authority. But not always, and never without limits or a foundation of respect—and certainly, she decided, not in the middle of a disaster like this. She had only so much faith in the general public to think clearly and for themselves. It was a weird feeling for a journalist, but, Genie explained, "we could not report the facts. We had to be a voice of assurance and instruction."

That said, Genie was no longer sure KENI *would* return to the air. The station's signal emanated from a radio tower on the western edge of the city, anchored in a marsh called Bootlegger's Cove. It wasn't far from the site of the horrendous landslide Genie had heard described on the police radio outside Penney's.

She was keeping a transistor radio tuned to KENI, but so far, nothing: only absent waves of static.

KENI's rival station, KFQD, had managed to start broadcasting again, however, returning to the air at 5:57 p.m., only twenty-one minutes after the quake. KFQD had been carrying occasional messages from city authorities since then, relayed to its studio from the Public Safety Building downtown; the mayor had even driven out to KFQD and broadcast a brief statement. But KFQD was more of a music and entertainment outfit, with a one-man news bureau. Genie decided she would go back to the Public Safety Building and provide KFQD with direct reports, using the shortwave radio in her car.

She headed upstairs to change into warmer clothes. Moving through the house, she saw that the disarray was spectacular and strange. The quake had somehow sent the living room furniture hopping inward from all four walls, leaving it clustered in the center of the room. The toilet in the upstairs bathroom was empty; the water had splashed out across the floor. Genie threw on the cold-weather gear—quilted underwear, electric socks— she'd purchased the previous fall before covering an army missile test in the mountains. When she couldn't find her boots, she spotted Albert's rubber ones by the back door and stepped into those instead. Winston had started pleading with her. "Don't go down to the Public Safety Building," he said. On his way back from work, he'd driven past several buildings that had cratered in on themselves. All of them, he told her, were new constructions, built of prestressed concrete, just like the Public Safety Building. "If you're in that one down there and the next quake hits, it'll just be gone," he said.

It was around then that an eerie sound materialized from the transistor radio Genie was carrying: warbling strains of music on KENI, warped by the fluctuating power from the station's emergency generator. Soon, Ty Clark's voice came on. "This is KENI, 550 on your dial," he said over the music, "returning to the air on an emergency basis. All rules and regulations of the Federal Communications Commission are declared void and invalid under this emergency."

Genie was heading to her car. Winston was following after her, and the kids were following him. "Baby," he was saying, "it's not going to be safe." But Genie was already breaking in on Ty from the VHF unit in her front seat, explaining that she was ready to make an initial report about the situation downtown. "Go ahead, Genie," Ty said. She spoke fast, taking sharp, quick breaths. She was astonished, later, when people told her she had sounded calm.

"It has become obvious that the earthquake that struck Anchorage less than an hour ago was a major one," Genie began. "A great deal of damage has been done throughout the city." She advised people to check their supplies and keep their doors closed to retain the heat in their homes. "But, uh, now another thing," she continued. She was making it up as she went along, warning about as many hazards as she could remember registering as she dashed through downtown: Avoid tall buildings, which may still be susceptible to aftershocks; stay clear of power lines; stay put. And most of all, don't panic—there was no need. "KENI will keep you informed throughout the night and bring you the official instructions from the Public Safety Building. So stay tuned to your radios. Check on your neighbors. See if they have transistor radios. If they don't, possibly they could move in with you and share one for the night. It seems like it's going to be a long, cold night for Anchorage, so prepare to batten down the hatches, and stay tuned to KENI."

Another tremor struck just as Genie finished—or possibly moments earlier, while she'd been on the air; the accounts are unclear. There would be fifty-two separate aftershocks over the next three days, eleven of which measured higher than 6.0 on the Richter scale. This one was particularly severe. The door of Genie's car, which had been hanging open, swung shut, sealing her inside. She watched her husband and children sprint out from under the whipping power lines, into the center of their street, and clutch one another to keep from wobbling over.

When the aftershock subsided, Genie told Big Winston, "I have to go." By now, he'd given up on convincing her to stay and was, instead, urging her to slow down, not to rush to the Public Safety Building unprepared. Did she have everything she needed, he kept asking.

"I'll just go the way I am," Genie said. "And don't worry about me." After all, Winston was lucky: many husbands in Anchorage were going to spend the night helplessly wondering where their wives were, whether they were safe. But Winston would know for sure, Genie told him: he could switch on the radio and hear her working.

Genie drove off. It was just after 6:40 p.m. Only one hour had passed since the quake. "For the next thirty hours," she would explain when it was over, "I talked constantly."

5.

"INFORMATION IS A FORM OF COMFORT"

GETTING ORGANIZED AT THE PUBLIC SAFETY BUILDING

THE ANCHORAGE PUBLIC SAFETY BUILDING WAS A BLOCK-long L-shaped structure that housed the headquarters of the city's police and fire departments. The building was three years old and one of several relatively new landmarks downtown signaling that the former frontier town had matured: the people of Anchorage had built an austere home for all the uniformed grown-ups in charge.

By the time Genie made it back, just before seven o'clock, the building's lobby was loud and packed with people. An emergency generator had switched on after the quake, but stopped running eighteen minutes later when a gas line ruptured. Now there was insufficient light and heat in the building. Some of the men clogging the lobby wore heavy coats and fur caps as if they were still outside. There was talk of a single working phone somewhere in the fire department, but even as more lines flickered open, the city's exchanges were overwhelmed. A ramshackle, substitute communications system was evolving in their place: people scampered outside to the police and fire vehicles in the parking lot, using their VHF radios to relay and receive messages from all over Anchorage. But it was impossible to get a handle on the overall scope of the crisis: how many neighborhoods were damaged, how many people might be missing or dead. The radio units used by each different city department were marooned on their own frequencies, making communication between them mostly impossible. Before long, one city worker explained, it became apparent that the best way to get ahold of someone was simply to "walk around and shout and wave your hand in the air until you found them."

Walking into the building, Genie found Anchorage's fire chief, George Burns, huddling with the chief of police and a police captain, and listened while the three men talked the situation through. Burns was fifty-eight years old—"a highly irascible but lovable old goat," Genie called him—and had been struggling with his health since suffering a stroke three years earlier. When the quake struck, he had been on his way to refill a prescription at the Rexall Drug Store, across the street from Penney's. After one of the department store's concrete panels crashed down next to his car, he sped back to the Public Safety Building and dispatched his first engine to the scene. Burns had been fire chief in Anchorage for fifteen years and was one of the most veteran city officials in the building; he had just put in for early retirement and was planning to move to Seattle with his wife and daughter the following June. In May, however, he would have another stroke and die. A plaque bearing his name would go up inside the Public Safety Building, not far from where he was standing right now, talking to the policemen and Genie.

Burns's firemen were already sweeping some of the damaged buildings downtown, calling out for survivors, though the department seemed far more focused on fighting and preventing fires. About an hour later, in fact, Burns would make the questionable decision to call in his men from the dark and pause the search-and-rescue work until sunrise. He wanted his firefighters rested and in one place in case any more blazes broke out.

Frankly, it was a miracle Anchorage wasn't already burning to the ground. As Burns explained to the two policemen, the city's water system was so debilitated that his men didn't have the capacity to put out a major fire. But thankfully, only a few small fires had sparked up so far. At three of the city's schools, chemicals in the science labs had combined and ignited. Another fire would soon be reported at the Charcoal Burger restaurant. There was a broken gas main on Post Road at Third Avenue. A fuel tank had split open at the port. And a battery of forty-foot missiles had broken apart at an army installation next to the airport; nearly a million gallons of jet fuel were now spilling out around them. Only later, after the spill was cleaned up, would the public learn that those missiles had been outfitted with nuclear warheads.

Genie told Burns and the police chief, John Flanigan, that KENI was on the air again, and that she had her mobile unit in her car outside, ready to go live. She'd come here to offer them a way to speak directly to the city; they were free to use her rig to broadcast announcements. Without much thought, Chief Flanigan immediately offloaded that job on Genie instead. He knew Genie—she was here at headquarters every morning, digging through the police logs for the morning news. *She* was going to be the one talking to Anchorage, he told her. The first announcement she needed to make was to tell everyone not to panic.

"We've already done that," Genie told him.

In that case, Flanigan said, urge them to stay in their homes. His primary concern was managing the people streaming into downtown to find loved ones, or just to take a look around. His officers were having difficulty working around the congestion and crowds, and he was worried even larger waves of civilians would wander downtown once, as Flanigan put it, everyone had had a chance to check on their families and straighten a few picture frames at home. Flanigan was already getting reports of downed power lines and gigantic fissures in city streets. There was debris everywhere, likely with bodies under it, and more hazards could appear with every aftershock. Buildings that were standing now might still collapse. He needed the people of Anchorage to know it wasn't safe to travel around the city right now, he said.

Genie hurried to her car and started reeling off the information she'd collected, taking uncertain stock of Anchorage's wounds. "City police report that a high-voltage power line is down on Northern Lights Boulevard," she said. "State police report that there is a large crevasse in the Seward Highway about two miles south of the city limits of Anchorage. It is impassable at that point." In fact, "Both highways out of Anchorage are closed to through traffic." She listed numerous roads within the city that were reported to be blocked, too. "You are urged to stay home," Genie said. "Do not drive around to see the sights. Stay in your places and await further instructions."

Soon, runners were rushing out of the Public Safety Building and appearing beside Genie's car with more announcements to broadcast. She periodically ran back and forth from the building, collecting others herself. She listed off the locations of public shelters opening up for the displaced and started directing equipment and personnel around the city. "A first-aid station is being set up at the old First Federal Savings and Loan Building," she said. "A doctor is needed there as soon as possible." An assistant fire chief came to tell her, with some aggravation, that his men were seeing lit candles in people's windows all over town. "This is a possible fire hazard," Genie explained on the air. "This could be very dangerous. If you are using candles, please light them only when it is necessary, and then use them with extreme care." Essentially, she was doing her job—or what most resembled it, refracted through the stress and strangeness of the emergency: she was talking to Anchorage on the radio. "I was responsible for reassuring them that the world had not come to an end," she said.

Think, for a second, about what it means to say a person feels "shaken." In Anchorage, this wasn't a metaphor: the whole city had been thrown. One woman explained that at some point during the earthquake, "my sense of reality and my connection to everything was just lost." For many people, a feeling of dislocation, of stupefied alienation, arose when the ground started moving—and it didn't necessarily resolve once that motion stopped. Looking around afterward, trying to absorb their scrambled surroundings, felt equally disorienting. At Presbyterian Hospital, one man watched blood seep slowly into the hall from a doorway, like a scene in a horror movie; it took a second for him to understand that the hospital's storehouse of donated blood had broken open and spilled.

Still, people were only able to take in so much of the damage before, about a half hour after the earthquake, the sun set and the city went dark. The electrical grid was down. Most phone lines were dead. As Anchorage staggered to its feet, each person, or cluster of people, was cut off from everyone else. There was no way to know exactly what had happened, or how thoroughly their world had been jumbled.

This feeling of vulnerability saturated the city. One man, discovering he'd fallen to the sandy bottom of a pit, explained, "You just wonder, 'Where are you?' You don't know if anybody else is alive. Maybe you're the last man." Another remembered taking stock of the erratic transfiguration of his neighborhood and assuming that no other part of Anchorage could possibly have gotten hit so badly. Others made the opposite assumption: that the devastation they couldn't see must be far worse. Both assumptions provoked loneliness. Each generated a slightly different species of despair.

It was reassuring, then, to hear another voice on the radio, talking to you—especially a familiar voice like Genie's. It urged your imagination outward, encouraged you to picture other people, still out there, listening to the radio, too. Very little of the information that Genie, or any of the other broadcasters, was reporting early that evening provided much comfort. But Genie's neighbor Joy Dresie, who was listening at home, would later point out that in the throes of such blindness, isolation, and disarray, every fact that Genie relayed had a stabilizing effect; each was a point around which reality could re-gather. "Information," she said, "is a *form* of comfort."

"Genie Chance," another man explained, "was telling everyone, 'You're not alone.'"

———

ONE OF THE FIRST people to approach Genie at her car with an announcement was Anchorage's city manager, Robert Oldland. Under Anchorage's charter, the city manager was the town's chief administrative officer, with total authority over city employees, and Oldland seemed exquisitely comfortable claiming that responsibility now.

Oldland was a slim, youthful-looking man, but carried himself with the stoicism of a veteran technocrat. He was a relative newcomer to Alaska, but had worked in city governments for thirteen years, last serving as the city manager of Champaign, Illinois. He would spend the first frantic hours of the evening working out of his car in the Public Safety Building parking lot, radioing his staff and passing Genie handwritten bulletins to read over KENI. He worked methodically, and began by asking Genie to call in all his deputies: "City Manager Robert Oldland," she broadcast, "asks that the heads of all city departments report to him at the Public Safety Building."

Beyond that, however, any discernible chain of command was unraveling. The city had no protocol for this kind of emergency. Organizationally speaking, Anchorage was still an excruciatingly young place; before the earthquake, one old-timer said, Alaskans "hadn't even learned how to cope with the ordinary day-to-day stuff yet." Within fifteen minutes of the quake, city employees had started spontaneously converging on the Public Safety Building, but were basically just flinging themselves at whatever facet of the emergency materialized in front of them. Many began to gather around a handsome, blustering young man from the public works department named Dick Taylor.

Taylor had arrived in Anchorage from the East Coast two years earlier, after working in the steel and oil industries. He liked working for the city—a lot. In Anchorage, when he disagreed with his coworkers, he told them to go to hell, and they told him to go to hell right back—all with the mutual expectation that they would argue out their differences, reach a sensible resolution, and get back to work, without any hard feelings. "I have been, at times, a very unpopular fellow," Taylor admitted. But no one could question his effectiveness. A colleague praised him as a "honcho." When he had to make a decision, there was "no hesitation and no mental agony." He snapped his fingers and made it.

Taylor oversaw the construction and maintenance division of Anchorage's public works department; when something busted in a city-owned building, his crews fixed it. But Taylor saw living in Alaska as similar to living on a ship at sea: official job descriptions were insignificant; each person had to pitch in wherever he could. His men moonlighted constantly for other departments, and even helped city employees who were building their own homes check framing details or foundations. If someone needed a particular kind of bolt or screw, the guys in Taylor's shop would machine one for them, avoiding the hassle of mail-ordering the part from Outside.

Taylor had taken to calling his troops the "Do It Kids," because, he explained, "we have always operated on the theory that there are certain jobs that have to be done. There's nobody to do them but us." They were like hard hat–wearing Argonauts. They worked Saturdays. They drank their coffee at their desks or on the move. They worked efficiently and autonomously and, ideally, without generating lots of paperwork. "We bounce in," Taylor said. "We get it done. We move out. Sometimes we don't even ask if it's all right to do it. We just do it." Skirting the proper channels didn't bother him. Overzealousness didn't bother him. Consequences didn't bother him. The only thing that bothered Dick Taylor was not doing it—whatever "it" happened to be.

Taylor had been among the first people to show up at the Public Safety Building after the earthquake. People were flocking in all around him; the confusion was wild. A few cops had taken up posts at the police counter in the lobby to intercept the crowd, but Taylor noticed that the officers had been quickly swamped, and had few answers to offer the scrum of civilians anyway. Taylor took over, commandeering the desk for himself.

Taylor saw himself, essentially, as the guardian of Anchorage's built environment, so he divided a map of the city into a grid and sent out teams of people—his Do It Kids, plus volunteers who were walking in off the street—to survey each section for damage. They looked for gas leaks, broken water mains, and structural hazards, then shut off the utilities and barricaded any dangerous areas. From there, Taylor's work kept expanding; he apparently had a way of making himself a part of other people's decision-making processes. Within an hour of the quake, he found himself in the middle of a conversation between Chief Flanigan and Anchorage's city attorney, both of whom were worried about the potential for looting. Those wrecked shops and bars on Fourth Avenue were just lying there, exposed. Elsewhere, a bank and a government building, which housed a repository of public records, had similarly split open. Flanigan wanted those sites protected, but didn't have enough patrolmen to spare.

Taylor had an idea. He headed to the other end of the Public Safety Building, then returned carrying a heap of white bedsheets from the city jail. He tore the sheets into strips and asked a parking attendant to write POLICE on them with her lipstick. Taylor passed these around to some of the civilians in the lobby to wear as armbands and presented Flanigan with his class of new recruits.

The city attorney advised Flanigan that he'd need to deputize these men, but any kind of formal swearing in seemed a little too fussy, under the circumstances, so they agreed that anyone wearing an armband was now automatically an officer of the law. Flanigan assigned a group of these volunteers to each of his available patrolmen and sent the units to stand guard downtown and keep the peace. Anyone who wanted a gun was given one; few of them did. It eventually dawned on Taylor that he wasn't keeping track of how many volunteers he was dispatching. He didn't even know who these people were. It all looked highly unusual, though no one had time to step back and look at it.

The shock that overcame Anchorage in those first couple of hours, and the complete breakdown of all bureaucracy, had freed Taylor and his Do It Kids to behave as they always did, but even more flagrantly. They started requisitioning generators and fire axes, shovels, hard hats, rope, and other supplies from building contractors and shops downtown, leaving a note if they couldn't reach the owner. They heard about a stockpile of medical supplies across the street, broke into the building, and transferred them to Providence Hospital. They outfitted old fifty-gallon oil drums with plywood covers and distributed them downtown as makeshift toilets for the workers. Ultimately, Taylor would work at the Public Safety Building for fifty-four hours straight before getting any sleep, and seemed, at one point, to have entered a kind of hyperfocused flow state. He later described simultaneously carrying on four separate conversations with four different people and managing to make some sense of each one—and, moreover, observing himself pull off this feat, as though he were watching the episode from above. "This man has a question, this one has a request, this one has some information to offer and all are talking more or less at once," he said. "And you're picking it up! It's amazing. I've never had that experience before."

Eventually, people would start calling Taylor's counter in the Public Safety Building "Disaster Control." And the more the Disaster Control team accomplished, the more volunteers gravitated toward it, eager to contribute. One of Disaster Control's earliest and most active members was the man Genie had seen leading the improvised rescue of the woman from her crushed station wagon outside J. C. Penney. His name was Clarence Myers and, as it turned out, he'd been a resident of Alaska for exactly one day—an enlisted man who had just been shipped to the army base outside Anchorage from North Carolina. Later, when asked how the earthquake compared to being bombed in a war zone, Myers would explain, "There's no comparison." In a war, you can fight back. But with an earthquake, "you don't have no control. You can't do anything about it. It was just there. That's it."

Two hours had passed since the quake, long enough that the character of the crisis was beginning to change. The stunned helplessness was wearing off, and something new was taking shape. People were determined to understand what, exactly, had happened to Anchorage—and to regain control. "All I remember is mass confusion but an awful lot being accomplished," a clerk working in the Public Safety Building said.

Then, at eight o'clock, a military commander told Genie to broadcast a tidal wave warning.

6.

"A CITY OF PERMANENCE"

---

*HOW KENI GOT BACK
ON THE AIR*

W HEN THE EARTHQUAKE HIT, MOST OF KENI'S STAFF WAS at the station's downtown studio, inside the Fourth Avenue Theatre building, preparing for the six p.m. newscast.

The building was a wide, four-story concrete colossus built as a kind of extravagant civic centerpiece by its developer, Austin E. Lathrop. Cap Lathrop, as he was known, was said to be the Alaska Territory's first homegrown millionaire, an eccentric riverboat captain from Michigan who'd become a shipping, railroad, and mining tycoon after coming north in 1896. Lathrop had arrived almost two decades before the city of Anchorage was founded, but it wasn't long after the first smudge of tents appeared on the landscape that he started talking about building a world-class movie theater for the town one day. After stops and starts in construction, he opened his Fourth Avenue Theatre in the spring of 1947.

Everything about the building was lavish: the walnut-and-etched-glass double doors, the travertine floors and serpentine baseboards in the lobby, the masterful wood carvings that ran up every post, the winding staircase leading to the balcony, and the grand murals depicting the industrial history of Alaska, its wildlife, and icons of its natural beauty like Denali. Across the theater's arching, dark blue ceiling, pinhole lights traced the shape of the Big Dipper and the North Star—the same image on the Alaska state flag; when you leaned back in your velvet seat and looked up, it was like peering into the night sky. Above the theater, the building's upper floors were given over to the lushly carpeted offices of Lathrop's business empire, including the new radio station, KENI, which he would launch shortly after the building was finished. Bram, then Lathrop's young right-hand man, would emcee the station's opening ceremony for a live audience in the theater downstairs.

Architectural critics celebrated Lathrop's theater as "the culmination of the Art Deco movement in the US." Yet it was odd to find such a masterpiece in a half-built backwater in Alaska. Walking around Anchorage in that era, one man remembered, "you had the feeling that everything was temporary. We weren't all going to leave, but, you know . . . We might." The night the Fourth Avenue Theatre opened, there was still only a single paved road in all of Anchorage—the one the building was on. The theater's 960 seats could accommodate nearly a fifth of the entire town.

But if Lathrop's theater seemed out of place in Anchorage, that was because it wasn't actually built for the city it occupied. It was instead built for the city Anchorage might become, the one Lathrop felt its citizens deserved. The Fourth Avenue Theatre was meant to give the city a foothold in its own future, and call everyone toward that future. Covering its opening night, the *Anchorage Times* hailed the building as "a landmark in the transition of Anchorage from a frontier community to a city of permanence." Lathrop's theater, the newspaper wrote, signaled that Anchorage was no longer some provisional outpost, but a "city in which families live, work, play and die."

The vaulting, vertical marquee became a landmark of the city's central thoroughfare: 4TH AVENUE, it read, in lights. And the portion of Fourth Avenue that surrounded it became a kind of de facto town square. The theater was directly across the street from Anchorage's titanic white Federal Building and one block from city hall. It anchored the stretch of Fourth Avenue where the city gathered for parades, or to wave at the motorcades of every visiting VIP, like President Eisenhower or John Glenn. It was where the Fur Rendezvous sled-dog races started and ended every year and where, after being honored by a national civics organization in 1956, the city rigged a tremendous neon sign, high over Fourth Avenue, proclaiming Anchorage an "All-America City." And it was where, on June 30, 1958, much of Anchorage spontaneously assembled after word reached the city that Congress had voted to grant Alaska statehood. A forty-by-sixty-foot American flag was unspooled down the facade of the Federal Building, and a glittering new star was added into its ranks. Dignitaries shook hands in front of the flag; families posed for pictures. Then a bonfire as big as a building—built symbolically with forty-nine tons of wood—was lit in a nearby park, and people on horseback cantered around the blaze. Parents hoisted their children onto their shoulders to watch it burn, and Bram and Ty Clark rushed out of the Fourth Avenue Theatre building with microphones, circulating through the crowd to cover the entire madcap jamboree for KENI.

As the statehood celebration went on that afternoon and well into the evening, radio networks in the Lower 48 pleaded with KENI for on-the-scene reports from the nation's newest state. It was a bizarre but welcome sensation, one station staffer later wrote, to suddenly have all of America paying attention to Anchorage: "All of us at KENI and KENI-TV were awed with the realization that we had been in the center of the nation's top story. Yesterday we had been part of a network in the 'Frozen North.' We were very far away and probably lived in igloos," as far as most Americans were concerned. But now, "all of a sudden, we worked for the biggest radio and TV network in the biggest state in the union."

Bram had been a bullish booster of Alaskan statehood. His mentor, Cap Lathrop, on the other hand, had been one of the long campaign's loudest opponents; Cap liked things in Alaska fine the way they were, and didn't care to pay federal taxes. But by the time Alaska's star was added to the flag across the street from Lathrop's theater, he had been dead for nine years—cut nearly in two by a train car in an accident at one of his mines. Bram still kept a painting of his old boss hanging near his office upstairs in the Fourth Avenue Theatre, and for decades after Lathrop's death, people who worked at KENI would swear they saw his ghost in the building: a tall, white-haired figure in a three-piece suit. "I actually wouldn't believe it if I heard it," one man confessed a half century later, "except that I lived it myself."

SEVEN HUNDRED CHILDREN, all off from school for Good Friday, were packed into Lathrop's theater, watching a matinee of Walt Disney's *The Sword in the Stone,* when the building first shuddered at 5:36. The theater manager ordered his ushers to block the doors, worried about a stampede. Then he leapt onstage and shouted at the kids to stay calm.

Up on the third floor, in the radio booth, a KENI disc jockey stopped in the middle of reading a commercial, scrawled EARTHQUAKE! on the broadcast log, and fled. In the building's original radio studio, which Bram had converted into offices, two KENI salesmen were still at their desks. The room was palatial—large enough to host a symphony orchestra—and built, for better acoustics, as a so-called floating studio, with the floor on springs instead of fixed rigidly to the subfloor. This effectively turned the room into a giant trampoline during the quake. Then the door jammed, locking the two salesmen inside.

The majority of the staff was directly underneath the theater, busy preparing for the evening news in the KENI television studio in the basement. First the lights flickered, then the space went dark. Then the churning intensified and the screaming started.

The station's cameraman braced himself in the narrow hallway, arms and legs flung out to either wall. A petite film editor wrapped herself around one of the engineers, as though the man were a load-bearing column. Ty Clark scampered under a desk. "I really thought it was the end," he'd confess a few days later. "We felt like corks bobbing in the open sea." The motion was nauseating. And the longer the shaking went on, the more likely it seemed to everyone in the basement that the four-story structure above them would collapse. One man pictured the television tower on the roof piercing downward through each story like a massive drill press until it reached the basement, crushing everyone inside.

A few minutes into the earthquake, there was a brief lull, when the shaking slowed but did not stop, as though the earth had momentarily gotten distracted or bored. The staff in the basement made a break for the staircase, scurrying above-ground in a single-file line. But by the time they reconvened in the alley behind the building, the ground was roiling under them again.

They could see crumpled facades and fissures in all directions, including one blown-open edge of J. C. Penney, a block south. Charlie Gray, a part owner of the network and its head of engineering, was surprised anything was standing at all. As soon as the shaking stopped, Gray looked behind him to see which way KENI's television antenna had fallen over on the roof. But he found, impossibly, that it was still standing up straight; in fact, the entire Fourth Avenue Theatre seemed to be mostly intact. On the opposite side of the building, children were flooding out of the theater's front door. Gray surveyed the situation, trying to figure out what the station's next move should be. He was, by nature, fairly unflappable, and if he betrayed any emotion at that moment, it seemed to be satisfaction: Gray had arrived earlier that day to find an unfamiliar car parked in his usual parking spot. Now he saw that a brick chimney had fallen and broken apart on its hood.

With Bram off on his tour of Japan, Gray was in charge. He was forty-two, an imposing, somewhat affectless man, equally at home alone in the wilderness or with his head buried in the wiring of one of his machines. He appeared to prefer technology to people. Sometimes, when other KENI employees arrived at work in the morning, they'd find Gray with his sleeves rolled up in the middle of some project—repairing, upgrading, tinkering— and get the impression he'd been there all night. Eventually, Gray would completely renovate KENI's studio; when he finished, one colleague would remember, Gray hauled a large bag of sand into the next room and fired at it with his .38. This was his method for checking that the walls were sufficiently soundproof.

Gray had lived in Alaska since 1955 and had helped build a significant share of the state's communications infrastructure— literally installed it with his hands. Recently, he and two of his engineering protégés at KENI had been climbing grizzly bear– riddled mountains across south-central Alaska to set up diesel- powered translators, which Gray had built himself, to bounce the station's television signal down to tiny towns in the bush. Everywhere Gray and his engineers went, they were regarded as Prometheans, bringing each dull and isolated settlement the life- sustaining flicker of *Bonanza* and Dick Van Dyke. "Any one of us could have been elected mayor in one of those towns," Gray's fifteen-year-old gofer, Michael Janecek, would later remember. They were told they'd saved marriages.

Even as KENI and its competitors pushed television deeper into Alaska, radio retained its relevance in the state. In 1964, many Alaskans still lived speckled across the wilderness, uncon- nected by any common infrastructure. Only radio could shoot through the empty space between them and close that distance. Every Sunday night, KENI continued a long-standing tradition of reading personal messages from ordinary people over the air, passing information to friends and family in remote regions of the state where phone lines hadn't yet reached: *Martha, your sister had a baby. Mike, the washing machine you ordered arrived from Seattle; come into town and pick it up.* They called this service the Mukluk Telegraph. (The word "Mukluk," a name for the sealskin boots made by Alaska Natives, was a common shorthand for everything authentically Alaskan.) Children growing up in remote villages or on family homesteads learned to be very still and not say a word while the Mukluk Telegraph was airing; there would be consequences if a kid made her parents miss a message.

Standing behind the Fourth Avenue Theatre building after the quake, Gray understood that everyone in Anchorage would be instinctually switching on their transistor radios, looking for information. Even if he could manage to get KENI's usual television broadcast up and running, it was unclear if anyone had the electricity necessary to watch it. He turned to his colleagues and said, "Let's get radio on the air!" Then he and one of his engineering sidekicks got in his car and bolted for KENI's radio transmitter across town.

The transmitter was housed in a smaller building three miles away, on a wooded hillside above a saltwater marsh known as Bootlegger's Cove. The station's three-hundred-foot radio tower was anchored in the wetland. Normally, it was an easy drive from Fourth Avenue. But Gray and the others who followed him found themselves groping for alternate routes around impassable cracks in the road and occasionally dragging the bottom of their cars on serrated, upheaved plates of pavement. When they arrived, they discovered the top forty feet of the antenna had snapped off; the broken segment was dangling upside down alongside the remaining portion. Gray did not consider this an insurmountable problem. He could shift the tuning on the transmitter and still make the thing work. Maybe he could eke out enough signal to cover the town.

The men fired up the generators and controls in the transmitter building. Before long, Ty Clark arrived and started warming up the KENI Kamper, the station's mobile studio, which was parked outside. Ty lowered the needle on a classical record and let it play as a test: when the music came through on the radio, they'd know they were on the air.

Clark seemed rattled; he preferred it when the earth stood still. Gray's young gofer, Michael Janecek, would later claim that when the quake was over, he'd been tasked with coaxing Ty out from under the desk where he'd taken shelter in the basement of the Fourth Avenue Theatre building. Now, alone in the Kamper, waiting for Gray and his engineers to retune the transmitter, it's possible Clark started drinking. But true to form, he managed to pull himself together—to become Ty Clark—the second the signal was up and his microphone went live. "This is KENI, 550 on your dial," he said over the music, "returning to the air on an emergency basis."

The problem was, Ty didn't have a lot to say. None of the men at the transmitter had solid information about the extent of the disaster. Ty did his best to spout general warnings and post-earthquake advice, then rigged up KENI's rhombic antenna to see what he could glean, secondhand, from civilian and military ham radio chatter. But virtually the entirety of what he knew for sure, and could report with any credibility, was merely what he and the others had observed on their frantic drive to the transmitter from downtown. "Genie was more the reporter," Janecek explained—the one who'd dig out the details of whatever was going on. "Ty was more the talent who'd sit there and say it."

Fortunately, it wasn't long before the men at the transmitter heard Genie's voice, cutting in from her driveway, ready to make her first report. "From then on," Gray would remember, "we were in business out there."

TWO HOURS LATER, around eight thirty, Gray pulled into the Public Safety Building parking lot towing the KENI Kamper behind his car, and immediately got snarled in a jumble of traffic and idling emergency vehicles. A crowd of people gathered around the little trailer and hoisted it clear off the ground, then walked it to a spot near the door.

Gray went to work quickly, unbundling the equipment inside the Kamper to get it operational so KENI could start broadcasting from the scene. Meanwhile, at various points around Anchorage, the rest of the station's staff was settling into the haphazard arrangement from which they would cover the disaster for the rest of the night. The sound of an enterprising, if slightly blundering, newscast was starting to take shape on the air, even though most of the people talking—everyone except Genie—still had relatively little definitive news to report.

The Fourth Avenue Theatre building was back online, running off a diesel generator housed in the basement. A few broadcasters were wedged into the cramped radio booth on the third floor, relaying damage reports radioed in by other staffers from their cars or passed on by ordinary civilians who were walking through the front door of the theater and up the stairs. Many of those arriving were worried about family members in other parts of town, and had come to KENI hoping to get more information from the announcers. But each had information to contribute as well. The upheaval in Anchorage was omnipresent and incomprehensible; everyone had seen something that counted as news.

Early on, two KENI announcers had agreed to play down the unnerving likelihood of mass casualties while on the air. Instead, they would insist to listeners that Anchorage would be living with total uncertainty about the death toll until the morning, when the city could be searched in daylight. Now, however, one announcer at the studio was trying to tactfully summarize a vague but harrowing secondhand report about the landslide in Turnagain from a man who'd shown up at the station looking for his sister-in-law. "There's one section of Turnagain which we understand is pretty badly devastated," the announcer said. "It sounds as though there are some homes in the crevasses down there. As far as I know, no one has checked these homes to see if anyone is in there and needs help." Then the announcer called on Ty Clark, who'd stayed behind at Bootlegger's Cove to man the transmitter with another broadcaster: Had they heard anything about Turnagain out there, the man asked Ty. But by that point, Ty seemed to have opened up the transmitter building as an impromptu shelter; he was taking in neighbors. A dog barked loudly in the background, and a woman started laughing, and no one heard the question.

Genie, meanwhile, was being inundated with detailed and credible firsthand reports from officials inside the Public Safety Building. The first survey teams that Dick Taylor had dispatched were starting to report back, feeding Genie updates to broadcast from her car. The picture she was assembling was grim; at times, her voice quavered with disbelief. After one update from fire chief Burns, Genie got on the air and exclaimed, "I have gotten word from an official source that the big apartment building that was under construction just behind St. Mary's Residence, there at Ninth and L Street, just completely *collapsed*! It just fell down to the ground and there's nothing left standing."

Another KENI announcer, Nat Brook, had arrived to help Genie. The two were sitting next to each other in her car, passing her VHF handset back and forth. Brook was a newcomer to Anchorage, a sharp-looking but paunchy young man with a faint mustache and hip horn-rimmed glasses who had, hands down, the smoothest, most sonorous radio voice on KENI's staff; his on-air nickname was "the Babbling Brook." But now Brook was floundering. Like Genie, he'd already put in a full day of work that Friday, and though his voice still sounded soulful and warm, his mind was struggling to furnish it with any meaningful combinations of words. "You sit here and you evaluate and talk to people," Brook began stammering, as feedback shrieked from his microphone. "We don't know how many people have been *killed* in this thing!" he finally burst out.

Genie felt bad for Brook. It was clear that the scotch he'd drunk earlier, to steady himself, was wearing off. And he soon gave up entirely, figuring he was better off going home to sleep so he could relieve whoever was still standing in the morning. Genie, however, stayed put. And it wasn't long after she'd outlasted Brook that Gray ran a long microphone cable from the KENI Kamper into the Public Safety Building and managed to get her broadcasting from inside the exact nerve center of the recovery operation. Genie Chance was alone in the middle of things again.

7.

"THE WORST THING
I'VE EVER SEEN"

GENIE KEEPS TALKING

"THIS IS GENIE CHANCE, REPORTING FROM INSIDE THE Public Safety Building," she began from her new post at the police counter, right next to the dispatcher and Disaster Control. The scuttle and din of everyone working around her bled into her microphone as she spoke.

The city manager swept through, ordering her to put out a call for diesel fuel. A public health official stood over her shoulder while she repeated his instructions for purifying snow for drinking water. An Anchorage police lieutenant requested that an electrician hurry to Presbyterian Hospital. While Genie made one announcement, others zipped onto the counter in front of her. "Providence Hospital needs six cases of six-inch plaster of Paris," she said. "All electricians and plumbers at Fort Richardson, please go to Building 700 immediately."

Chief Flanigan told Genie that she was now effectively the

city's public information officer: it would be up to her to decide whether to put the information and requests people passed to her over the air. It was stressful; the responsibility was daunting. The highways out of Anchorage appeared to be impassable. The airport and railways were closed. Genie understood that everyone would be trapped together inside this crippled city for the foreseeable future—in the snow, in the dark, with no electricity, in below-freezing temperatures. Under those circumstances, she felt, "mass hysteria would have meant total destruction." She continued to worry about the possibility, even the inevitability, of such a breakdown of civil society, and felt it was her responsibility to stave off that mayhem.

She found herself scrutinizing each new bit of information that reached her: Was it knowledge the public could handle, or would it generate panic? And how much could she withhold before listeners turned suspicious and stopped trusting her? It also seemed possible that the accuracy of any given piece of information could have slipped, as messages made their way from the far corners of Anchorage into the building like so many games of telephone. Lots of people bringing Genie messages were volunteers, after all—ordinary citizens, many of whom seemed no more qualified to handle such a crisis than Genie was—and everyone was working so quickly that much of the knowledge circulating was imperfect or incomplete. Earlier, for example, the city attorney informed Genie that the municipal court building could be opened up as a shelter for those who'd evacuated their homes, but also asked her who was in charge of inspecting the structure to ensure it was safe. Genie had no idea. It was unsettling, in retrospect, that Anchorage's city attorney was asking her.

She wondered how she had wound up in this role. Shouldn't authority figures, like the police chief and the city manager, be talking over the radio themselves? The public might trust those men's voices more than hers. The previous June, Genie had covered the crash of a Northwest Orient Airlines flight chartered by the military to transport nearly a hundred soldiers and their family members from Washington State to Anchorage. The plane had gone down in the ocean en route, killing everyone aboard. Genie had reported on the search effort tirelessly for three days. But when a correspondent for NBC's national newscast called KENI from New York, looking to air its coverage of the crash, he asked the station to send a male reporter to redo all of Genie's interviews. It felt too unorthodox, or unserious, for a woman's voice to inform the American people of a tragedy. Only after taking it up with his bosses did the correspondent agree to put Genie on the air.

Yet here she was in the middle of a disaster—without any instructions or guidelines. People kept coming into the building and hurrying straight to Genie's counter, entrusting her with the starkest damage reports and updates. "I don't know why," she later explained; merely standing behind a microphone seemed to give her a sufficient air of authority. As the night wore on and information kept raining in sideways, everyone seemed to move around the building so quickly, "with this brilliant, tense look in their eyes," Genie said—"everybody doing a job." Then, around nine thirty, a sturdy-looking, middle-aged man in the uniform of a high-ranking military officer walked calmly out of that feverish blur of bodies and beamed a small, confident smile in Genie's direction. He sat down beside her and watched patiently as she stood talking, waiting his turn.

The man seemed to occupy a different atmosphere than everyone else in the lobby, to have coasted toward her in a small depressurized pocket of his own. Genie knew many of the commanding officers at the two military bases outside Anchorage. Together, Elmendorf Air Force Base and the army's Fort Richardson housed about 7,500 troops; the bases were part of the fabric of local news that Genie reported on every day. Once she'd even tagged along on an Arctic training exercise, deep in the backcountry, trundling behind a line of soldiers as they crossed rope bridges over terrifyingly deep ravines. The previous summer, she'd called in a favor and arranged for Wins and his friend to launch a model rocket on an actual firing range at Fort Richardson, with an ordnance officer supervising and a fire engine standing by, for effect. Still, this officer at the Public Safety Building was unfamiliar to Genie. Finally, when she could spare a second, she turned and asked him, "Who are you?"

"I'm Carroll," he said.

Major General Thomas P. Carroll was adjutant general of Alaska's National Guard. He happened to be overseeing a training encampment north of Anchorage that week and had immediately ordered his soldiers onto trucks and led them into town. "I have one hundred fifty men here," he told Genie. They were waiting outside, ready to pitch in.

The military had been working with the city since earlier that evening, deploying drivers and vehicles and tanks of potable water—whatever resources it could. Still, something about Carroll's appearance at the Public Safety Building felt viscerally reassuring for Genie, and seemed to generate the first surge of genuine relief she'd experienced since finding her two younger children unharmed at home. Carroll just projected competence.

The man had once single-handedly gunned down eighteen ambushing Nazis at once; he was prepared to tackle this mess, too.

Carroll told Genie he needed her help as well. He was looking for a way to reach Juneau, the state capital. Lines of communication were still scarce, and Carroll wanted official permission from the governor to keep his guardsmen on duty. Genie told him to go out to the parking lot and find a ham radio operator named Walt Sauerbier.

Among the many citizens of Anchorage who'd leapt into action that evening was a small legion of amateur ham radio operators. Anchorage was said to have more hams per capita than any other state at the time; it was an amusing hobby to get people through the winter, and an easy way for Alaskans to stay in touch with family Outside. A number of hams in the city had previously organized themselves into a preparedness group and practiced emergency communications during nuclear war simulations. After the quake, many flocked to the parking lot of the Public Safety Building or took up posts at other critical locations around Anchorage, hunkering in their radio-equipped cars to function as a kind of substitute telephone service. The man Genie had hooked up with, Walt Sauerbier, had been among the first to show up. He was a sixty-one-year-old mechanic who'd been driving around, idly chatting on his mobile unit with someone in Hawaii, when the quake struck. His call sign was KL7ESR. His QSL card, which he mailed to everyone he made radio contact with, featured a polar bear yanking a seal out of an ice hole and a cartoon Eskimo paddling a kayak. He would work at the Public Safety Building, sending and receiving messages, for sixteen hours straight.

Carroll went outside to find Sauerbier and returned to the

police counter a few minutes later. He told Genie he'd reached the governor's office, and everything was squared away: Carroll's National Guardsmen were now officially at Anchorage's disposal. Genie reported this news over KENI, then pulled Carroll in for an interview on the air.

"You got here so quickly!" she began. "You got your group right in the spirit and you arrived at the Public Safety Building in such short order."

Well, Carroll explained, it was lucky that the earthquake struck during the Guard's annual two-week training at Camp Denali. "This is the one time of year when all of the guardsmen, from approximately seventy-five villages and cities in Alaska, are here in Anchorage," he said. Many of Carroll's men were Alaska Natives from remote villages around the state: so-called Eskimo Scouts, drawn from the Aleut, Athabascan, Inupiat, Tlingit, and other ethnic groups that had been disproportionately represented in Alaska's National Guard since World War II, when the military armed and organized Native men to protect the territory's coastlines from a potential Japanese invasion. "This was our last day of camp," Carroll said. "We were all starting for home at midnight tonight—though those plans have been canceled."

He spoke into Genie's microphone with dry, unbothered stoicism. Genie, meanwhile, kept marveling at the serendipity of the situation. It comforted her; after the savage arbitrariness of the earthquake, here was a small coincidence swinging in Anchorage's favor. She was eager to spread some of that comfort around the city. "Well, we certainly are grateful that your men are here."

"Anything we can do to help, we will make it available," Carroll told her.

You could imagine that this, finally, was the sort of well-trained and unflappable authority figure Genie had expected to find at the Public Safety Building all along, someone who was *supposed* to carry the monumental responsibility that seemed, instead, to be dispersing, haphazardly, onto the shoulders of so many ordinary people like herself. Carroll appeared impervious to the ruthless disorder that had swallowed Anchorage. Four weeks later, however, that randomness would rear up again and claim him: Carroll would plummet into Prince William Sound aboard a C-123 twin-engine cargo plane after taking off from the town of Valdez. He had just dropped off the governor to examine the earthquake and tsunami damage there. All four people on board were killed.

Carroll left behind a wife and four children. One of them, Thomas C. Carroll, would eventually become adjutant general of the Alaska National Guard like his dad. In 1992, he too would die in an airplane crash, in another twin-engine National Guard plane—this time on approach to Juneau. It flew into a mountain.

THE MILITARY WAS STILL projecting that a tsunami might shoot up Cook Inlet and strike the city of Anchorage. Tidal waves had already thrashed the towns of Valdez, Seward, and Kodiak, and the villages of Kaguyak, Old Harbor, and Chenega, and would continue radiating outward from Alaska all night, barging down the coast. The water shattered a small town in British Columbia, wiped out a bridge in Washington State, and carried houses away in Oregon, as well as drowning four children who'd been camping on a beach there with their parents. The town of Crescent City, California, at the Oregon border, sustained a direct hit:

a series of four waves, escalating into a monstrous wall of water, which leveled the downtown and killed eleven people. The wave action in the Pacific would still be ferocious enough, as it traveled south, to sink boats in a marina near San Francisco and damage a dock in Los Angeles—until, finally, twenty-two and a half hours later, the last of its energy petered out in a few four-foot-high swells slapping the banks of western Antarctica at the bottom of the world.

In the hour since Genie had first broadcast a tsunami alert for Anchorage, two fire trucks had been patrolling the city's coastal neighborhoods, blasting orders to evacuate. Now a police dispatcher pressed Genie to warn Anchorage again; another radio station, he explained, had been mistakenly announcing that the danger had passed. Genie leaned into her microphone. "Please," she warned, "any of you in the lowland areas, get out of the lowland areas and head for the hills! Please, don't be overconfident!" There was pleading in her voice, as though, if she said it forcefully enough, it might repel that other, incorrect information off the airwaves.

Other times, when the station's broadcasters clicked over to her for an update, she tried to smooth the frantic churn of announcements into something more conversational, interviewing more people who, like Major General Carroll, passed by her post in the building. "I have here a very interesting person who can tell us about some of the damage out at International Airport," Genie said at one point. Then she stumbled clumsily over the name of the Scandinavian Airlines sales manager standing next to her—Chris von Imhof—and brought him on the air.

Von Imhof told Genie and her listeners that he'd been at his office, on the second floor of the airport, when the earthquake started. He described smashing a window open with his foot, then leaping out of it just in time to turn and watch the control tower behind him "crack like a match" and crumble. Von Imhof and several others immediately rushed toward the wreckage to dig people out. It sounded exactly like the scene Genie had witnessed outside Penney's. They cooperated to ratchet up the rubble on jacks and had been clawing into the debris for at least a half an hour, von Imhof said, before they managed to extricate the first survivors: a waitress and cook from the flight kitchen. Another man emerged bleeding badly from his head. Another was "completely covered with rocks." They found at least one fatality, von Imhof explained. The body was gnashed too tightly into the ruins for them to recover it.

"Altogether, when I left, it just looked worse than after the war," von Imhof said. "It's just—it's a terrible mess. It's the worst thing I've ever seen."

As awful as this sounded, the same truth held: information was a form of comfort. Each stunned, eyewitness account on the radio that night appeared to help people in Anchorage find the contours of this sinister abstraction they were living through— and to locate their places in it. For nearly five minutes, the earthquake had overpowered everyone. But now so many stories, like von Imhof's, described people switching back on and spontaneously helping one another—reclaiming their roles, collectively, as protagonists in the disaster. "Anchorage has sustained a large amount of damage," Genie would eventually tell her listeners, "and it's been a shattering blow to a very proud people. However, many of us have enjoyed—actually, taken a great deal of *pride* in—seeing the way the people of Anchorage can rise to the occasion."

Before letting von Imhof go, Genie asked him if all his own employees were accounted for and safe. Yes, he explained, everyone was fine. They were over at the hospital now, donating blood.

8.

"THE CHANCE FAMILY
IS ALL RIGHT"

———

*MILD RELIEF, THEN CREEPING
UNEASE BEFORE DAYBREAK*

THE CITY FELT SEALED IN, AS THOUGH IN A TERRARIUM. Nearly six hours after the quake, communication with the Outside was still sporadic and disjointed. A kind of claustrophobia was setting in. "It was terribly dark and dismal," Genie would write. "We were living in a world unto ourselves—one that had suddenly, and without warning, turned topsy-turvy."

Occasionally, the KENI announcers found themselves in the awkward position of trying to extract a fuller picture of what had happened to their own city from snippets of news they picked up from ham radio operators in the Lower 48. Some of what they heard was obviously and horrifyingly exaggerated: radio stations in San Francisco and Vancouver apparently believed that Anchorage was completely flattened; elsewhere, the city was being described as overtaken by a sea of flames. But KENI's staff was largely helpless to correct those rumors, and to stamp out any panic or despair. They were isolated. They could only shout into the sky.

Charlie Gray, KENI's chief engineer, had gone to see about solving this problem. After positioning the Kamper in the Public Safety Building parking lot, and Genie at her microphone inside, Gray and a colleague had taken off for Government Hill, on the northern edge of Anchorage, to check on the Alaska Communications System, or ACS: the military hookup that ordinarily connected Anchorage to other cities in Alaska and the outside world. It was through ACS that phones in Anchorage were patched in to long-distance calls, and that news flowed into the city from the Lower 48 over the Associated Press wire, spooling out of the Teletype machine at the KENI studios.

Much of the neighborhood surrounding the ACS building had been mangled by the quake. Inside, two 15-ton battery plants had turned over and sparked an electrical fire. But Gray walked in to discover that the air force's engineers already had the operation up and running again. Some people in the building were even making long-distance phone calls. Moreover, they told Gray, they'd discovered that the hardline connecting KENI's downtown studio to the ACS building was still intact and functional. The engineers had already taken it upon themselves to start relaying that night's radio broadcast, through their statewide hookup, to KENI's sister station in Fairbanks.

This was incredible news. Until then, the announcers at KENI weren't even certain how much of their own city could hear them talking; in reality, they were being heard three hundred and fifty miles away from Anchorage, in Fairbanks, too. And because the damage in Fairbanks was minimal and phone lines were operable, they presumed that people there would be passing on their reporting to the Lower 48 as well.

Gray fired up the shortwave radio unit in his car to tell the rest of his staff. KENI's lead announcer, Bob Fleming, was anchoring the broadcast from downtown when Gray's voice broke in on him abruptly and wound up live on the air. "You'll be interested to know, Bob," Gray explained, "that ACS is feeding Fairbanks, simulcasting the bulk of our broadcast to Fairbanks right now."

The relief this revelation generated was instantaneous; it pricked the intolerable loneliness that had stretched tight over Anchorage like a lid. But Gray didn't care to pause and bask in having delivered it. As soon as he was done talking, he hung up on Fleming with a loud, brusque *clunk*.

"Boy, when he stops, he stops," Fleming said with a chortle. "Oh, that's wonderful. That's really good to hear. "

Genie didn't appear to be tracking what was happening on the air when she was off-mic. Her work at the Public Safety Building had only gotten more hectic as the night went on and, even an hour or two later, she'd seem unaware that their broadcast was reaching beyond Anchorage, to the outside world. The Outside, however, started reaching her. Around two a.m., Genie picked up the phone that was ringing on the police counter in front of her and was surprised to find a man in Nebraska on the other end. "This is Bill Addison," he said, from radio station KOIL in Omaha. "Will you give me a news story?"

Addison explained to Genie that he'd been waiting on the phone for forty-five minutes, dealing with four different operators, before finally finding this open line. It was deeply comforting for Genie to hear a voice from Outside. Other long-distance calls had started reaching the Public Safety Building erratically by then; earlier, a police officer had even handed Genie a phone call from London's *News of the World* newspaper, but she could only offer a bit of basic information before a dozen dismayed city officials and volunteers had clustered in front of her desk with urgent announcements to broadcast. Genie had excused herself and hung up. Right now, she said, her responsibility had to be to Anchorage, not to London.

This time, though, when Addison asked for an eyewitness account, Genie found she had some breathing room and unloaded the entire story on him. "To begin with," she said, "it was exactly five thirty-six p.m. Alaska standard time when the first little motion was felt. I myself was sitting in my car, stopped at a traffic light, about two blocks from the city police station. My first thought, as I hit my brake to stop at the red light, was that I had a blowout. But I realized the car was continuing to rock harder and harder. And I realized the other cars around me were rocking, too."

Genie told him everything. She described Wins running back to her, screaming that the J. C. Penney building was crumbling; recounted the moment she'd discovered that one half of Fourth Avenue had "fallen into a hole"; relayed the tentative reports from Turnagain where, she was told, "most of the houses are a mass of nothing"; and summarized news she'd gathered from elsewhere in the state. Genie spoke quickly and diligently, continuing for nearly forty minutes before she was called away from the phone. Before hanging up, she reached for a striking, uplifting conclusion: "Anchorage, Alaska, was injured on Good Friday," Genie told the reporter, "but tomorrow is another day, and the people of Anchorage, Alaska, are banding together to save those who need help, offer housing to those whose homes have been swept away from them, and offer condolences and assistance to those who have lost their loved ones."

SHORTLY AFTER THE CALL with Omaha, Genie's colleague Bob Fleming paged her from the KENI studio downtown, asking for another on-air update from the Public Safety Building. Fleming was a genial, square-jawed man of forty-two who hosted KENI's morning show; he was among the most popular radio personalities in Anchorage—a local celebrity. He'd come to Alaska after working for several big-market stations in the Lower 48, including one in Los Angeles, where he'd once interviewed Bing Crosby and taught Jimmy Stewart to bowl. There was a photo floating around of Fleming with his arm around Elvis in Spokane.

Still, Fleming was modest. He came off as even-tempered and easy to get along with; the other men at KENI were among his closest friends. His on-air persona might be described as completely self-assured and mildly bumbling. Earlier that Friday night, he had reported on KENI that a police car was driving through downtown warning people to evacuate because another earthquake was imminent. A colleague leapt on the air and told Fleming firmly, "Bob, there is no way to predict an earthquake whatsoever. This is one of these rumors that we've absolutely got to stop right now." Fleming agreed; yes, of course, he said, "this is my thought, too—that there's no way to predict an earthquake." Fleming's point, he claimed, was merely that someone ought to find this policeman who was driving around and stop him from inciting panic. And maybe that *had* been Fleming's point, though it didn't sound terribly convincing.

In the two hours since Gray had revealed that their broadcast was reaching Fairbanks, the mood on KENI had depressurized. Fleming sounded looser, chattier—like he was doing his regular morning show—and he and Ty Clark and the other men were going around on the air, trading their own stories of the quake. Fleming explained that he'd been in the basement cafeteria of Presbyterian Hospital, waiting for his wife, Dolly, to finish her nursing shift, when everything smashed to the ground: dishes, silverware, coffeemakers, the Coke machine. "It looked like the entire basement of that concrete building was on a swing," Fleming said. He grabbed two nurses and pulled them into a doorway. One screamed at him that she needed to run to her children, but Fleming kept her pinned against the doorjamb—clearly, in his mind, protecting her and chivalrously squelching her panic. Still, the whole experience unnerved him. Many decades later, Dolly Fleming would sit with her cat across from a framed portrait of her husband—the same photograph that had run with Bob's obituary in the local paper seven years earlier—and recall that the earthquake had disrupted the equilibrium of both of them so severely that, even weeks later, they would get dizzy whenever they leaned over the sink to brush their teeth.

By the time Fleming paged Genie, he sounded so chatty and relaxed that he might as well have been in Omaha himself. It was as though he were patching in from an altogether different, more tranquil universe than the one Genie had been spinning in for hours. "Is Genie there?" he said suavely on-air. "Genie, could I have a conversation with you?"

Fleming was curious if she'd heard any reports from the Aleutian Islands. And, all at once, Genie whipped herself back into a rigorous monologue like the one she'd performed on the phone with Omaha, offering Fleming and KENI's listeners the spare and uncertain information she'd learned about the destruction of communities on the island of Kodiak. It was all miserable and shocking—"We have had one report that Kodiak was virtually demolished," she said at one point—and Fleming listened silently as Genie detailed tsunamis and evacuations.

The problem with Genie's report, however, was that Kodiak Island is not part of the Aleutian chain. Kodiak Island is just southwest of Anchorage; the Aleutians are the long string of islands all the way at the western reaches of the state, nearly eight hundred miles away.

"Genie," Fleming started in, "there's an old saying that says, 'Never underestimate the power of a woman.' And I never will again, because you have just done what nobody else has been able to do: You have just added a new link to the Aleutian chain! Kodiak has just now been added to the Aleutian chain!"

Maybe it was a sign of how acclimated people were getting to the direness of the emergency at that point in the night: the sarcasm and chauvinism of ordinary life were sliding obliquely back in. Fleming let a beat of silence pass, as though it were Genie's turn to talk. She didn't talk. He said, "I'm teasing you, Genie . . . Are you there?"

"I'm telling you!" Genie said good-humoredly. "That earthquake gave me a jolt! I've been on the air ever since it hit at five thirty-six, and—now I feel a slight tremor once again! Either that, or I'm getting a little bit dizzy from lack of sleep."

A short while later, Fleming tried to page Genie at the Public

Safety Building for another update but couldn't reach her. "Maybe she's mad at me for teasing her about the Aleutian chain," he said over the air, to no one in particular.

A staffer in the Kamper interjected, "I wouldn't blame her a bit."

"I wouldn't either," Fleming said. He sounded momentarily defeated. It was very late. "Actually, I don't know why I do things like that," he said. "I just hate myself."

SOMETHING ELSE WAS HAPPENING that Friday night—a thread of this story that, as time passed, would come to feel almost like folklore. Everywhere in Anchorage, a certain latent energy was being released, a force equal and opposite to that of the earthquake itself.

At the Public Safety Building, ordinary people who were separated from their children or other family members began stumbling up to Genie's counter and asking her for help. They arrived anxious, or solemn, or outright distraught.

"They were heartbreaking," Genie remembered. All night, without the haziest sense of the disaster's death toll, any person in Anchorage with whom you hadn't been in touch directly was considered a potential casualty. The people converging on Genie were desperate to know if somebody they loved was safe, or to let a loved one know that *they* were safe—to find one another, to shout across their fractured city in the dark. They hoped that Genie might amplify their voices with her own.

Among the first to arrive at her counter, around nine o'clock, was a couple from Turnagain. "Mr. and Mrs. Fisher have lost their children," Genie said, relaying their message over the air.

"They can't find them. They said they will be waiting at the home of Charles Ball." More people came. And, as the telephone lines in the Public Safety Building reopened, many more called in as well, quickly overwhelming the switchboards. "Mel Fleeger," Genie said, "we've received a call here at the fire station. Mel Fleeger who lives on Eighty-Sixth Avenue: The fire department dispatcher said it sounded like children calling, and they said please come home.

"Howard Forbes would like it to be known that he will be at Mike Whitmore's. A message to Kenneth Saddler: Mrs. Saddler is fine. Kenneth Saddler is out in the bush and listens on a transistor radio. Mrs. Saddler is fine. A message to Walter Hart: Lee Hart is fine. Jim Murphy and Bill Sarville at Point Hope: your families are A-OK. The Boy Scout troop that went overnight to McHugh Creek—they left at four o'clock yesterday, due back tomorrow: Bill Noble would like to get a message as to their whereabouts, if they are all right.

"We have a message here from Northwest Airlines, saying the crew cannot locate stewardess Beverly Johns. Beverly Johns is requested to contact them at the YMCA building.

"A message to Clyde Wythe at Homer: Your daughter is OK. Damage at Fourth and Cordova is light. Signed, Melba.

"We have another message that Bob Deloach is all right. He's been working here at the Public Safety Building all along—his family doesn't know where he is. Bob Deloach is all right.

"We have a message here to Ruby Meigs and family, and also Bethany Jones and family: Ted Kepenach and family are all all right and at home.

"We have received a call from Whitehorse, Yukon Territory, from Bill Tamarin Sr. and Mrs. Tamarin. He informed us that he and his wife left Anchorage yesterday en route to the South 48. They would like their daughter, Mary Chapman of 825 I Street, or their son, Bill Tamarin Jr., who stays at the YMCA, to call them collect at the Cathay Hotel, room 111.

"We have received a call from Joe Fernbeck who said that he'd gotten word on his radio from the oil crews at Beluga and Tyonek. They want their families to know that they are all OK. They have received no damage and there were no injuries. However, the men in the oil crews at Beluga and Tyonek would like to get some word about their families to find out if their families here in Anchorage came through this earthquake all right.

"We have word here that Mary Sweet is asked to contact her mother. Mother is at home. Mary Sweet's mother is looking for her, and the mother is at home.

"We have a message about an elderly lady at 216 East Eighth Avenue who lives alone. We have no name on her, but we do have a request for somebody in that neighborhood to please check and see if the sweet lady is all right."

It wasn't just Genie through whom these messages were flowing. People were knocking on the door of the KENI Kamper in the parking lot and walking into KENI's studio on Fourth Avenue with announcements for the other broadcasters to put on the air, too. KENI's rival station in Anchorage, KFQD, was inundated as well.

Jack Thornton wanted to know who was looking after Georgia Sparks. If Mrs. Martha Walker was listening, could she please report in. Basil Hanson wanted to alert any available rescue crews that a party of twelve people were southwest of Anchorage, at the air strip at Lake Clark. Captain Smith and Harold Honeyball were safe, asleep in an office at the Fourth Avenue

Theatre building. Anyone knowing the whereabouts of John Manders, please call. The family of seven-year-old Michael Baskett was looking for him. A few minutes later, Genie reported that little Mike Baskett was waiting there at the Public Safety Building, safe and sound, with twelve other friends; she would gather a complete list of their names, she said, and broadcast it as soon as she could.

Meanwhile, that first couple from Turnagain continued to check back with her at the counter. "Mr. and Mrs. Dick Fisher are still here at the police headquarters at Sixth and C, waiting for any word of their children," Genie said. "Their home went off the bluff. They're out there in the Turnagain area, where we understand a great deal of damage took place."

Everything about the undertaking was instinctual: that the people of Anchorage would turn to KENI, but also that the staff of KENI would throw open their airwaves for them. It was just like transmitting messages to remote homesteads in the bush over the Mukluk Telegraph every Sunday night, only now it was the city people who were suddenly unreachable and disconnected from one another; Alaska's largest metropolis had been reduced to a wilderness.

"An estimated four thousand messages were carried on KENI in the three critical days following the temblor," Bram would write. They came in quick. Late on that Good Friday night, a staffer at the studio could be heard pleading, off-mic, for some airtime to broadcast seventy-five messages he'd collected. In the time it took the announcer to segue to him, he'd taken a seventy-sixth.

Once KENI's sister stations started picking up its signal, staff members in Fairbanks and Juneau began relaying these messages to the Lower 48 by phone. And around Anchorage, people converged on the homes of amateur ham radio operators, the same way they were swarming to Anchorage's commercial radio stations, asking them to reach their families Outside and let them know they were safe. Walt Sauerbier, the ham operator Genie had been working with, would finally decamp from the Public Safety Building parking lot on Saturday morning, catch forty-five minutes of sleep, and then spend the next eighteen to twenty hours transmitting messages from his living room for whoever showed up at his home. ("It got to be a regular Grand Central Station up there at the house," Sauerbier said.) Another ham operator claimed to have relayed six hundred messages for friends and neighbors before he finally quit sometime the following Wednesday or Thursday. Several others worked forty-eight hours straight. "Five men stuck by their mobile units all night Friday," one report noted, even though "their homes had been destroyed."

Details would eventually surface, too, about the Outside hams who were receiving these messages from Alaska and disseminating them across the country. In Seattle, for example, a man named Harris C. Hug became a key conduit for information coming out of Anchorage into the Lower 48. Hug would stay in contact with the city for sixteen hours that Good Friday night, and twenty more hours on both Sunday and Monday. After that, he kept going, passing messages from Alaska to his wife, June, who dialed more than four hundred different people around the country and read them their messages over the phone. Eventually, other ham operators in Seattle shut down their own channels and started sharing shifts at Hug's house, to keep his hotline going. "Sandwiches, coffee, babysitting and all the other chores so essential to a successful operation became a neighborhood project of tremendous magnitude," one observer wrote.

One man, listening to KENI at home, would later describe the station as "our only beacon of light in a night of terror." The improvisational, communal nature of the entire project communicated a kind of reassurance itself. Even people in Anchorage who were listening at home with their families, together and safe, found comfort in the sheer volume of announcements they were hearing on the air—all the people, one after another, calling in to report they were OK. You could hear the potential death toll in the city gradually ticking down. And with each small declaration of survival that aired, you could imagine a constellation of affirming flames slowly lighting the emptiness outside.

"To me, nothing could be more dramatic than the *actual sound* of KENI during that tense, frantic night," a woman named Jo Butler would later write to Genie, "when the messages started pouring out that people were all right." As another woman put it, listening from the remote community of Clam Gulch, "It made us who were fortunate realize that no matter what powerful forces nature unleashes, it also releases similar forces in our men and women to cope with them."

A few Alaskans recorded what was happening on their radios that Good Friday night. If you try hard, you can track their old reels down. More than a half century later, those tapes are muddled by age and afflicted with hiss, but if you listen closely, you can still catch a trace of the euphoria and awe those listeners described feeling. It was as though the voices on the radio were spooling across Anchorage like wires, dividing and crisscrossing until they thatched together like a net. A kind of human infrastructure was snapping into place where the built environment gave way.

IT WAS NEARLY TWO THIRTY in the morning. Genie was spitting out a few last pleas for information about missing family members before scuttling away from her microphone at the police counter for the first time all night. She would be going down to the basement to cover a meeting called by Anchorage's mayor and city manager.

For the past nine hours, people in the Public Safety Building had been fielding fragmented damage reports from all over the city. But it was impossible to assemble those details into any systematic overview. "Somebody would come in from one area and we'd see a little picture," Anchorage's mayor, George Sharrock, explained, "then somebody would come in from someplace else." This uncertainty exacerbated the sense of helplessness: they were helpless to even know what had happened, the extent of the crisis they were facing. They still had no idea of the death toll, or how dramatically the geography of their city had been slashed apart. Twice that night, Mayor Sharrock had attempted to drive around Anchorage himself, to make his own survey, but found it was impossible to see much, through the darkness and snow. After returning from his second reconnaissance trip, the mayor had consulted with the city manager, and they decided to gather everyone in one place—to pool information and formulate a plan for the morning. Up to this point, the city had only been reacting; now it was time to take charge.

The meeting was called for three a.m. "I will be sitting in as an observer on this conference," Genie explained to listeners, "and offering the services of KENI radio in any way possible." But before stepping away, she added, "I understand that KFAR in Fairbanks is monitoring us and is relaying messages to the South 48. I wonder if the person at KFAR would take down a message for me and get the word to my family in Bonham, Texas, that the Chance family is all right. I've been so involved trying to assist down here . . . in the coordination of the message service. I really hadn't stopped to think how worried and concerned *my* parents must be. So if my friends in Fairbanks would please call collect to Judge A. S. Broadfoot, in Bonham, Texas, and tell them the Chance family is all right." She spelled her father's name, very slowly, then reiterated: "The Chance family is all right. The Chance family is all right. All five of us are safe. None of us received a scratch."

By then, a slight lull had set in around Genie at the Public Safety Building. Workers who'd shown up immediately after the quake were taking the opportunity, before the three a.m. meeting, to check on their families for the first time. Running home, some discovered displaced neighbors or even complete strangers asleep on their sofas or living room floors. According to one estimate, three thousand people in Anchorage had been suddenly left homeless. One hundred and seventy-five people had bedded down in the Federal Building downtown. Others clustered in the lobby of Providence Hospital, or found unused rooms in the Alaska Methodist University dorms. Two hundred were asleep at a nearby YMCA, including a fifteen-person flight crew from Northwest Orient Airlines, marooned in Anchorage during their stopover.

The traffic that plagued downtown earlier had subsided. The

streets were quiet and dark. A local freelance writer named Betsy Woodman, the first reporter to file a wire story out of Anchorage after the quake, would describe downtown as consumed with a foreboding stillness that weekend. "The buildings had lost their familiarity," she wrote, "their bodies twisted, broken, sunken, collapsed." The Eskimo Scouts deployed by the National Guard appeared as "bundled blurs looming at street crossings, keeping their eerie vigil. The pain of broken buildings, shorn of their people, is almost beyond endurance." One man described the city as "a wounded thing, lying here, waiting for some light to come on." Until the sun came up, all everyone could do was brace themselves. Their determination was mounting, but so was the terror of what they might find.

A bit of space had opened up, before daybreak, for that unease to linger and grow. It was as though between the earthquake at 5:36 p.m. and this meeting scheduled for three in the morning, exact time became garbled—even ceased to exist. The hours went fuzzy, grew elastic and irrelevant. Snippets of terrible information cascaded by without being fixed on any contiguous timeline, without a chance for clear story lines to build or resolve. Only as an afterthought, for example, had KENI's staff realized, around one a.m., that the tidal wave projected to hit the city apparently never materialized.

Similarly, only after midnight had come and gone did it occur to someone to note that trivial swivel in history on the air. "Well, it's now another day," Bob Fleming said. "The earthquake was yesterday."

Then, having noted it, he moved on to other announcements. Apparently, small patches of the city's electrical grid were switching back on; someone had just contacted the studio to report that Maxine's Beauty College, out on Fireweed Lane, was all lit up. "Every light in the place is on!" Fleming said, astonished.

It must have been beautiful: the lone illuminated building in the darkness—like a lost boat, or the lighthouse calling it in.

SATURDAY

MARCH 28, 1964

9.

"A NEW WORLD"

TEXAS TO ANCHORAGE

I T WAS STILL DARK, EARLY ON SATURDAY MORNING, WHEN
the telephone rang at the home of Judge and Mrs. A. S. Broadfoot in Bonham, Texas. Genie's sisters and their families were
visiting her parents for Easter, and it was Genie's older sister
who reached the phone first.

The caller was a local acquaintance named Dave Ray. Ray
explained that he'd just received a phone call from his son, who
lived in Fairbanks. There'd been a terrible earthquake in Alaska,
Ray's son told him, but—believe it or not—he was listening to
the Broadfoots' daughter, Genie Chance, covering the disaster
on the radio right now. The station in Fairbanks was carrying her
voice, live from Anchorage. He'd just heard her ask for someone
to phone her parents in Texas and tell them "The Chance family
is all right."

The crowded house in Bonham shot to life. All the Broadfoots were up. They switched on the lights and the radio. The phone rang again. This time, it was a perfect stranger—a military officer in Fairbanks named Smith—calling collect, just as Genie had instructed on the air. He was passing on the same message: The Chance family is all right.

"From then on, the phone rang constantly," one family member wrote. Friends in Bonham who couldn't get through simply showed up at the Broadfoots' door, where they found the entire extended family red-eyed and weeping, relieved but also broken from the shock. Genie's mother, Jessie, confessed that as soon as it sunk in that her daughter and grandchildren were safe, "I just let down and bawled in a boo-hoo of all time."

Jessie Leona Butler Broadfoot—"Den," as her family called her—was a loquacious and obdurate elocution teacher who claimed to be the daughter of distinguished early Texan pioneers. She'd lived outside the state only briefly before marrying in 1921. Genie's father, Albert Sidney Broadfoot, was a retired judge who was now haplessly sinking himself, and his savings, into a hobby cattle ranch that had been in his family for a century.

The Broadfoots were not a tranquil couple. Den seems to have easily overshadowed her husband; she blazed at a higher wattage than the judge. She was adventurous and restless— erratic, but always decisive. The judge was a lanky and somewhat morose-seeming homebody. Once, when he was away for an extended period, touring his judicial circuit, Den bought the smaller lot next to their prime corner property in Bonham, hired house movers to move their home onto it, then started construction on a brand-new house, which she'd designed herself, on the original parcel. When Genie moved to Anchorage, Den wanted to visit, but the judge was afraid of flying and ruled it out. Den suggested driving to Anchorage, up the Alaska Highway, instead. The judge ruled that out, too. Finally, one morning, she packed up their car and was readying to make the nearly four thousand mile drive herself when, at the last possible minute, the judge backed down. He assumed, with this dramatic stunt behind them, they'd now sit down and plan a proper trip. Instead, Den told him to pack a suitcase and waited in the car.

The Broadfoots had four children. The first three, Albert, Jesse, and Emma Gene—Genie—had always been known within the family as Brother, Sister, and Baby. Their fourth child was Alice; everyone called her Alice. The Broadfoots instilled in their children a commitment to being themselves—authentically and without compromise, but also without any trace of arrogance. "I had been reared to believe that each person is given talents by God," Genie remembered. "Since those talents are a gift from God, you have no reason to be proud of them, but you do have the responsibility to use them for the benefit of mankind." Pretending to be someone other than who you are, or conforming to someone else's expectations, meant stifling those gifts and defaulting on your duty to the world. The Chance children were also taught to be insatiable strivers: "The mandate of our family was 'Whatever you do, be the best,'" Genie said.

By the time Genie was in college, at North Texas State, she'd grown into a driven and alluringly extroverted young woman. She joined the Camera Club, the Modern Dancers group, and the Quintilian Club for public speaking. She performed in a continuous string of theater productions and was profiled in *Who's Who in American Colleges and Universities*. She also fell in love with a baby-cheeked and barrel-chested football player named Winston Chance.

Winston was five years older than Genie, but a stint in the navy had left him lagging behind her in school. Genie had to wait for Winston to graduate after she'd finished her own degree. While she waited, she taught seventh-grade English and high school speech, coordinated fashion shows, and produced variety programs for a local radio station. In 1947, when Winston took a summer job in a different town, he wrote Genie cornball love letters almost daily, fantasizing about their future children and the house they'd live in one day, with an aromatic lilac bush erupting under a bay window. Genie stacked his letters and tied them in lace. That August, they married.

Genie applied herself to being an equally overachieving wife and mother. She hosted book discussion groups and joined the Toastmistresses and the PTA. When their first child, Wins, turned six, she staged a hobo-themed birthday party at a local park, with a tiny boxcar on top of the cake and refreshments bundled in blue and red bandanas tied to the ends of sticks. After Jan was born, in 1955, Genie posed for a Mother's Day portrait holding her new daughter, dressed as the Madonna and Child. "I am glad that I am a mother," Genie told the *Bonham Daily Favorite* when the photo ran in the paper's society pages, "and am privileged to do the things a mother has to do."

Winston, however, struggled to support the family as it grew. All he knew was selling cars. He spent his days chasing commissions, but didn't always handle the money well when he landed one, habitually stopping on the way home from the lot to celebrate with a steak dinner and drinks. Winston worked up to owning his own dealership and body shop but was forced to file for bankruptcy in 1958, after slipping too deeply into the red. After that, the Chances moved to Littlefield, Texas, where Winston tried working in a factory. He drove a gravel truck. He scrounged. The financial strain seemed to destabilize their marriage; their faith in each other appeared to be slipping. Winston could only absorb so much discouragement, while Genie felt pressure to hold the family together and make their precarious life feel safe. "We're not poor," she'd often tell the children, "we just don't have any money." Her sister sent her a little cash, just enough to buy bus tickets back to Bonham for her and the children. Genie kept it hidden in her bra, in case.

A wave of young Texans was decamping for jobs in Alaska, and a friend of Winston's who'd already moved there, a heavy equipment operator named Cleve Keaton, filled Winston's head with seductive stories about the territory. Keaton talked about Alaska as a promised land: anyone willing to work construction would wind up flush. Slowly, Winston became convinced he'd run out of other options. He left for Anchorage in March 1959, three months after Alaska became a state.

He went alone at first. Genie was hesitating. The life in Alaska that Keaton described did not sound like a fun adventure to her; it sounded dreadful and alien. Genie loved Winston, but felt conflicted as to whether their marriage, at this point, was worth such a sacrifice. She had watched friends send their husbands north to find jobs and houses for their families, then decline to join them. But those women's lives in Texas wound up seeming just as desolate and sad. "They were nursing elderly parents," Genie wrote, "or already alone in huge, dreary homes that echoed with the ghosts of past generations of growing, prosperous families." She might have looked to her mother as another kind of cautionary tale as well. Den, a fiery and freethinking suffragette, had gone to Emerson College in Boston, then somehow gotten hemmed into a static, domestic life back in Bonham. (As she got older, Den would disappear for weeks at a time on what she called her "genealogy trips," driving around the South ostensibly to research her family tree, but primarily to get time away from her husband.) The truth was, Genie had never fit that comfortably within the strictures of Texas society. She seemed to understand that there might be new opportunities for her in Alaska, too—more freedom to be herself. And if life didn't improve for her and Winston in Anchorage, maybe divorce would at least feel more feasible there: she'd be at the edge of the world; nobody would know.

Genie resolved to go. Her decision was hurtful to her parents. For years, Genie and Winston had lived next door to the Broadfoots in Bonham. Wins, Albert, and Jan had grown up moving freely between their two houses; if Genie failed to get lunch ready for the kids quickly enough, they'd climb into chairs at their grandparents' table, then curl up on a sofa for their nap. Now Genie's parents were left crestfallen, but also anxious. Their impressions of Alaska seemed as dismal as Genie's. They told her they would not contribute a penny to helping her family get established in Anchorage, but would happily pay to fly her and the children home to Bonham if she changed her mind.

Genie left Texas with her three small children on June 11, 1959. She had seven dollars in her purse. Her father walked them onto the airplane in Dallas and helped buckle in the kids. The judge had counted the steps up to the plane. There were thirteen of them—the same number that sheriffs used to build up to the gallows before hanging a prisoner, the judge realized, though he kept that thought to himself.

———

THEY TOUCHED DOWN IN Alaska the following morning, after twenty hours of travel and four connecting flights. Jan, who was only three years old, had slept through much of the journey, nestled in her seat, or with her head on Genie's shoulder while they stood in the cold on a runway in Denver in the middle of the night. The instant they landed in Anchorage, Jan perked up and squealed, "Where's my daddy?"

They spotted Big Winston through the window, waiting with a crowd on the opposite side of the plane to meet their flight. The kids started waving madly, then tore off their seatbelts and ran to him, scrambling down the steps of the aircraft so recklessly that Genie worried Jan would go tumbling. She'd assigned each child a piece of luggage to shepherd through the trip. In their excitement, they'd left Genie to carry it all.

Outside, Genie saw a sky plugged with clouds. The air was heavy with dust. As Winston drove the family from the airport toward town, the car jounced over potholes, and Genie cringed at the gaudy signs for bars and dancing girls that ran the length of the road. "I felt heartsick," she would later write, "but blamed my disillusionment on my fatigue." As they approached the little house Winston had rented, city workers were breaking open the neighborhood streets. Their new basement had filled with two inches of water. Genie announced that she was going to lie down.

Winston and the children woke her up at seven that evening; it was time to take a drive, they told her. No thank you, Genie said. She'd already seen enough of Alaska's dreariness; all she wanted was to sleep for the next twenty-four hours. They fed her a cup of coffee. She agreed to get in the car.

The Chances went out for hamburgers, then headed into the country south of town to visit some friends from Texas at their mobile home. On the way, Winston got the car stuck in a muddy trench on a remote stretch of Northern Lights Boulevard and couldn't push it free. It was past nine thirty at night by then, but the summer sky was still bright. Even an hour later, Genie would see people watering their meager front lawns or working in flower beds as though it were the middle of the afternoon. Winston set out for help on foot, and disappeared. "I sat there in deep despair as I looked at the desolate scene about me," Genie remembered. There was no escaping how ugly the city was. At the same time, there wasn't nearly enough of it.

She would quickly settle into a routine in Anchorage, pressed by necessity. The lease Winston had signed on their house was temporary; they needed to move out by the middle of the following month. So, after finishing the housework every day, Genie would throw the three kids into the car, drive to the *Anchorage Times* building downtown, and wait outside for the first copies of the afternoon paper to come off the press. Standing in the doorway of the building, she'd scan the classifieds for affordable apartments, unfold her city map, then race between various neighborhoods for the rest of the day. The search was discouraging. Most landlords gave preference to the military families rotating into Anchorage's air force and army bases that year. Others were only renting rooms to single men. "They seemed to think I was the most contemptibly brazen person in the world, to propose bringing three children into their property," Genie complained in a letter to her sister; some looked at her kids like they were an exotic, communicable disease. She also learned not to mention where they had moved from. Many longtime Alaskans resented the influx of newcomers, and looked down on Texans especially as screwups and hicks.

Genie had her own knee-jerk pretensions to work through as well. Often, people arriving in Anchorage from the Lower 48 carried themselves with a kind of unspoken superiority complex, a conviction that they were from the *real* world and that nothing in Alaska quite measured up or mattered. For Genie, it was a struggle to accept life in Anchorage as fully legitimate. She complained in her letters home that the store clerks didn't bother to wait on you, and the grocers didn't carry out your bags. ("If you smile sweetly," she explained, they might plunk the grocery bags into your arms, but "otherwise you just wrestle with them yourself and hold up the line.") She resented the strange, ashy gravel that people put in sandboxes in lieu of actual sand—how filthy it was, how it stained the children's skin. She mocked Alaskan politics as a "naïve game of beginners" and vented that watching a local community theater production felt like "someone hurling a dare at me. I'd like to show them how to stage a play."

She also seemed, that first summer, to be fighting back depression. Winston was working all the time, even on weekends. Alone with the children all day, Genie often wound up feeling dejected and defeated by nightfall—"convinced," as she once explained to her sister, "that I was just barely mediocre." She wrote long letters home to Texas every day or two while Jan took her nap.

What seemed to win Genie over slowly, that first summer, was the natural beauty surrounding the city. She would stand at her kitchen window staring at the Chugach Mountains, observing the subtle, ever-altering details of that fantastical landscape at the horizon. She watched the mountains' auburn and black silhouettes phase into bronze as the sun shifted; the soft blue haze as it poured past them; the pale, clumpy clouds that hung at their peaks, then broke apart slowly and coasted off, towing shadows across the foothills. One afternoon, late in the summer, the family took a drive into those mountains. From a lookout point near a Nike missile site, Genie could see the entire city of Anchorage wrapped against the curving tongue of Cook Inlet. Everything looked more delicate from so high up. "It felt as though all you had to do is lift your hand above and feel the floor of heaven!" she wrote.

Several weeks later, Genie and Winston left the kids with a babysitter and went out to the Idle Hour Country Club, a center of Anchorage's nightlife. There was no cover charge, and the orchestra was surprisingly decent. By eleven thirty, they had exhausted themselves dancing and were calling it a night when, outside on the street, they looked up, and saw manic ribbons of light, streaking and surging from all directions in the sky: the northern lights—an incredibly rare sight in the summer, but there they were, "as big as life," Genie wrote. Returning home, they stood in the yard, watching the sky awhile longer with some neighbors, until everyone finally got cold and said good night.

There was a feeling of togetherness in Anchorage that slowly drew Genie in as well. Young families were arriving from all over America, effectively to start over. Some people likened it to moving to Mars: no matter where you came from, you were hopelessly far from home. That dislocation fostered genuine openness in town. Everyone was eager to build friendships to replace the families they'd left behind.

"It's a new world being built," Genie explained. "People don't lock their doors at night. You stop for a car in trouble on the road. You stop without fear. If there's no one in it, you start a search party." There was a spirit of independence, strangely mingling with a sense of interdependence, that Genie found appealing: everyone was being themselves, together. In Anchorage, you immediately discovered "the opportunity to do what you want to do when you want to do it, rather than doing it because it's expected of you or because it's considered the thing to do," she wrote. "Every family has its own dreams and ambitions and people don't have time or inclination to condemn the next fellow for what he does." This freewheeling egalitarianism was written into the cityscape. There were still shoddy shacks next door to lovingly designed modern homes on landscaped lots. Many families built their houses themselves, or cobbled together small, rustic cabins, just to get a roof over their heads, then slowly improved them. Genie noticed how neighbors always helped neighbors, taking advantage of the extra daylight to lay foundations, frame houses, or shingle roofs late into the night.

Still, at times, that freedom from tradition and expectation merely struck her as crudeness. She kept stumbling into reminders that she'd chosen to live at the far horizon of ordinary society, where the norms and etiquette she'd been raised with didn't necessarily hold. One night, at the end of that first summer, Winston took her to dinner for their twelfth wedding anniversary at the Hofbrau, a German cafeteria downtown where the staff dressed like peasants and huge chunks of roast beef hung on chains in the window, rotating over glowing heat lamps. It was a romantic evening; Winston gave Genie a necklace and earrings made of sterling silver and hematite—a glassy black mineral the local merchants called "Alaskan black diamond." But as Genie and Winston left the restaurant, they walked straight into a fight between two young women on the sidewalk outside. The girls were scratching each other viciously, pulling hair. More disturbing was the fervor of everyone watching, the crowd of men stumbling out of the bars on Fourth Avenue for a better view. Traffic stopped in both directions.

The street fight was a disquieting bookend to their date earlier that summer, when they'd walked out of the Idle Hour to discover the northern lights drowning the darkness overhead. But this was what those early days in Anchorage seemed to be like for Genie: even the happy moments could be chewed through, without warning, by a kind of random unruliness that you sensed was always there.

WINSTON'S TROUBLES WITH MONEY turned out to be chronic. He couldn't escape them by leaving Texas. After hearing Cleve Keaton's stories about the Alaskan building boom, he had promised Genie that he would give up selling cars and find work in construction. But he went straight to work at the General Motors dealership in Anchorage instead, once again selling on commission. The decision was perplexing to Genie, and she was discouraged when Winston sold only two cars the week after she and the children arrived. Still, in a letter to her parents, she blamed herself: she must be a jinx, she said.

To save money, Genie sewed clothes for the kids. She furnished their bedrooms with cots from a military surplus store. She borrowed power tools and built tables and bookshelves for the living room. Every week, she would spend an hour and a half poring over the grocery store circulars, scrupulously planning meals around what was on sale. The food prices in Alaska were shocking: fifty-nine cents for a loaf of bread; $1.25 for a pound of ground beef. Occasionally, Cleve Keaton would return from a hunting trip with cuts of caribou or moose for Genie's freezer. But mostly, she sustained her family with instant milk, macaroni, canned tuna, and dried beans.

Genie would need to find a job. It had been eleven years since she'd worked in broadcasting, briefly, after college. But as far as she could tell, "the Anchorage stations were about fifteen years behind the times, so I figured I'd fit right in." The first two stations she approached turned her away; she was overqualified for the jobs they had for women, they explained. "But I was desperate," Genie would later remember. "I had three small children and I didn't want to break their habit of eating regularly." So that fall, applying at a third radio station, KBYR, she chose not to mention her work experience or college degree. She was hired to run the telephone switchboard for $100 a week. She had never worked a switchboard before.

Friends from Texas, Dottie and Johnny Snodgrass, were building an apartment house near the radio station, and Dottie was running a day care out of a trailer on the property. Genie made a deal to drop her children with Dottie on her way to work every morning; in exchange, she would spend four hours installing drywall or doing other construction work at the apartments when she picked up the kids at the end of the day. Then, once she finally got everyone home at night, it was a scramble to make dinner and the next day's lunches, followed by laundry, baths, and bedtime stories. The kids were always cranky and unreasonable by then—exhausted, but also desperate for her attention. All

Genie wanted was to get them to sleep; there'd be no relief as long as they were conscious. She took to calling this torturous phase of every evening "the arsenic hour."

At KBYR, Genie worked six days a week, upward of fifty-two hours, hoping to prove herself and advance. "I made no waves, just did my job," she wrote, "and any other task that was thrown my way." By the following spring, the station owner had recruited her to help set up a second, FM station. For six weeks, Genie studied what she called "the psychology of the time of day," compiling purportedly scientific research about how the typical American's mood fluctuates throughout the day, to craft the station's programming schedule accordingly. Eventually, she was rewarded with her own morning show, *This Is Genie*, which aired every weekday at nine thirty.

Genie's boss had asked her to put together a program for women, but Genie preferred to imagine her target audience as all intelligent and tasteful adults. Still, when *This Is Genie* debuted on KBYR-FM, the station marketed it as "a special program for the fair sex," featuring "everything from the latest tasty recipe tip to local events that women will be interested in," and hosted by "a veteran radio performer, a homemaker and mother—and a nice-looking one, too." Before long, the success of *This Is Genie* earned her a second morning show, a story hour for children called *Playmates*. The two shows that Genie created were among KBYR's most popular and commercially successful. "This is an opportunity I could have never got in Texas," she wrote to her parents. When she asked for her first raise at KBYR, however, the station's program director rebuked her. "After all," Genie would remember, "I was just a woman."

The program director, Merrill Mael, was a celebrated broadcasting veteran in Anchorage who had been in the business since 1939. But for as long as they'd worked together, Mael had seemed unreasonably irritated by Genie. She would later describe him as short, insecure, and weaselly; he seemed particularly threatened by women but was "easily jealous of anyone who did well." At work, Mael often turned spiteful, distracting Genie from across the studio to throw her off in the middle of an unscripted segment or scheming to undermine their boss's confidence in her. It was shocking, Genie complained in a letter to her parents, how "one petty, jealous little man can really tear up an organization." She saw him only as a sad and elfin one-dimensional creep. When Mael died forty-eight years later, however, a man who worked with him at the end of his career would tell a reporter: "I considered Merrill Mael to be one of the most moral and finest men I have ever had the honor of knowing. The world needs millions of Merrill Maels."

Mael's behavior toward Genie wasn't just maddening. It felt unfair. Genie had wanted to work in radio most of her adult life, and had trained to be a broadcaster in college, but she'd never been given a genuine opportunity to use those skills before. This job wasn't a game to her; it was infuriating to be sabotaged constantly while trying to achieve something real. Still, Genie put a large share of the blame on herself. Tolerating Mael's abuse, and winning his respect, seemed, to her, like one more challenge she should be able to master, and she felt ashamed for failing at it. Then again, her other option—quitting—felt like an even more shameful failure; she didn't see herself as a woman who backed down. That is, Genie was trapped. All her choices were bad. By the spring of 1962, she wrote, "the atmosphere was getting unbearable."

Until then, Winston had always encouraged Genie's career. He seemed genuinely proud of her, and told her how much happier and more energetic she seemed at the end of her workday than she had as a schoolteacher in Texas. But Genie would recount years later how Winston turned unsympathetic as she became increasingly agitated by Mael's harassment. "Well, you just ought to quit and stay home where you're appreciated," Winston would snap. He couldn't understand why it was so important to her not to give up; he considered her radio shows fundamentally less important than her real job, at home. In truth, Genie did too, but struggled to make Winston understand that, given his troubles at the dealership, earning a second income *was* her way of serving their family. Winston just kept telling her to walk away. "It seemed that everything I did was wrong," Genie wrote. "As hard as I had been working, I had been all wrong. I was a failure as a woman."

In April 1962, after two and a half years at KBYR, Genie finally quit. "Winston had convinced me that he was the only one with my best interest at heart," she wrote. "He had insisted that I devote my life to being his wife and the mother of his children. If I would be the right kind of wife and spend all of my energies being supportive of him, he could be a success."

Six weeks later, they were unable to pay their rent. Winston said not to worry—he'd sell some cars soon. Genie worried.

"And this is what a good wife is supposed to do?" she wrote. "Just wait at home for her man to bring money in to pay the bills and feed the family? If other wives do it all the time, why can't I learn to relax and let it happen? What right do I have to expect so much of life, and of another human being? Who do I think I am to believe that the standard of living I aspire to is the right one? I was convinced I was going insane. I wept in despair one day hoping that Winston would give me comfort. But his response was: 'Well, if you're so worried about paying the rent, why are you sitting on your fat fanny? Get out there and get a job.'"

Genie was speechless. Two weeks later, she got herself hired at KENI.

10.

"NO PATTERN"

———

THE SUN RISES ON SATURDAY

DAYBREAK WAS CRUEL. THE WORLD LOOKED WRONG.
As light seeped over the horizon on Saturday morning, formerly symmetrical structures appeared gravely contorted. Spindly fissures forked through facades like cracks in ice, and the ground had split open just as randomly. Ragged crevasses tore through the tidy X- and Y-axes of the downtown grid on disinterested diagonals. All over Anchorage, so many rectangles and squares had become shapes with no names.

KENI scrambled its correspondents around town at sunrise, and one reporter, driving down D Street, would confess that he couldn't tell whether a row of buildings there had been shoved upward six inches or if the pavement had sunk instead. Where there'd once been an empty lot, there was now a deep pit with half a dozen cars foundered at the bottom—and remnants of a hardware store, too. On L Street, a monolithic six-story apartment building was eleven feet away from where it had stood the day before.

More than fourteen hundred properties in the greater Anchorage area suffered significant damage. More than nine hundred homes were destroyed. Much of downtown, one reporter wrote, "looks like the devil ground his heel into it." But it was eerie: some structures had crumpled, imploded, or been pulled underground while neighboring buildings, across the street or even right next door, were left perfectly undisturbed.

"There's no pattern with this earthquake!" another KENI broadcaster, Darrell Comstock, marveled on the air. "Absolutely no pattern!" And trying to decipher one only left you feeling more defeated—because any hints of logic you could identify in the wreckage seemed only to suggest a certain spitefulness at work: some infuriated god, deliberately choosing its targets.

All the most celebrated symbols of Anchorage's progress had been struck down. "It's as though the best of our buildings—the proudest of our buildings—were the ones that were hardest hit," one prominent businessman lamented. The city's beloved J. C. Penney was largely rubble. A gaping, Y-shaped crack ran up one side of the prominent Westward Hotel, while a new luxury apartment house had pancaked completely. The building hadn't even been completed yet; it was still in its last phases of construction, marketed to tenants with the aspirational name The Four Seasons. Now its concrete elevator shaft was propped up at a violent angle, resting on a heap of broken material. It looked like a derailed boxcar.

It would take some time to understand how all this random-seeming destruction fit together. Viewed from overhead, you could see that much of the damage had been caused by five distinct slides triggered by the quake: long, blobby bands of land where the ground had split apart and the earth on one side simply spilled downhill or sank. The slide that dragged down the bars and shops along Fourth Avenue ran for fourteen blocks and tore through thirty-six acres of land. Another, on L Street, was roughly twice that size, extending for five thousand feet.

The most catastrophic slide by far wrenched apart the crown jewel of Anchorage: Turnagain, the new high-end subdivision where many of the town's most dignified citizens had built their homes. The neighborhood had been constructed on a gray, silty sediment called Bootlegger Cove Clay, which had shaken apart during the quake. Originally, Turnagain sat on a ridge overlooking Cook Inlet. Now the portion closest to that edge—a ribbon of land more than a mile and a half long and twelve hundred feet across at its widest point—had simply sloughed into the inlet some thirty-five feet below. Everything had come careening down: the shoreline was a debris field of saw-toothed, shattered homes, inundated by the tide. Overhead, houses that had previously been several blocks inland were now perched at the lip of a new ridge, or flumped halfway off it.

The KENI reporter Darrell Comstock offered what appeared to be the first descriptions of Turnagain from the air. He was one of two broadcasters at the station who were recreational pilots, and by midday Saturday, both men would be up in small airplanes, surveying the greater Anchorage area and calling in live reports from overhead. Comstock was the longtime anchor of KENI's nightly television news, a classically handsome man and polished performer who didn't get easily rattled. He'd often light up a cigar behind the anchor desk when they went to commercial and seemed to have an impeccable sixth sense for just when to extinguish it before they returned. Once, when the TV camera fell on its side in the middle of a newscast, Comstock simply tilted his head at the equivalent angle and kept reading. Now, however, as he made his first approach over Turnagain, Comstock could barely spit out the words. "The shoreline!" he said. "It's a huge bulge of dirt and mud. It's cratered like the surface of the moon! It's just incredible to see."

Soon the houses came into view—except they weren't houses anymore; they were flotsam on the beach. "I've seen so much today that this just takes my breath away," Comstock said. "These beautiful homes, and all they meant to their owners— they're just lying in the water, toppled over." Anchorage was a small enough community that Comstock knew whose home had been whose; presumably, he knew many of their owners personally. He called out some of the names, identifying the scraps: the Atwoods, the Rasmusons. "It just has to be seen to be believed," Comstock said. "And if you see it, you just can't hardly believe it. It's just indescribable." He spoke with befuddlement and grief, and seemed unnerved, himself, by the plaintive quaver creeping into his voice. "I'm doing my best," he said apologetically.

Twelve and a half million cubic yards of earth had broken away and collapsed onto the shore in Turnagain. Residents reported hearing a rumbling, like an avalanche, then the creaking and snapping of the beams of houses and the sound of exploding glass. Dozens of people fled their homes only to find the landscape heaving up and down maniacally ahead of them. They were left to leap over fissures that raced toward them through the ground, or to climb aboard stable-enough-seeming boulders of earth that rose out of the weaving chop ahead of them like volcanic islands.

Robert Atwood, the fifty-six-year-old publisher of the *Anchorage Times,* had been at home, practicing his trumpet, when the chandelier in his living room started swishing like a circus aerialist overhead. He ran outside. "It was then that I discovered I was falling," Atwood later explained. He dropped into a V-shaped chasm that opened under his feet. Trees and fence posts poured in around him. He noticed he was still holding his trumpet.

He landed on something soft—sand, maybe—and eventually climbed back up to daylight: a soiled mole-person in a suit coat, slacks, and oxfords. Atwood presumed he was on the shoreline below Turnagain, but it resembled a mountain range. He was nested within slopes of disfigured terrain and debris. He heard a voice shouting, asking if anyone was alive, and soon caught sight of his fifteen-year-old neighbor, Warren Hines, holding his four-year-old sister, Mitzi. Atwood moved toward the kids, scaling craggy new hills and sinking into patches of clay up to his knees before reaching them. Eventually, the little group collected another woman and her four children, too, then happened upon the Hineses' mother. She was standing high above them, unharmed, stranded next to her car on a small, standalone pillar of earth. It was a patch of their driveway; the rest of their home had fallen away, she explained. She had just pulled in when the quake hit.

Atwood started scanning for a route up to safety. There was no telling how many bodies might be buried in the ragged hash that he and his companions were traversing. Mitzi was crying, wearing only her pajamas; Warren wasn't even wearing shoes. Atwood was among Anchorage's wealthiest and most esteemed citizens—one of a handful of Alaskans to make a fortune in the territory's first, limited wave of oil discoveries in 1957, and a guest at the White House two years later, when President Eisenhower officially made Alaska a state. Now he was just a tiny figure stranded in a ruptured wasteland, trying to keep a few even tinier figures warm.

"It's interesting how values change," Atwood later explained. "Right at that moment, it occurred to me that the most valuable thing in the world would be a piece of wool—anything wool."

11.

"HOLD A KIND THOUGHT"

GENIE ATTEMPTS A
SHIFT CHANGE

"THIS IS GENIE CHANCE, REPORTING FROM DISASTER headquarters in the Public Safety Building. The meeting of representatives of federal, state, and city agencies who have surveyed the damage in Anchorage has just been concluded. Plans have been mapped out for the work that will get under way at daybreak this morning."

Genie had hustled back to her microphone and resumed broadcasting as soon as the three a.m. meeting ended, and was now moving through her notes, giving a meticulous summary. Close to a hundred people had been called in for the meeting, all of them lumbering to the basement of the Public Safety Building in their overcoats and hats or hard hats, passing a conspicuous crack in the cinder-block stairwell on the way down. Anchorage's mayor and city manager had requested that the heads of each city department and utility attend the meeting, plus officers from the military and state police and representatives from the state highway department, the airport, the Federal Aviation Administration, the Salvation Army, and the Red Cross. As everyone settled in, the atmosphere was grim; as one official later explained, "We were still not sure what we had left in the city. Everyone, of course, was thinking the worst." The basement was still without power. The room was lit only by a fire department searchlight that someone had laid on a table. It threw strange shadows on the weary people around it. "Fatigue had carved new lines in their faces," one reporter wrote.

The men started going around, each one giving a damage report from his particular department's point of view. Then they began, collectively, to work up strategies for tackling those problems when the sun came up. The fire department would take responsibility for search and rescue. A public health official outlined a plan to give typhoid inoculations. Someone else was assigned to salvage a stockpile of food from a collapsed warehouse. The commander in chief of Alaska Command, who oversaw the army and air force bases in Anchorage, explained that he'd been in touch with the chairman of the Joint Chiefs of Staff in Washington, and that relief supplies would start flying out of a California air base in a few hours.

Genie took notes furiously. She could feel everyone's confidence rising as they spoke, the momentum ricocheting around the room. Then, after the meeting had been going on for nearly two hours, the basement started shaking mildly and the conversation stalled. Genie said a prayer. The shaking stopped. A few minutes later, another aftershock struck: a deep, rolling motion, far more severe than before. People in the basement turned restless until, finally, the earth quelled its tantrum and the room resettled. "Not one word was mentioned about the tremor," Genie later noted, "but the meeting was quickly adjourned." The sun was about to rise anyway, and it was time to get to work.

It would take Genie almost an hour, maybe more, to report all the details of the meeting on KENI. At that point, many people in Anchorage were still in the same predicament as those city officials had been a few hours earlier, heading into the meeting: helpless to assimilate whatever random fragments of information had reached them over the radio or by word of mouth throughout the night. Now, for the first time, Genie was giving the city the entire picture at once. She was also ticking off the many requests for help from the public that she'd been told to broadcast. She asked grocers to open their stores; assured the public that there was no danger of a food shortage, to discourage hoarding; and asked anyone who'd taken in people needing shelter overnight to bring a list of their names to the Salvation Army headquarters, where volunteers would be setting up a makeshift missing persons bureau. As soon as Genie got through all the information in her notebook, she turned to the personal messages that had meanwhile accumulated on the counter in front of her: "We have a message here from Robin, daughter of Mr. and Mrs. Augie Hiebert. Robin is with the Smith family at the Olden home in College Village," she said. "We have a message here asking Barbara Capstick to please go to the Alaska Native Services Hospital as soon as possible and stay with Mary Wolcott."

Before long, Dick Taylor, the bombastic honcho from Disaster Control, appeared with another request for Genie to put over KENI. Taylor was preparing to dispatch his Do It Kids to repair Anchorage's streets and needed another two hundred able-bodied volunteers to come down to the Public Safety Building with hard hats and shovels. No problem, Genie told him; she'd make the announcement. Then she took a look around the lobby and asked Taylor where he expected to put all those people once they arrived.

Overnight, the Public Safety Building had gotten crammed with civilians, and hundreds more showed up in anticipation of daybreak, or in response to Genie's broadcast, eager to pitch in. Initially, the fire department tried stocking these volunteers in a large room upstairs, but people were now lingering everywhere, smoking cigarettes, drinking coffee from the percolators the Salvation Army had placed in the lobby, and plugging up the police counter, repeatedly checking back in for assignments. Many arrived offering up their own construction equipment, too: earth-movers, dump trucks, cranes—all the semi-dormant machinery of Anchorage's diminishing building boom since statehood was revving up again.

Eventually, two of the volunteers decided their job would be to organize everyone who'd come in looking for a job. They carried tables down from the firemen's quarters upstairs, enlisted a few secretaries to record everyone's names on index cards, then sorted the volunteers, by trade, into different corners of the building so that Disaster Control could more efficiently deploy them: carpenters in one spot, plumbers and electricians in another, and so on. This ad hoc human resources operation in the lobby would eventually become known as "Manpower Control."

No one in the city government had anticipated the convergence of such a crowd, or put any system in place to manage it. The conventional wisdom, in a disaster, was that authorities had to worry about hordes of civilians chaotically fleeing the hardest-hit area. Here everyone was piling in to help.

———

AT SUNRISE, KENI BEGAN sloppily executing a shift change. A new crew of announcers gradually relieved those working at the studio on Fourth Avenue, and Ty Clark, having apparently slept off whatever drinking he'd done the previous night to steady his nerves, straggled back to the Public Safety Building parking lot from the transmitter to take over the controls in the KENI Kamper. Getting settled, Ty put a bleary call over the air for someone to please bring him a sandwich and cigarettes. Then again, he added, "I'm not really too hungry, but I could certainly go for some cigarettes."

Genie had been broadcasting from the Public Safety Building for almost fifteen hours, hadn't slept in twenty-eight, and appeared to still be wearing her son's rubber boots when, around nine o'clock, her bosses finally sent over her ostensible replacement. Theda Conley worked on the television side of KENI, doing the weather on the nightly news and hosting her own talk show, *The Woman's Touch,* every afternoon. She was several years younger than Genie and, Genie felt, better-looking. The men at the station seemed more accepting of Theda, too, if only because she appeared to tolerate their cracks and mischief more amiably than Genie did. As far as Genie knew, Theda had never studied broadcasting in college like she had, or even had any prior experience in the field. "I guess she just has the idea that all she has to do is be pretty and that makes her tops," Genie had sniped in a recent letter home.

Still, Theda was talented; her job wasn't as demanding as Genie's, but she nevertheless made it look effortless. One afternoon, she brought a chef on *The Woman's Touch* to demonstrate

Mexican recipes, and the sample bite the man gave Theda was so spicy that she wound up having to finish the segment with tears dripping off her chin. Still, she finished the segment; people noticed professionalism like that. Now, she arrived at Genie's counter ready to get to work. "Well," Theda said, "tell me what to do."

Genie couldn't answer. There was no way to explain what she'd been doing since the previous evening. Her job didn't even have discernible parameters. Like everyone else who'd toiled in the Public Safety Building overnight, Genie was improvising, and purely by accident, she seemed to have become central to the operation. Every time someone showed up at the police counter announcing, for example, that he'd brought four hard hats, one wire cutter, one screwdriver, one pair of pliers, and one hammer, only Genie knew where to direct him—because she was the one who'd broadcast the original request for those supplies and knew who in the building was waiting for them. "None of the departments knew what the other was calling for," Genie later explained. "Only I did." The police department set up a second desk, in front of Genie's counter, hoping to divert some of the foot traffic surging toward her, but the officer manning it could frequently only turn and yell "Genie!" then wait for her to come and sort through the problem herself.

Initially, the previous night, Genie had questioned whether she was supposed to be playing such a big role. But now she was irreplaceable. The pace and the pressure were unendurable. "I wasn't equipped for it," she would remember, "emotionally, physically, or anything else." Her responsibilities, and the idiosyncratic systems she'd worked up to manage them, couldn't be easily explained or handed off to Theda. And every time Genie started to explain them, the phone rang or the counter got mobbed. "Just start working with me," Genie finally told her, "and you'll find out."

Several hours after Theda showed up, the two women were still working together at the police counter, side by side; the workload had simply expanded into a two-person job. Theda caught on quickly, however. It was obvious, in retrospect, that she was far more resilient and competent than Genie gave her credit for. Theda would host *The Woman's Touch* for another two decades after the quake, in fact, and evolve into a beloved, almost Oprah-like icon of local broadcasting in Anchorage. She was especially fearless about covering difficult subjects on the program if she felt it would benefit the women watching. One afternoon in the mid-seventies, Theda would bring a radiologist on *The Woman's Touch* to discuss the importance of mammograms. To illustrate, the doctor showed the audience a scan, and pointed out where that particular patient had clearly developed a malignant tumor. At no time during the program did Theda mention that it was a picture of her own breast.

Theda beat the breast cancer, then later contracted lung cancer. When she died, in January 1998, her family told a local newspaper that if Theda could have left the people of Anchorage with any last words, it would be the same sign-off she'd offered the city every weekday afternoon for twenty-five years: "Hold a kind thought."

12.

"THE GUY IN THE SHADOWS WHO MAKES THINGS WORK"

SEARCH AND RESCUE BEGINS

THE ANXIOUS CALLS STILL CAREENED THROUGH THE AIR-waves: "John Doran of 1557 Eighth Street is trying to contact Genevieve Moffitt of Palmer," Genie announced. "She was in Anchorage yesterday, and he has not heard from her since the earthquake." Anyone knowing the whereabouts of Patty Scott should immediately call her father. "Mr. and Mrs. Sommers of Turnagain," another broadcaster said, "please contact your daughter. She is extremely concerned about you. She has been looking for you." As those names scattered over Anchorage on the radio, a man in a cramped office at the back of the Public Safety Building—another volunteer who'd walked in off the street that morning—was finally organizing a systematic effort to scour the city for those still missing and to collect the dead.

William E. Davis was an assistant professor of psychology at Alaska Methodist University, the upstart liberal arts college on the east end of town. He was thirty-five years old, a tall, spindly man with glasses and a balding, conspicuously egg-shaped head. He was known to stand on his desk during lectures or contort his rubbery body for emphasis. "A nutty professor," one of his students said.

Bill Davis had been recruited to join AMU's tiny faculty from the University of Denver three years earlier, when the college was only one year old. The job suited Davis fine, but he'd come to Alaska primarily for the adventure. As a child in Colorado, he'd spent his summers playing in the foothills of Mount Evans and had grown into an accomplished mountaineer, making some of the first-ever ascents of the Saint Elias range. Davis's audacity and proficiency as a climber sometimes surprised people who only knew him from the classroom; he was too modest to brag. Besides, soon after arriving in Anchorage, Davis had fallen in love with AMU's professor of anthropology. Now Nancy Yaw Davis was six months pregnant with their first child, and Bill was committed to being a more prudent, low-altitude family man from now on.

He was, however, still the chairman of the Alaska Rescue Group, a loose association of volunteers in Anchorage who got together periodically to practice plucking people from the sides of mountains or rescuing them from avalanches. The Rescue Group had been founded by other transplanted Coloradans who'd modeled it after an organization back home. For Davis, it was an excuse to spend time in the mountains with friends and maintain his climbing skills; though they set up a phone tree for emergencies, the group seldom performed more than one or two genuine rescues a year. Still, part of the fun came from taking their training seriously and staying ready. The group kept a storehouse of climbing gear at Anchorage's municipal airport, in case the Civil Air Patrol—a similar organization of volunteer pilots—needed to fly them out to an accident in the backcountry. Together, the two outfits could cover thousands of square miles beyond what the city's professional first responders could. "The ethos of the frontier was, you looked after your neighbor," Davis explained.

After the quake on Friday night, the Davises had driven from their home to the university to check on their students, but got stuck in a tangle of cars at an intersection leading to Anchorage's largest hospital. The traffic lights were dark, so Bill leapt out of his jeep with a flashlight and wound up directing traffic there for several hours, while Nancy waited in the passenger seat, listening to Genie on KENI. Bill kept scampering back to check on her, asking if she was too uncomfortable, too cold. Eventually, Nancy stuck her head out of the car window and hollered for him: they'd just put out a call for mountaineers to help with search and rescue.

It wasn't clear from the announcement on the radio whether the city wanted those volunteers to report to the Public Safety Building immediately or the following morning, but Davis figured they'd need fresh bodies once the sun rose regardless, so he drove himself and Nancy home, got two hours of sleep, then left again before dawn. Later, he'd confess that his reasoning was probably only a justification; the truth was, Bill wasn't ready to leave Nancy that night. He would have liked to have been more selfless, but they had lost a baby the previous year, and although Nancy had relaxed once they'd passed the same point in this pregnancy, Davis's anxiety, and protectiveness of her, never relented.

Davis came through the front door of the Public Safety Building around five thirty that Saturday morning, just after the meeting in the basement adjourned. He found an assistant fire chief who explained that his department had been working on the missing persons problem only haphazardly; one observer would later explain that any search and rescue conducted in the first twelve hours after the quake had happened "more by accident than by plan." The night before, firemen had covered whatever ground they could before Chief Burns suspended their work for the night at eight. It was unclear how many bodies the city had managed to reclaim. Only three deaths were reported at the three a.m. meeting.

In retrospect, it was hard to believe, particularly since authorities had moved so quickly after the quake to guard the broken storefronts on Fourth Avenue. Arguably, the city was protecting its ruins from looters more conscientiously than it was looking for people trapped in them. Because there was no analog for that search-and-rescue work in ordinary, non-emergency life, no specific agency emerged from the initial shock of the earthquake focused on it, the way the police department instinctually restarted policing the streets. Some of the only people to lock on to the problem right away, in fact, were the owners of two of Anchorage's mortuaries. The two men were among the first civilians to arrive at the Public Safety Building on Friday evening, interrupting Genie's initial huddle with the police and fire chiefs. Knowing the city owned only two ambulances, the morticians had begun positioning their hearses outside—six vehicles in all, with volunteer drivers, ready to go. They'd also come equipped with embalming fluids and other supplies, and were already hashing out plans for potential mass burials or perhaps even for a large refrigerated truck to store as many bodies as possible, if the city's power wasn't soon restored. "We felt it better to be overprepared than underprepared," one mortuary manager explained.

Still, it was only after the three a.m. meeting that the fire department finally focused on looking for those bodies in a methodical way. And now the assistant chief seemed to be confessing to Davis that they didn't know where to start. Davis knew exactly what to do, however; this search wouldn't be so different from the work the Rescue Group trained for. He agreed to take over the enterprise. And just like that, he was in charge: "The great impostor," he said.

The fire department cleared out an office for Davis at the rear of the building and he quietly got to work, cloistered far away from the crowds in the lobby—an unassuming, accidental authority figure. "I've always perceived that my role in life was to be a factotum," Davis would later explain. "I'm the jester that follows the king around—the loyal aide-de-camp. I've always wanted to be the guy in the shadows who makes things work." It amused him that, at some point, people had started referring to him by the exaggeratedly austere title "Coordinator of Search and Rescue Operations" and the little room he'd taken over as the "Central Search and Rescue Operations Center."

Right away, Davis recognized how much he didn't know. In fact, because there'd been no procedure for searching the city or a centralized accounting of which areas had been searched, he knew almost nothing definitively. Scores of people were likely missing in Turnagain. Word circulated that a couple hundred kids might have gotten trapped inside the Fourth Avenue Theatre while watching *The Sword in the Stone*. You only had to look at Penney's to wonder how many victims might still be buried inside. Just moments earlier, in fact, city workers had extracted a survivor from the rubble there—a child they'd been working to free since the previous night.

Davis started getting organized, applying standard wilderness search-and-rescue procedures to that ruined urban environment. First, he hung a large map of Anchorage on one wall of the office, rolled some adhesive plastic over it, and drew a grid over the entirety of downtown with a wax pencil. By this time, more members of the Rescue Group had shown up, and Davis gradually absorbed firemen and military personnel into his ranks as well, along with any capable-enough-seeming volunteers who floated into his office. Davis recognized one young man from class at AMU. Another was the fellow who sold him cigars at the Texaco station. He wrote down each person's name on a little pad in his pocket—a master roster, in case anyone went missing—split the men into teams, numbered the teams, and wrote each team number on the portion of the grid they'd be searching. Then he gathered everyone up and issued his instructions.

Davis told the men to pick apart every square inch. He told them to stay together. Listen for tapping, he said—for cries, for yelling; pause every once in a while to listen in silence. If they found someone alive, they should do whatever it took to get her or him out; if a survivor was badly pinned, Davis could call in a crane or other heavy machinery to clear debris. He also prepared his troops for the morbid reality ahead of them: Whenever they found a dead body, he said, they should remove it, too. But they shouldn't try to identify anyone until a mortician arrived.

By seven o'clock that morning, Davis was dispatching his first crews. Over the next three hours, he would deploy roughly a hundred and fifty people into Anchorage. That number quickly passed two hundred, and before long, Davis gave up counting. A layman might have found something uplifting about the willingness of so many ordinary people to do such dangerous and grisly work, but Davis felt uneasy. Nine years earlier, his mountaineering group in Colorado had traveled to assist other recovery workers in Wyoming after a United Airlines flight crashed into Medicine Bow Peak. It was the deadliest commercial airline disaster in history at the time, killing everyone aboard. The wreckage was strewn wildly across terrible terrain; it took Davis's cohort five full days to recover all the bodies. By the third day, when the sun came out and the temperature rose, the stench had become intolerable.

Sixty-six people died on Medicine Bow—but *only* sixty-six. Now, in Anchorage, Davis explained, "I began thinking that if we had four, five, six hundred dead, we were going to have a hell of a mess to clean up." He was bracing himself: "I was concerned that there wouldn't be enough people."

DAVIS SENT FOUR OF his first teams to Fourth Avenue and instructed them to work through the wreckage in opposite directions, two teams from the east and two from the west, until they met in the middle. He sent another to Turnagain, where firefighters and the military had already begun rooting through the ruins that had cascaded into the inlet. He assigned a final team to the J. C. Penney building to search the department store's interior, floor by floor.

The Penney's team was led by one of the founders of the Alaska Rescue Group, a thirty-one-year-old veterinarian from

Colorado named Jim Scott. Scott was a friend of Davis's; not only were the two men in the mountaineering group together, Scott took care of Bill and Nancy's golden retriever. Two decades later, Scott would convert his veterinary clinic into a rehabilitation center for injured wild birds and become somewhat famous as the "Birdman of Alaska." After the *Exxon Valdez* oil spill, he would perform numerous surgeries on bald eagles and execute numerous bald eagle blood transfusions, saving the lives of many birds. "He saw that there was a need and nobody was filling it," a colleague would remember in 2017, after Scott passed away at age eighty-four.

Scott was exhausted. He had been up most of the previous night. Around eleven o'clock, he and fifteen others had made an impromptu search of the shoreline under Turnagain after hearing that two neighborhood children, the brothers Perry Jr. and Merrell Mead, had gone missing in the slide. Scott's crew had descended into the debris field in the dark, roped into teams of three, and pried their way into the splattered houses on the beach.

In the wreck of one home, Scott picked up a photograph of a German shepherd standing with its owner, and felt suddenly destabilized. "I know this guy," he said; the man in the picture always talked to Scott about that dog at Rotary Club meetings. It was an experience his crew would have repeatedly: some familiar artifact would surface in the upended ruins and they'd realize they were standing in the decimated home of a friend—and thus be hit all over again with the demoralizing epiphany that this vicious dreamscape was, in fact, real life. "It always came as kind of a shock," Scott explained. "I managed to come out of there with a tremendous depressed feeling."

Scott's crew searched the Turnagain wreckage as thoroughly as they could in the dark. Some structures had been so hideously warped that it was physically sickening to walk through them; one man compared it to the disequilibrium one feels while moving through a fun house. In the end, they were unable to find the two missing brothers—or anyone at all. Around the time they climbed up from the shore on Friday night, a team of army specialists arrived on the ridgeline. But looking down, they decided it was either too dangerous, or too futile, to search the inlet before sunrise, and turned back.

Now, on Saturday morning, Scott's team moved diligently through Penney's, freezing to listen for any faint tapping or wails in the dark. A few times, someone caught sight of a body part in the passing beam of his flashlight and stiffened, only to realize it was just a mannequin buried in piles of merchandise or rubble. They searched the entire building—all five floors. They found nothing: not a single person, dead or alive.

They headed over to help the others on Fourth Avenue. Starting with the camera shop, Mac's Foto, they searched the long strip of storefronts and bars that had dropped underground. But again and again, each structure they crept through or crawled under was empty. The rooms were flooded with silence. In some of the bars, Scott and his team found beers still somehow upright and full on slanted bartops. In the absolute stillness, it was as though the men were divers exploring old wrecks.

Eventually, in one sunken tavern, they were shocked to find another human being. The man was sitting comfortably on a bar stool, in a suit, with his back to the mountaineers as they entered. He had a shot glass in his right hand and a bottle in his left, and was refilling the one with the other. It took a moment for him to realize that Scott and his men were behind him—to catch their reflections in the mirror over the bar. The man turned around and said, "There's nobody in here, boys. Nobody in here." After some discussion, Scott convinced him to make his way aboveground.

Soon, Scott's crew was crawling through the Denali Theatre, which had plunged deep into the far end of the Fourth Avenue crevasse. The theater's second-story marquee rested level with the street. Inside, the ceiling had crumbled, then dropped into the auditorium, crushing the seats. Still, Scott's team didn't turn up a single body. When they were done searching, the men lingered in the lobby of the theater, as though trying to wrap their minds around what wasn't there. None of them had eaten anything since the previous afternoon. "I undertook it upon myself to release a few candy bars from the candy stand," Scott said.

The other search-and-rescue teams were largely reporting back the same results to Davis: the dead were nowhere to be found. By nightfall, after several rounds of searches, the city believed there'd only been twelve fatalities; Genie would read their names over the air. The low body count was a tremendous relief, but still not necessarily easy to make sense of, or trust.

Scott's crew searched one last building on Fourth Avenue, a two-story restaurant called the Anchorage Arcade. Then, feeling they'd picked the area apart, they accepted it was time to pack up and report back. A few minutes after they left, the Arcade shifted violently and settled two feet deeper into its crater. Later that afternoon, the building gave way entirely and collapsed, pulling down a streetlight and utility pole with it. One of them landed on Scott's Volkswagen, which he'd left parked at the corner. The other pole had Frank Brink's *Our Town* banner tied to it. The banner went slack, then floated into the street.

13.

"A PLACE TO RECOGNIZE ONESELF
AND OTHERS"

---

*FRANK BRINK'S
COMMUNITY THEATER*

HISTORY HAS FORGOTTEN FRANK BRINK. IN TRUTH, FEW outside Anchorage knew his name while he was alive.

Brink was forty-seven years old in 1964 and carried himself with a beguiling air of total self-assurance: he moved quickly, spoke quickly, and wore his conspicuous ego about him like an opera cape. In the mostly conservative city of Anchorage, one colleague said, Brink stuck out as "the very avatar of a creative person."

The man's every instinct seemed to be maximally expressive. "He was naturally always staging," a collaborator explained—subtly directing the scenes of his life. "He'd walk into a room and sit in the most pronounced area of that room." At a time when some people in Anchorage still lived in jury-rigged starter cabins, Brink's home, which he had designed himself and built with a friend, rose out of the woods south of town like a mid-century-modern apparition. It was the sort of jewel you'd expect to find in Big Sur or Malibu, fronted by two walls of windows cresting to an arrowhead-shaped roof. Inside, a spiral staircase wrapped around a colossal spruce trunk, and white sheepskins were spread around the orange shag carpet in the living room.

When writing or speaking publicly, Brink seldom let a breath go by without cramming it full of adverb-bedazzled stentorian flourishes. Later, he would make a documentary about the earth-quake that included this sentence: "Incredible are the stories of people who have known the awful power of the earth, straining to adjust to the ever-moving forces beneath its rocky crust; sto-ries of people who desperately fought for their lives and mar-veled at the unexplainable miracles that literally snatched them from death; stories of tragedy, human dignity, and bravery that symbolize the events and the attitudes of the buoyant, persever-ing people who survived America's greatest natural disaster."

This overblown aesthetic may seem at odds with the slow and plainspoken simplicity of the play he was producing that Easter weekend, but Brink had always loved Thornton Wilder's *Our Town*. He called it "the greatest play ever written in Amer-ica" and seemed to identify deeply with its characters and themes. Brink grew up in Eagles Mere, Pennsylvania, a small, isolated community that resembled the one Wilder had invented for the play. "I was raised in a poor logging camp and a poorer farm in Northern Appalachian Pennsylvania," Brink wrote, "where I learned to love the smell of a dank cow barn on a rainy morning, and sour pine cuttings on a mill floor. Where I learned to eat molasses balls in cow feed and swamp frog thighs smoked in willow bark. Where I learned to drink silo juice strained through a loaf of bread—'depression whiskey.'" Brink was the last, conspicuously accidental child in a family of five kids; his closest sibling was eight years older. The Brinks had no money— often literally not a nickel to their name. Frank was an unexpected burden on his parents, and grew up feeling like one.

As a boy, Brink taught himself to forage for ginseng roots and trap muskrats for their pelts, which he sold to Sears, Roebuck and Company. He learned to track a deer all day and kill it at night, with a bow and arrow, so that the game warden, who lived nearby, would not hear him hunting out of season. His best friends, he said, were "an old race horse, a blind sheep dog and an uneducated grandmother." That is, he seemed to have been growing into as feral and uncultivated a creature as Huck Finn. But at some point in Brink's childhood, someone made the mistake of taking the boy to a movie, and after that, he was devoted to the performing arts. At fourteen, he hitchhiked to New York City on the egg man's truck because he wanted to see an opera. At eighteen, he left home for good with a battered suitcase and fifteen dollars.

When World War II started, Brink served in the navy and was shipped to the South Pacific, where he suffered through a heinous tropical disease. When his deployment was over, he vowed to settle somewhere cold. "I always had a desire . . . to experience the adventure of Alaska," he explained, and he and his new wife, a New Englander named Jo, decided to try homesteading in the Eagle River valley outside Anchorage.

The Brinks found little culture in the city when they landed there in 1945. Anchorage's first movie houses pandered to unsophisticated tastes; other entertainment included going to church, getting drunk, or fighting. In the spring of 1946, however, an army officer at Fort Richardson decided to stage a one-off production with the USO of a play called *Ladies in Retirement,* and Brink started turning up to watch rehearsals. The show was floundering. Eventually, the director decided to take over the male lead and find a new director to take his place. The way Brink later told the story, the man tried to recruit an aerial gunner with some acting experience named Charlton Heston, but Heston declined. Brink won the job for himself.

Brink rehearsed the cast endlessly and managed to shape the scraps he'd inherited into a legitimate piece of theater. After rescuing *Ladies in Retirement,* he and his collaborators decided to forge their partnership into a proper community theater—the first in Alaska. They called it the Anchorage Little Theater, and Brink started planning its debut for the summer of 1946. It made sense to choose something simple, a feasible first success. He turned to *Our Town.*

Thornton Wilder had written *Our Town* in such a way that any theater company, anywhere in America, could stage it easily and cheaply. He explicitly stipulated that the stage should be virtually bare, except for a couple of tables, ladders, trellises, a bench—scenery that could be borrowed, or hammered together after a trip to the local hardware store. According to Wilder's stage directions, there shouldn't even be a curtain.

Brink had zero interest in such austerity, however. "When Frank first staged *Our Town* in 1946," a friend recalled, "he made it a religious experience!" There was a military band blaring an overture, a choir singing, a marathon of opening remarks by civic leaders and military dignitaries, and recitations of congratulatory telegrams sent by notable people from Outside. This was Anchorage's first real production, after all, and Brink wanted to show his new city what the theater was capable of. Then, while an air force major performed a ceremonial ribbon cutting onstage, Brink delivered a speech that, in retrospect, could be seen as an aspirational mission statement that would guide his work in Anchorage for the next thirty years. He called his talk "To Bring the Miracle of Theater."

BRINK ENVISIONED THE VALUE of community theater similarly to how Bram, the head of KENI, envisioned local broadcasting. A functioning theater, Brink claimed, was an integral part of any thriving municipality, "as necessary as food." And the experience of performing together—"community-wide playmaking," as he called it—would cohere the people of that community as their city grew.

A good theater "must be truly a place to play, a place to create and re-create, a place to commune and contemplate, yes, even a place where one might have the opportunity to recognize oneself and others," Brink wrote, "so that some of the truths still available to mankind may be discovered there." As a director, he had an almost despotic commitment to excellence. But in the end, the quality of the production was less important to him than the simple fact of people joining together to put it on. Eventually, on his résumé, Brink would start listing himself not just as "Theater Director," but "Community Leader," too.

Brink went out of his way to cast his plays inclusively, drawing from nearly every demographic nook and ethnic cranny of Anchorage. His productions included students, housewives, judges, military officers, local celebrities, children, and tradespeople—everyone from the powerful to the unemployed.

And though many of these volunteer actors arrived at Brink's rehearsals exhausted at the end of a long day, he worked them hard, leaning on them to read their Stanislavsky and Uta Hagen, rehearsing them late into the night, while he paced with his clipboard and barked direction. If one of his actors seemed stuck, or wooden, Brink would simply repeat a particular line reading, mercilessly, until the actor could mimic his inflection. "There was no faking it with Frank," one actor said. "He didn't stand for any shtick or B.S. You had to do your sensory and imagination homework." Another called Brink "a tyrant." Yet his ambition was magnetic; people strove to please him. As one woman put it, "Frank Brink *was* the theater."

After that first *Our Town* production in 1946, Brink was everywhere in Anchorage, putting on *Macbeth* and *Hamlet,* and musicals like *Man of La Mancha* and *South Pacific*. He would stage *The Crucible* and Robinson Jeffers's *Medea,* and more avant-garde work like *The Persecution and Assassination of Jean-Paul Marat as Performed by the Inmates of the Asylum of Charenton Under the Direction of the Marquis de Sade.* Brink's production of *The Miracle Worker,* a play about Helen Keller, was so uncannily perfect, one actor remembered, that "it touched the face of God."

In between these larger productions, Brink also produced flurries of one-acts, staged readings, variety shows for Fur Rendezvous, and Alaska's first radio dramas on KENI. Brink even managed to lure a few stars to town, like Boris Karloff and Will Rogers Jr., often to reprise roles they'd originated on Broadway. He wanted to give audiences in Alaska—which is to say, his own pool of actors—an appreciation for the magic true artists could conjure. When Karloff starred in *Arsenic and Old Lace* in a school auditorium in 1957, the people of Anchorage called him out for eleven consecutive curtain calls. "He projected a sense of solicitude and tenderness that went beyond ordinary courtesy," Brink wrote. Karloff ultimately donated his fee for the production back to the theater and, at the cast party, told Brink he wanted to leave him with a personal thank-you gift as well, but could not think of anything meaningful. Brink asked the maestro for his shoes: "To have the shoes of the first great theater talent to walk on the Alaskan stage would be the most wonderful gift I can think of," he told Karloff. Fifty years later, a distant relative of Brink's would find one of those shoes in her father's attic in Ohio, track down Karloff's aging daughter, and mail the shoe back.

By the end of the 1950s, Brink had hit his stride. Then, in 1960, came his opus—an epic of Alaskan history, which he wrote himself, called *Cry of the Wild Ram*. The play took three and a half hours to perform and the list of its cast and crew stretched across four pages of the program. Soon, Brink was busily adapting it into an even bigger production—a musical version, despite the fact that he did not play a single instrument or read music himself. (A colleague would sit beside him as he worked, transcribing his humming and whistling.) He tasked his wife, Jo, with stitching more than two hundred costumes. Another collaborator had to figure out how to build a harpsichord. As for the quality of the play, one crew member remembered, "It was so damn long. I had mixed feelings."

Cry of the Wild Ram told the story of Alexander Baranov, the Russian trader who shipwrecked on a remote Alaskan island in 1790 and was subsequently promoted to run the Russian American colonies for the czar. Baranov would wind up governing

Russian Alaska for almost twenty years. By the end, he was miserable. "Baranov didn't want to be here, either," Brink's longtime collaborator, Robert Pond, pointed out. Brink, he added, probably identified with him.

In fact, it became easy to wonder what Brink was doing in Anchorage—why he'd stayed so long, and whether he was truly content there, artistically. Brink had tried to break into the New York theater scene as a young man, before going to war, but rarely spoke about that brief period of his life. An acquaintance later remembered how "overwhelmed" Brink had seemed in New York; beneath all his erudition, he was still "a naïf," the man said—"the most sophisticated primitive I ever knew." Brink landed a few jobs, but seemed to find the competitiveness of Manhattan intolerable. He left without ever truly testing whether he had the talent to make it. "That weighed on him," said Robin Niemann, a close friend. What Brink was building in Anchorage was monumental: not just the Little Theater, but a broader culture of the arts blossoming around his example. Still, it was tempting to see his perfectionism, and the self-serious ostentation of his productions, as springing from some insecure or over-compensatory craving for something bigger—or, more poignantly, from regret.

By 1964, the so-called Golden Age of Anchorage community theater that Brink had catalyzed during the previous decade had withered and collapsed. For a time, there'd been five separate theater groups in the city. But now, after a confluence of artistic disagreements and fund-raising difficulties, only one was standing. It was an incarnation of Brink's original Little Theater, though it was without a building of its own, or even reliable access to a theater in which to stage its work.

Brink had taken a job on the inaugural faculty of Alaska Methodist University in 1960. The teaching gig offered him stability. It also provided him with a new, hassle-free home for his plays: a 233-seat circular lecture hall in the college's central building, Grant Hall, with a small stage built into one end. The room had concrete walls, and no scenery shop or backstage to speak of; an actor who had to exit one side of the stage, and reenter a subsequent scene from the other, was forced to walk outside and scamper around the exterior of the building in the cold. It wasn't quite a theater, in other words, but it was all Brink's— a place, like he'd always wanted, where he was free to create and play.

This is all to say, at the time of the earthquake, Frank Brink was essentially starting over. Putting on *Our Town* again—scaled back this time, as Thornton Wilder intended—seemed like a sensible first step.

OUR TOWN DEBUTED AT the McCarter Theatre in Princeton, New Jersey, in January 1938. Within three years, it had been performed by amateur theater groups in nearly eight hundred different communities and every state in the union but one (Rhode Island). By 1964, it was an icon, a classic. And yet it was also on its way to becoming "the most misunderstood and misinterpreted of American plays," as one *New York Times* critic put it: "a pioneering work of experimental theater" disguised as a sappy slice of small-town life.

The unnerving strangeness of the play hits you right away, first with the glaring absence of scenery, and then when the Stage Manager character appears and speaks the first lines right at the audience: "This play is called *Our Town*. It was written by Thornton Wilder"—and so on. But even beyond his immediate breaking of the fourth wall, there's something disruptive and irreconcilably weird about the Stage Manager as a narrator. He interacts with the characters onstage as easily as he does with the audience, but doesn't seem to be wholly part of either world, or situated in any specific time. Instead, we discover, he's endowed with a kind of breezy omniscience about the past and future, able to see the full sweep of time around each present moment that unfolds onstage. Just minutes into Act I, for example, as the sun rises on the small town of Grover's Corners, New Hampshire, and a character named Dr. Gibbs returns home to his wife from an overnight house call, the Stage Manager interrupts the couple's conversation to explain to the audience how and when each of those characters in the kitchen behind him will eventually die. "Mrs. Gibbs died first," he says.

It's startling, morbid, eerie—and it happens again and again. The play keeps lavishing lapidary attention on the most mundane details of people's lives, only to be undercut by the Stage Manager's asides about their deaths. Other times, he goes on odd tangents about the vastness of the universe, or the breadth of recorded history, against which this relatively tiny drama, and these individual people, barely register. The play keeps toggling our focus between the everyday and the cosmic. Those lives, and everything we see happen in that town, come to feel both infinitely rich and infinitely fragile.

From there, a kind of ambient bleakness gradually consumes the play. Nothing evil or cataclysmic happens. The people onstage just live their lives. Yet the drama slowly turns wrenching.

(Eleanor Roosevelt wrote that by the time she left the theater she was depressed "beyond words.") One critic would identify *Our Town*, ultimately, as a story about "how mankind confronts overwhelming disaster."

The play centers on two teenagers in Grover's Corners. George Gibbs is the innocent, somewhat lunkheaded son of the town's only doctor. Emily Webb is the bright and introspective daughter of its newspaper editor. They are next-door neighbors. We watch them do their homework, fall in love, get married, grow up. The story's outlines are generic, and Wilder highlights that ordinariness in a way that's almost cruel.

The first scene, for example, opens on an ordinary morning in Grover's Corners. On the bare stage, George's and Emily's mothers pantomime lighting invisible stoves in their adjacent houses, readying invisible breakfasts for their kids before school. The milkman leads an invisible cow down their street, making invisible deliveries. When Act II starts, we're shown the same routine—except now, three years into the future, the paperboy who enters is the little brother of the paperboy we saw in Act I. The point is, existence in Grover's Corners has always been like this: over time, the rhythms of the community subsume individual lives. Even the oldest tombstones in the cemetery, the Stage Manager explains—and some are more than two centuries old—bear the same last names as people walking around town now. Zoom out, the Stage Manager is saying, and all the moments of our lives appear fused into one endlessly repeating cycle. Even in the middle of George and Emily's wedding ceremony, the Stage Manager turns to the audience and confesses, cynically, that he's seen hundreds of weddings and isn't particularly impressed with this one. "Almost everybody in the world gets married—you know what I mean?" he says. Later, he adds, "Once in a thousand times it's interesting."

Wilder was fixated on this kind of vulnerability: the way time inevitably swallows all of us. He remembered visiting a few mundane archeological sites while living briefly in Rome: the tomb of a typical first-century family, the ancient plumbing on the Palatine Hill. "And ever since," Wilder wrote in a preface to *Our Town,* "I find myself occasionally looking at the things about me as an archeologist will look at them a thousand years hence." He walked around New York wondering how they would interpret the bronze wall plaques that had survived the disappearance of the city's brownstones—the ones reading TRADESMEN'S EN-TRANCE or NIGHT BELL. The minutiae of daily life begins to look very different if you spiral forward in time and glance back: somehow, every scrap feels both precious and meaningless. "An archeologist's eye combines the view of the telescope with the view of the microscope," Wilder explained.

In *Our Town,* he wanted to bring that way of seeing to the stage. The Stage Manager explains this outright toward the end of Act I. A new bank is being built in Grover's Corners, he notes, and they're sealing a time capsule in its cornerstone to be dug up a thousand years in the future. The Stage Manager expects that they'll put a copy of the Constitution and a Bible in the time capsule, but worries those documents won't reveal the texture of ordinary life in town—"real life," he says, like the stories we've been watching onstage. After all, the Stage Manager explains, "Babylon once had two million people in it, and all we know about 'm is the names of the kings and some copies of wheat contracts . . . and contracts for the sale of slaves.

Yet every night all those families sat down to supper, and the father came home from his work, and the smoke went up the chimney—same as here." So the Stage Manager decides he'll put a copy of this play in the time capsule, too: *Our Town* by Thornton Wilder.

Suddenly, the Stage Manager starts talking to those people a thousand years in the future. His logic here is convoluted, but sound: knowing that he is a character in Wilder's play himself, he knows that what he says to us, in the theater, will be preserved in the script for those future humans to read. "So—people a thousand years from now," he says. "This is the way we were in the provinces north of New York at the beginning of the twentieth century. This is the way we were: in our growing up and in our marrying and in our living and in our dying."

It's among the most famous passages in *Our Town*—a kind of existential credo whose mix of determination and desperation echoes the feeling in Anchorage in 1964. The Stage Manager is saying: Remember us. *Recognize* us. It's one community's simple insistence that it mattered, made urgent by a suspicion that, ultimately, it might *not* matter. In other words, the overwhelming disaster everyone in *Our Town* is confronting is irrelevance: a creeping awareness that no matter how secure and central each of us feels within the stories of our own lives, we are, in reality, just specks of things, at the mercy of larger forces that can blot us out indifferently or by chance.

The ground is moving under Grover's Corners, shrugging people off—not in a sudden and violent spasm, like it would in Anchorage that Good Friday, but in the steadiest, most predictable way imaginable: by pushing away from them, traveling forward in time.

Every once in a while, the earth rears up and shakes. But it's always, always spinning.

BRINK'S *OUR TOWN* CAST, in March 1964, was a motley cross section of greater Anchorage. There was a silver-haired middle school English teacher, an African American prizefighter who worked for the Army Corps of Engineers, an aging maintenance man, a plumber, a handful of kids, a young navy veteran who'd auditioned mainly to meet girls, and a young gay man with coke-bottle glasses named Bob Deloach who'd been acting for Brink since he was a boy, latching on to the director as a kind of surrogate dad. ("Frank had a gift for seeing the hurt in people," his friend Robin Niemann would later explain, "partly because he had some of his own.") Mr. Webb, the newspaper editor, was played by a tradesman named Chick Sewell, who'd been roped into his first Frank Brink production by his wife six years earlier. Sewell had initially seemed irredeemably stiff as a performer, reciting his lines as though he were a schoolkid reading a report. But Brink had worked the man over into a proficient character actor.

Brink had also taken one big and unexpected risk with his casting. To play the lead, Emily Webb, he had recruited Susan Koslosky, an Alaska Methodist University freshman with no prior acting experience. Koslosky was a third-generation Alaskan from one of the state's earliest pioneer families. She was eighteen and stunning, with dark eyes like a doe and a tall tangle of brown hair; a year earlier, she'd been crowned Miss Fur Rendezvous at the annual winter carnival, then first runner-up in the

Miss Alaska pageant. Brink saw Koslosky as radiating a kind of fragility and innocence—exactly what he wanted for Emily—and bet on her to carry much of the play's emotional weight. He considered her inexperience an asset. She would bring that guilelessness to the role.

In Koslosky's mind, this air of virtue was merely a persona she had scrupulously crafted, or built up like scar tissue over her wounds. Koslosky's parents separated when she was three years old. She saw her father only occasionally, when he came to argue with her mother about child support. Her mother, meanwhile, seemed emotionally unwell: sometimes she was loving; other times she'd snap at Susan ruthlessly, calling her worthless or a slut. To cope, and to prove her mother wrong, Koslosky had gradually affected a kind of divine poise. She got active in student government. She represented Alaska at a youth conference at the White House at age fourteen. She turned herself into a beauty queen. Then she enrolled in Frank Brink's speech and drama class in her first semester at AMU. She had never before met someone who seemed so genuinely free and comfortable with himself. She decided to try acting herself.

Unfortunately, Koslosky wasn't particularly good onstage. Brink had to push her, relentlessly, through the early rehearsals for *Our Town* that winter, and his dissatisfaction with her left her feeling dejected and trapped. One evening, they were rehearsing a scene between Emily and her father in Act II—a turgid but emotionally loaded conversation before he gives her away at the wedding. The scene had to be played subtly. Koslosky wasn't getting it. Suddenly, Brink exploded at her from the back of Grant Hall, shouting over the heads of the rest of the cast. "I don't believe you!" he screamed at her. "I don't believe you!" She hadn't convinced Brink that this man standing next to her was her father.

What happened next surprised Koslosky: someone screamed back at Brink. What surprised her, specifically, was that *she* was the one screaming. How could she believably relate to her stage father, she shouted, if she didn't know what it was like to have a *real* father? Once she was done screaming, she started crying. Brink sent everyone else out on a coffee break and walked her down the hall to his office, to talk.

Koslosky told him everything. She explained how cripplingly inauthentic she felt—not only as an actor, but as a human being. Nothing she did was unselfconscious or unrehearsed, she told him. She'd even worked up a rigorous protocol for conversations on dates, a list of appropriate, enchanting things to tell a boy on a first date, a separate script for second dates, and so on. She knew Brink was asking her to reach inside herself for this role. But she worried that her mother was right and there was nothing inside.

Brink responded quickly, without hesitation. He told Koslosky that he saw a real person under her veneer—a person of value—even if she didn't. *That's* who he'd cast as Emily, and who he wanted to see step forward in this play and be expressed. Decades later, at age seventy-two, Koslosky would explain: "To survive my childhood, I had to become invisible. That was the first time anyone actually recognized me. The first person, ever, to acknowledge me was Frank Brink."

From then on, Koslosky devoted herself to the production— and to Brink. When the earthquake struck, she was with her younger sister at home on Twenty-Third Avenue, waiting for her mother to return from the grocery store and drive her to the theater for their Friday-night performance. It was two and a half hours before curtain time, but she already had her stage makeup on, and her hair in the long braid she wore for Act I. When the quake was over and her mother got home, Koslosky stood in front of their rattled house arguing with her, adamantly, that she still needed a ride to the theater, right away. Frank Brink was counting on her, Koslosky insisted, and she would not be talked down. Just trust me, her mom kept saying, today is different: the show didn't actually have to go on.

Brink himself seemed to have the opposite reaction to the earthquake. He was driving home for a rest before curtain time when the Seward Highway cracked open in front of him. The pavement on one side of the breach dropped abruptly by a foot or more, then the two halves started to twist and scrape against each other.

Unlike so many others in Anchorage, Brink seemed to understand the momentousness of what was happening right away: his dramatic imagination was equipped, or maybe even predisposed, to recognize that, during those four and a half minutes, he was passing fitfully through some severe inflection point in history. Normal life was disintegrating around him. There would be no community theater that night; his community's very idea of itself was now under threat.

"Even in those moments while the earthquake was still shaking the earth," Brink would remember, "watching the road sandwich and scissor itself and break open, I kept thinking: 'What will Alaskans do now?'"

14.

"THE WAY WE'RE GOING TO DO THINGS HERE IN ALASKA"

THE OUTSIDE COMES IN

GENIE WORKED FOR SIX MORE HOURS AFTER THEDA ARRIVED, ostensibly to relieve her. At one point, Big Winston drove Jan down to the Public Safety Building to see her, and Genie put the little girl to work with the Salvation Army, making sandwiches for all the exhausted volunteers. Genie finally stepped away from her microphone around three o'clock that Saturday afternoon, more than twenty-one hours after the quake. Two hours later, she was back to work, claiming to have taken a nap.

By then, Anchorage was swarming with Outsiders. The reporters had started landing around lunchtime, as the first tentative trickle of inbound air traffic resumed, and they multiplied throughout the day. They came from local newspapers around the Lower 48, from *The New York Times, Los Angeles Times,* and *The Washington Post,* from *Newsweek, National Geographic,* and *LIFE.* They arrived brandishing cameras, notebooks, and tape recorders, eager to translate the confusion in front of them into intelligible copy. Even before touching down, they would describe Anchorage International Airport's collapsed control tower coming into view as "a sickening jumble of steel girders and shattered glass," and the runways as buckling "like thin pie crust." The City of Anchorage had no public relations office, and no one at the Public Safety Building had the foresight to manage the press corps as it grew. Instead, at eight o'clock that evening, the city called a press conference at the Public Safety Building. They would wrangle everyone together and do their best to knock out some initial questions.

More than a hundred people showed up. Mixed among the Outside reporters were Alaskans like Genie who'd been grinding away in the building for more than twenty-four hours with little to no rest. Occasionally, workers had slipped upstairs to the fire department's barracks to curl up on the floor, but sleep proved elusive. One man explained that as soon as he drifted off, a fire alarm blared, and all around him the roused firemen hit the floor in their heavy boots, jolting him awake in a panic; he assumed the vibration was another quake. As everyone settled in for the press conference, one woman noticed that although many of the workers seemed dazed, not a single one was yawning. She watched one man absently picking at the whiskers sprouting on his chin and found something so poignant about the emptiness on his face—this utterly depleted trance into which the man had driven himself—that she would remember the image for the rest of her life.

Robert Oldland, Anchorage's city manager, began the briefing by asking several of his department heads to give a report, just like they had at the three a.m. meeting the night before.

Overall, the situation was stabilizing: Electricity had been tenuously restored to much of the city. Military airlifts of food and other supplies were arriving from Outside, and field kitchens around town were feeding the displaced. So far, the public had been generally tranquil and cooperative; police chief Flanigan was insisting, however, that Anchorage's bars and liquor stores remain closed awhile longer, to make sure it remained that way.

Just then, the governor, William A. Egan, walked in. Egan was Alaska's first governor—and still, at that point, the only one in state history. Prior to politics, he had run a grocery store in Valdez, a tiny, beleaguered town whose mining economy had gone bust while Egan grew up there. He had been one of two students in his graduating high school class, in 1932, and was said to be so meek as a young man that he couldn't bring himself to look his customers at the grocery store in the eye.

Egan had been propelled into office after two years in Washington lobbying for statehood, and though still a quiet man who spoke in a slightly high-pitched quaver, he now conveyed an ineffable steadiness. He was a true believer in Alaska—and in Alaskans, too. He had a habit of sitting in the governor's mansion around ten o'clock every night and dialing random numbers from the phone book. He would introduce himself to the unsuspecting Alaskan on the other end and just ask him or her questions: How are things going? Do you have a family?

After the quake on Friday night, Egan and his staff had tried to fly into Anchorage from the capital in Juneau, but were turned back by fog. He finally arrived at noon and had spent the afternoon somberly surveying the damage alongside Alaska's two senators, who had raced in from Washington. "God almighty," one muttered when Egan and his entourage got to J. C. Penney.

Now, at the press conference, Egan tried to offer encouragement. "I am happy to note the attitude of the people toward the terrible disaster," he said. The calamity "had not overtaken them." He relayed what information he had about ravaged outlying towns—the military was arranging to fly him and the media to some of them first thing tomorrow—and offered a few uplifting, forward-looking generalities about reconstruction. Everybody he was meeting was already determined to rebuild a better town than they'd lived in before, Egan insisted. "Let's not consider this a beating," he said. "We are not licked."

The governor's words were met with bursts of applause. Then, all at once, questions started firing from the reporters in the gallery.

IT APPEARED THAT ANCHORAGE might be overmatched. The makeshift emergency organization at the Public Safety Building had only just started to restore some sense of order in the city. Now the surge of Outsiders, and the nation's attention, threatened to shake Anchorage again.

In the twenty-six and a half hours since the earthquake, the energy of nearly everyone in the city had aligned behind the same basic priorities: food, water, safety, locating survivors, finding the dead. The media had different priorities. One reporter wired a note back to his bosses after visiting evacuees from the Native communities on Kodiak Island that had been washed out by tsunamis. The reporter snagged a great photo, he wrote: "Shows Eskimo youngster bawling her head off with remainder of her family in background. Excellent copy."

"We had a real problem with the press corps," one city worker later explained. Some of the tension centered on access to the damage downtown. The area around Fourth Avenue was still sealed off, barricaded and patrolled by the army troops and the National Guard's Eskimo Scouts. But the journalists, accustomed to special press privileges, demanded to see it for themselves and got agitated when such access wasn't immediately granted to them. City officials started giving the reporters passes to show to the guards downtown, but the passes were issued in an uncoordinated, scattershot way that would, ultimately, only lead to more frustration. As the weekend wore on, some city workers were handing out blue passes, while others gave out pink ones. There were white passes, too. It was rarely clear which color, or colors, were valid at any particular time.

The situation quickly turned senseless, infuriating. The enlisted men at the barricades were accustomed to following orders, not making judgment calls. Moreover, a report later noted, some of the Eskimo Scouts spoke limited English and had difficulty reading what was written on the passes. As journalists found themselves turned away by this blockade of Native men, it's likely that some of their self-righteousness and outrage over the situation was exacerbated by racism. One aggravated reporter would finally bark at the city manager, "Will these little soldiers be told that we are free to work in these areas?"

Distrust mounted on both sides; the dynamic was turning toxic. Many in the media seemed to look down on the Alaskans as amateurs and rubes, in over their heads, which made the Alaskans understandably defensive—or led them, in turn, to look down on the media as prissy and entitled, in over *their* heads now that they'd set foot in Alaska. For the first time, Outsiders were scrutinizing and second-guessing decisions that Alaskans had made in isolation, in the throes of an emergency. At one point, a particularly testy reporter confronted Mayor Sharrock, unwilling to accept the mayor's claim that Anchorage had not been placed under martial law on Friday night, as had been mistakenly reported several times, including on KENI. Moreover, the reporter argued, if martial law *hadn't* been declared, was deploying these armed National Guardsmen into the streets even constitutional? A worker at the Public Safety Building would later describe how Sharrock finally lashed out at the journalist, rebuking him: "The mayor said he didn't know," the man remembered, "but that's the way they were going to do it here in Alaska."

The reporters were under pressure to gather facts quickly. So many Americans had migrated to Alaska in recent years that most newspapers in the Lower 48 understood that they'd have readers concerned about family members there. The disaster was national—even global. One typical plea for information, wired into the city from an Outside editor, read: "Flooded by calls from anxious people worried about relatives in Anchorage or lots of smaller towns. Story tremendous interest here and completely dominating newspapers." This editor was in Norway.

The first wave of reporters to take off for Alaska on Friday night had gotten bottlenecked in Seattle for hours, waiting for the fog in Anchorage to lift and the runways to reopen. Many spent those hours gathering whatever secondhand information they could. Macabre rumors about fires and tidal waves slowly coalesced in their minds into facts, some of which proved difficult to unlearn once the reporters touched down. They arrived bracing for unthinkable horror. It seemed only logical that the death toll would be catastrophic in the greater Anchorage area; it was the city closest to the earthquake's epicenter and had the largest population of any municipality in the state—nearly half of all Alaskans lived there. This made it especially baffling when, at the press conference that Saturday evening, city officials announced that they'd recovered only twelve bodies so far. Dr. William Davis, the oblong-headed psychologist who'd somehow become the city's "Coordinator of Search and Rescue Operations," insisted to the incredulous media that, after sending out more than two hundred searchers that day, he was personally convinced no survivors remained to be found; some areas of the city, he explained, had been combed three or four times. Whether there were fatalities still unaccounted for, however, was a more complicated question. Later, when Davis was asked about Turnagain specifically, he would concede that when the high tides plowed through the wreckage on the shore, it was possible the water had carried the dead away.

Twelve dead defied common sense. The reporters were skeptical. Many people were. There were whispers about faint cries still echoing from the rubble on Fourth Avenue, about bodies still sealed inside Penney's. Around the time the press conference was getting under way on Saturday night, word spread that one of Disaster Control's emergency demolition crews had, in fact, uncovered another body on the street outside the department store. A West Anchorage High School senior named Lee Styer was found crushed in his Chevrolet. The car had been a gift from his father, for getting into UCLA.

LATE THAT SATURDAY NIGHT, a city official named Douglas Clure called Genie to the back of the Public Safety Building to foist another responsibility on her. Since Genie returned from her break that afternoon, her role in the building had continued to shift and expand. With Theda now broadcasting from the scene as well, Genie was devoting a fair amount of her time to getting the Outside media oriented—helping the reporters navigate Anchorage, finding locals for them to interview, and even arranging places for them to stay.

Clure had another gaggle of new arrivals to hand off to Genie now, a group of journalists who'd just reached the city all the way from Europe and had missed the press conference earlier that evening. He explained to the reporters that this woman would get everyone up to speed; whatever information Genie Chance shared with them, Clure said, could be attributed to him in their articles. Genie would later remember being taken aback when the Europeans instantly recognized her name: "Oh yes," they told her. "We've heard you on the radio."

Without realizing it, Genie had become famous. In the last twenty-four hours, her voice had traveled around the world, spraying out of Anchorage on an array of convoluted, sharply skewing paths. One originated at KENI's sister station in Fairbanks, which, after starting to simulcast the feed from Anchorage late on Friday night, also relayed that signal to a radio station in Juneau. Then a man in Juneau telephoned a radio station in Seattle and seemed to simply hold his phone up to the radio and let the broadcast play. The announcer in Seattle threw that call onto his own airwaves. The sound—relayed and relayed and relayed again—was thin, distant, and hissy, but there was Genie, unmistakably, calling in city employees for the three a.m. meeting and churning through personal messages from Alaskans separated from their loved ones: "Frank Smith," listeners in Seattle heard

Genie say, "your family is safe, and at the home of Red Dodge." Like that, Genie's voice had touched the Lower 48: the first proof, for many Americans, that the city of Anchorage was still there.

It would be hard, a half century later, for Americans living in an age of instantaneous information to appreciate how desperate the Outside world was for firsthand accounts of the disaster that night, and how long they were left in the dark. But keep in mind that they, too, saw themselves as living in an age of instantaneous information. By early 1964, live radio and television coverage of historic events like the Kennedy assassination, but also comparatively trivial ones, like the Fur Rendezvous sled-dog races, had acclimated the nation to what felt like a reliable onrush of unlimited news. That Good Friday night, it was obvious that something horrific had happened; even fifteen hundred miles away in Seattle, the Space Needle had swayed. But to go hours without any genuine knowledge of the earthquake's toll was maddening. And even as details trickled out, there was a dearth of perspective to anchor them, or to translate those random facts into a story. The disaster had no narrator.

Later, another radio station employee would describe Genie's reports as "instrumental in avoiding panic and wholesale confusion." The information was a form of comfort, but so was the voice delivering it. It was encouraging to hear someone inside the black box of Anchorage—and particularly a woman, the man added—"maintaining such calmness, withstanding such pressures and assuming such heavy responsibilities for such a long period of time, and without her voice showing the strain." Even while fielding the brief phone call from London around midnight, Genie had passed enough precious scraps of eyewitness information out of Alaska to wind up quoted in several newspapers on the other side of the Atlantic. KOIL, the radio station in Omaha she'd spoken to, immediately fed a recording of its long interview with Genie to its sister stations in Indiana and Oregon, then pushed the tape across NBC's nationwide network. Genie's parents had heard it on their local affiliate in Bonham that Saturday morning, after being woken up by the ringing phone. The instant Genie's voice hit the air in Texas, the Broadfoots' phone started ringing more ferociously. "We're listening to Emma Gene's broadcast! Call later, please!" Genie's mother kept hollering into the receiver before impatiently hanging up.

From there, other radio and television networks reached out to KOIL to air Genie's interview as well: CBS, ABC, the Canadian Broadcasting Corporation. The Associated Press and other wire services quoted excerpts. Reporters stuck at the Seattle airport on Friday night, en route to Anchorage, listened to Genie on the radio and showed up at the Public Safety Building on Saturday asking for her by name. "It was a weird feeling," Genie later explained. "State officials arrived from Juneau with tears in their eyes, embraced me, and thanked me for keeping them informed."

By the end of the day on Saturday, Genie's interview with the Omaha radio station had been rebroadcast on one hundred and eleven other stations around the world. Her boss, Bram, had only just arrived in Tokyo with the delegation of Alaskan businessmen when he learned about the earthquake. When he switched on a radio, he heard his own reporter talking to him.

15.

"THE KEEPER OF ALL
THINGS CHANCE"

———

*THE REST OF GENIE'S LIFE
FLASHES BEFORE YOUR EYES*

ONE YEAR LATER, ON GOOD FRIDAY 1965, THE THREE
Chance kids had the day off from school and Genie took
Jan to do some shopping at J. C. Penney—a new J. C. Penney,
rebuilt on the site of the old one, which had been demolished
after the quake.

All day, Genie felt off. That morning, after the boys left for
work with Winston, she'd thrown herself into cleaning the
house. She did the dishes. She did the laundry. She shampooed
Jan's hair, then her own hair, then found herself tidying room
after room with increasing compulsivity. "For some reason," she
later wrote, "everything had to be clean." Now, around three
o'clock, in the Girls Ready to Wear department of Penney's,
Genie realized she'd been here with Jan at the same time last
year, too: "Unconsciously, we were repeating our actions." It was

as though she'd come back to remember, to test that the orderliness of the world had truly been restored. Maybe this was how trauma worked. Maybe it didn't knock you back, like an earthquake, but infiltrated and destabilized you slowly, like rot.

Genie took Jan home. She started cleaning again, filling the dishpan with mountainous suds just to wash a couple of drinking glasses and a coffee cup. She scrubbed and scrubbed. She turned on music, then flipped it off. It was almost five o'clock now. The house was too quiet. "I just couldn't stand it," she wrote.

She decided to vacuum. She started in the living room. She knew one of the boys had vacuumed there that morning, but told herself he probably hadn't done a thorough job. As she vacuumed, she checked her watch. The time was sliding closer to 5:36, the moment of the quake. She kept vacuuming. She kept looking at her watch. Soon, she purposefully *stopped* looking at her watch. More time passed. Then: "I got down on my hands and knees and attacked the carpet under the sofa with a vengeance." She was on the floor cleaning like this for a long time— until it was safe to stop. "The next time I glanced at my watch it was 5:40," she wrote: it was over. She put away the vacuum cleaner and started supper.

Genie was no longer working at KENI. Life at the station had become intolerable for her after the quake. As the story of the disaster started to be written, Genie became one of its recurring characters. "Few Alaskans will ever forget the cool calm voice of Genie Chance," one magazine explained. The media called her the "Voice of Hope" or the "Voice of Alaska"—a stand-in for the resourcefulness and composure of an entire state. She began receiving mail from around the country, thanking her. Governor

Egan told her, "I will always remember what a grand person you were at all times, despite the continuous and tremendous pressure you were under." An army colonel praised the "selfless devotion" with which Genie had stayed at her microphone, "even though obviously fatigued to the point of collapse." A woman in New Hampshire explained that her little grandchildren had been so impressed with Genie when they heard her on the radio that they now danced around the house, doing a kind of modified twist they called "the Genie Chance."

Some of the praise came laced with condescension. There was persistent, backhanded disbelief that a woman could work so hard and proficiently during a crisis. A federal official who'd listened to Genie from Washington noted that she "did indeed give lie to the expression 'the weaker sex.'" Another Alaskan dignitary compared "Genie Chance's well-modulated, calm voice" to "the tired but ever-loving voice of a mother." The man was impressed; her broadcasts, he said, were "not the usual simpering prattle I associate with many women's programs."

Many of the men at KENI already saw Genie as self-important. Her fame only exacerbated that friction, widening the rift. Genie actually felt ashamed by the attention. She knew the entire staff of KENI had worked just as tirelessly, as had the staffs of two other radio stations operating in Anchorage after the quake, particularly KFQD. Besides, Genie had only talked into a microphone that weekend. Her own suffering and sacrifices were minimal, compared to those of the rescue workers and police. And unlike all those people in Anchorage whose messages she had relayed over the air, she'd known her own family was safe the whole time. She was only getting recognized for her supposed strength and courage because, she wrote, "it was my voice that went round the world."

Genie downplayed her importance, but it was never particularly convincing. ("I don't *feel* famous," she said on NBC. She wrote to an editor in London: "Just a little old housewife and mother helping out with family finances being heard around the world? How crazy can this world be!") She tried to disappear into her job, but her job was different now; reporting the local news in Anchorage had turned exhausting, as the city was swallowed by planning and disputes about its reconstruction. That summer, Genie lost fifteen pounds from the stress. After taking two weeks off in August, she wrote: "I can feel my emotions again." But one of those emotions was dread: she dreaded returning to work.

She asked for a raise. She knew the reporters at Anchorage's other stations made twice as much as she did. Her boss, however, told her she was already making the highest salary "for a woman." The exchange convinced Genie she could never again feel fulfilled at KENI, only taken advantage of. "I was only being used because I worked hard and cheap," she wrote. She quit that same day.

She started hustling, reviving the same entrepreneurial energy with which she'd broken into radio initially. Within weeks, Genie was taking on clients as a one-woman public relations firm. She spoke at banquets around Anchorage and emceed benefits. In May of 1965, she was flown to New York by *McCall's Magazine* to receive a national award for women broadcasters called the Golden Mic, honoring her coverage of the earthquake. Wire stories about her ricocheted around the country again. The

Anchorage Chamber of Commerce took the opportunity to name her its "Goodwill Ambassador" to the East Coast and furnished her with samples of Alaskan king crab, reindeer steaks, and whale meat to pass around Manhattan. The TV game show *To Tell the Truth* invited her on as a guest. A few months later, she flew back to New York to stage a fashion show at the Waldorf Astoria to promote an Alaskan clothing company. "Genie has some spirit!" one newspaper profile exclaimed. When she returned home to Anchorage, civic leaders began cornering her at social events, asking if she'd ever thought about running for office.

Genie was growing more comfortable with her prominence and her place in the lore of the earthquake. She'd learned how to spin and channel that reputation. She regularly claimed, for example, to have stayed on duty at KENI for fifty-nine hours that Easter weekend, with only a few intermittent snatches of sleep—which was true, but only, it seemed, if you included the hours she'd worked during the day on Friday, before the quake. Still, by the time Genie launched her first political campaign, for a seat in the Alaska statehouse, in 1966, she hardly talked about the earthquake anymore; she didn't have to—it was an indelible part of her aura. One of her first campaign posters showed her posing in the glamorous fur-lined sealskin parka that was becoming her trademark, holding a radio microphone.

The parameters of her life were rapidly expanding. But since the earthquake, she seemed also to be privately wrestling with the conspicuous fact that she was outgrowing her husband. In one journal entry, Genie described herself as being in a class of women "who are individuals, who are independent, who love the very vibrations of life around them." Too often, a man is attracted to such a woman solely out of an impulse "to conquer and subdue this wild creature and make her do his will." Genie considered herself lucky: Big Winston had always allowed her to be herself. Still, she wrote, "it is unfortunate that the very man who can grant me such freedom to continue to grow and to live has no interest in continuing to grow and live himself." But the full truth, which she apparently could not bring herself to write, was more harrowing: Winston was an alcoholic. He beat her when he was drunk.

Years later, the details of that abuse could only be reconstructed indirectly, from people close to Genie and from Winston's own apologetic letters; not once did Genie discuss it explicitly in writing herself. It's unclear how frequently Winston hit her, or when the violence began. Clearly, the more accomplished Genie became after the earthquake, the more Winston smoldered. She lost that first race for the statehouse, but would be elected two years later in 1968 and serve in the legislature for the next eight years. The earthquake had propelled her life, irreversibly, onto a different trajectory, while Winston remained a car salesman, scrapping to make a living. "I think, at some point, he began to feel overshadowed," a family member would explain. It was true that Winston encouraged Genie's ambition. But when he drank, he punished her for it, too.

The breaking point came in early 1971. That winter, Genie took Jan with her to Juneau for the four-month legislative session, while Winston stayed in Anchorage. He was convinced that Genie was cheating on him and arrived one night, unannounced, at Genie's apartment in Juneau and began beating her furiously, grabbing her by the hair and tearing open her nightgown. Jan was fifteen years old. She hid under the covers in a back bedroom, clasping her puppy, as the violence escalated. At one point, Winston tried to throw Genie out the eleventh-floor window.

For Jan, the abuse was torturously hard to make sense of. It violated fundamental qualities of her parents that she'd always loved. Jan knew her father as a generous, affectionate man— a nurturer and caregiver; she'd adored Winston since she was a little girl. When he drank, he terrified her, but she also recognized his drinking as a sickness he couldn't overcome. Meanwhile, Jan revered Genie for her preternatural toughness and self-possession, her relentless insistence on her own dignity— qualities that seemed irreconcilable with being victimized by a man for so long. In short, Genie had instilled enough of herself in her only daughter that Jan couldn't understand how her mother could stay in an abusive marriage—why any woman would. Later, as an adult, Jan would press Genie for an explanation, and Genie would confess that her own feelings about Winston had been similarly confusing and fraught. She'd still loved her husband—truly. And he'd always seemed genuinely sorry afterward. Also, she was scared: Winston had once threatened to kill her, or hurt the kids, if she left him. Still, the morning after the assault in Juneau, Genie took Winston to the airport and put him on a plane back to Anchorage. She filed for a restraining order soon after and asked for a divorce.

Months of messiness and uncertainty followed. Winston turned regretful and desperate, which seemed to eat away at Genie's resolve. "Everything I will do will be to build you up into the perfect woman you are," he wrote to her. "Your mind and body will be all yours—you do not need to answer to me for anything." He confessed that his pride had been hurt, but not anymore: "I would be so proud to take you anywhere and show you off, tell everyone I have the prettiest, smartest, best wife in the world." Genie ultimately proceeded with divorce. Winston moved out. Then, one Friday night that August, he appeared outside the family's kitchen while Genie was having dinner with another man, a gentlemanly former Speaker of the Alaska House of Representatives named Bill Boardman. Winston wrenched open the bay window, barged through it, picked up a chair, and started shaking it, yelling, "I'm going to kill you, Bill Boardman, and everyone in this house!" He eventually calmed down, sulked off; the altercation went no further. Genie married Boardman the following month.

She felt liberated. In a way, her private life was aligning, belatedly, with the air of independence she'd been projecting as a lawmaker. There were only two other women in the statehouse when Genie was first elected, and some of the men, she wrote, "seemed dedicated to proving that I was out of place." They tended to be tough, old, and staggeringly lazy, and to regard their seats as a perk to which they were entitled after other distinguished careers. Genie made it her business to ram as much progressive legislation through the chamber as she could, and with none of the ladylike deference those men expected. ("She was not a glass of warm milk," one lawmaker would remember.) She championed what she called "people programs," often focusing on the needs of women, children, and other marginalized constituencies, like Alaska Natives, African Americans, and the disabled. She worked on subsidized day care, and on training police and EMTs to better assist rape victims. She had a hand in liberalizing abortion law in Alaska, three years before *Roe v. Wade*. In 1972, she helped get the Equal Rights Amendment ratified in the state. ("I don't think it will change my life a great deal," she explained to a reporter, "because I've gone ahead and lived my life regardless of the legislative and statutory restrictions. But it will certainly improve the rights of women all over the state.") She started wearing a frosted-blond wig, short skirts, and fashionable knee-high white go-go boots—not just around Anchorage, but on the floor of the capitol as well. When one of her colleagues sniped at her in the hallway, explaining—loudly enough so that everyone else could hear—that his wife wore more clothes to bed than Genie wore to work, Genie wheeled around and shot back, "No wonder you're such a grumpy old man!"

"There was a clear sense that she'd had a tragic past and now she was making up for lost time," her legislative aide, a younger woman named Barbara Brinkerhoff, would remember. One of Genie's touchstone issues was domestic violence, which was particularly prevalent among the military wives in her district. She worked to support the spread of domestic violence shelters around Alaska in the mid-seventies, holding low-key meetings in her living room, over drinks, to bring together advocates, social workers, and victims. Still, Genie never seemed interested, or perhaps comfortable enough, to share her own story; in public, she rarely spoke about her first marriage at all. She only wanted to know what concrete legislation and programs she could put her energy behind that would help people now.

Fifteen years had passed since Genie had reluctantly joined Winston in Anchorage, reassured by the hope that she might, at least, find opportunities on that dank frontier that were inaccessible to her in Texas. But before the earthquake, she'd seemed to only rediscover the same sexism and agonizing limitations—

injustices society considered normal, or too shameful to discuss, much less resolve.

By the mid-seventies, though, Genie appeared to be finding some of the happiness and ease that had eluded her. And in the legislature, she was retroactively building the new world she'd expected to find in Alaska when she first arrived. "At the time she was doing what she was doing, it was incredible," Brinkerhoff would remember. "She was giving younger women the opportunities she had missed. That's the whole women's movement, in a nutshell."

THIS MIGHT HAVE BEEN a fairy-tale ending to Genie's story. Except that story is fundamentally about the deceptiveness of such endings—the potential, given enough time, for circumstances that feel conclusive and stable to randomly come apart.

The first disturbances could be felt in 1976, when Genie lost her seat in the state senate to a Californian transplant named Bill Sumner. Even decades later, Sumner would be bitterly described by Genie's political allies as almost a cartoon villain: a brazen, bare-knuckled campaigner with, as one former legislator put it, "ridiculous hair." Meanwhile, as Sumner dragged down Genie's legislative career, Genie's son Al was struggling with drug and alcohol addiction in Anchorage, and her mother, Den, was succumbing to dementia in Texas. Den had violent hallucinations, tried to escape the hospital at one point, and lashed out at Genie. Genie wrote to Den, distraught and pleading: "I need your love, Mother, not your scorn . . . There are days I feel that if one more pressure pops up—one more unpleasant thing happens to me right now—I'll just collapse."

In 1985, Genie's second husband, Bill Boardman, suffered two heart attacks. Instantly, her world reoriented, exclusively, around his care. Genie's days became insular and lonely, wrenched by a sense of precariousness that only intensified two years later when Boardman had a stroke. Al, meanwhile, was in and out of rehab. Genie's older son, Wins, was diagnosed with a peculiar soft-tissue cancer, which shot through his body and metastasized quickly; he died in 1990, a month shy of his fortieth birthday. Boardman passed away three years later. Al would die suddenly three years after that, in 1996, of congestive heart failure.

When it was all finally over, Jan would be the only Chance child left. She wasn't Jan Chance anymore, but Jan Blankenship, happily married to a sweet-tempered man named Chuck. She was working for the local government in Juneau, while also raising two children and earning two degrees. (For a time, Jan oversaw the construction and maintenance of public buildings in Juneau, and would often drop her kids at day care with two baby bottles holstered in her tool belt.) Jan could remember one or two times prior to Boardman's death when she'd caught her mother seeming momentarily disoriented or adrift. But after Boardman was gone, whatever disarray Genie's mind had been suppressing suddenly rushed forward. Genie appeared to be changing, shedding facets of herself—nothing particularly dramatic, at first, but habits that nevertheless made her Genie Chance: She stopped mailing Jan packets of unsolicited newspaper clippings. She flew to visit friends in Toronto without leaving Jan one of her signature, preposterously meticulous itineraries. When Genie came to stay with Jan's family in Juneau that first Christmas after Boardman's death, Jan was shocked to dis-

cover that Genie had abandoned the elaborate facial care regi-
men that she'd followed every morning and night for her entire
adult life. Genie insisted it was no big deal; those creams weren't
so important for your skin after all. But then Jan watched Genie's
makeup getting strangely garish, like Bette Davis's, and noticed
that Genie sometimes didn't remove it before bed. Then Genie
stopped washing her face altogether. She stopped changing her
clothes. She didn't seem distressed by any of this. That burden,
instead, fell on Jan.

It took a year to get a diagnosis. By then, Genie had agreed to
move in with Jan, her husband, Chuck, and their two children in
Juneau. Genie's doctor called Jan to apologize, crying. Genie
had been her patient for years, the doctor explained—they'd become close—and she confessed that knowing Genie for so long
as such a fiercely capable woman had kept her from registering
how vulnerable she'd become. But the doctor had finally ordered an MRI, and the truth was indisputable. Genie's condition
was called multi-infarct dementia: the brain is rattled so persis-
tently by tiny strokes that pinholes begin to open in its surface
like sinkholes in destabilized ground. Even the idea of it was dis-
maying, this disintegration of the one reality we assume to be the
sturdiest: the city of the self, built in our minds.

After the diagnosis, Genie broke apart quickly. She angered
easily. She turned paranoid and hostile, particularly toward
Chuck and the kids. Jan's voice was the only one Genie seemed
to trust, her source of sense-making information in a world that
had scrambled. "I was her connection," Jan would explain.

Eventually, Genie's anger faded. She slid so deeply within
herself that her mind could no longer manufacture agitation or
stress. For a time, she seemed happy. Then she stopped talking.

Following the instructions Genie had left her, Jan moved her mother into the Juneau Pioneer Home, one of Alaska's state-owned assisted-living facilities. One morning in 1998, after a caretaker at the home finished doing Genie's hair and makeup and was leaving to fetch her breakfast, Genie looked straight at the woman, smiled, and spoke her first words in months. "Thank you," she said. When the woman got back, Genie was dead.

Jan was angry. She felt cheated. The 1990s had been an exquisitely painful decade for her, and after the long, onerous final chapter of Bill Boardman's life, and the deaths of both her brothers, she'd at least looked forward to finally spending concentrated time with her mother as two adults. Now that time was gone. Genie was gone. All Jan had left was a roomful of cardboard boxes—thirty or more of them, labeled year by year—into which Genie had assiduously packed thousands of letters and other documents from her life. Genie had planned to use those resources to write her memoirs, but after Boardman's first heart attack, she'd never found the time. Jan was supposed to sort through the boxes and send anything that looked important to the university library in Anchorage. She couldn't bring herself to do it.

Years passed—a decade, more. To everyone's surprise, most of all Jan's, Jan had gotten ordained as a minister in the Presbyterian Church (USA). In 2013, she was given the opportunity to lead her own church in upstate New York, and she and Chuck relocated, taking Genie's boxes with them. Seven years later, they decided to return to Juneau and shipped the boxes back. They resettled in their old home, on a hillside overlooking town and the Gastineau Channel, and stacked the boxes in an unfinished storage room off the basement. Their two children had grown up, gotten jobs. One moved away to the Lower 48. Jan and Chuck lived quietly, mostly happily, with three dogs, two cats, and one mind-bendingly articulate parrot named Misty Grey, who lived in a huge cage behind Chuck's recliner in the living room, absorbing dialogue and sound effects from the movies Chuck watched and regurgitating them at random. Misty Grey did an uncanny Jack Sparrow from *Pirates of the Caribbean*. She did R2D2. She beeped like a truck backing up. And every once in a while, out of nowhere, she would call "Hell-o!" in a bracingly clear, mellifluous woman's voice. This was the call Genie had always made, announcing herself at the front door.

Meanwhile, the boxes remained downstairs, cloistered under the action of their lives like sets from an old play stored under a stage. Jan was learning about similar cases of dementia in her family and feeling a disquieting suspicion, or even resignation, that she was probably next. This made the job of going through those boxes feel more urgent to her—but it did not make it easier. She would open one, poke around, and stop. For Jan, the boxes had become both a burden and a wound.

It was a feedback loop with no way out—until one afternoon in the fall of 2014, sixteen years after Genie's death, a writer named Jon Mooallem called Jan out of the blue and explained that he was thinking of writing a book about the Great Alaska Earthquake and had come across her mother's name. Did Jan happen to have any of Genie Chance's letters or keepsakes lying around?

Yes, Jan said, and started telling him the entire story. "I became the keeper of all things Chance," she said.

———

MOOALLEM WAS A WRY and sometimes laconic-seeming magazine writer with an off-kilter jaw. He was phoning Jan that afternoon from his kitchen table in the cramped San Francisco
apartment that his young family was increasingly unable to fit in
or afford. He and his wife had had their second child a few
months earlier; there was now a crib in the living room where his
desk had always been.

He was thirty-six years old that fall—born fourteen years after
the Good Friday Earthquake. The quake was still the most powerful one in American history, and the second most powerful
ever measured in the world, yet Mooallem couldn't remember
ever once hearing about it until recently, and only after a circuitous chain of coincidences, which were too hopelessly complicated to explain, had led him to one of Genie's reports about its
aftermath. It was enough to say—as Mooallem said to Jan on the
phone—that he had discovered the earthquake, and Genie, by
chance.

He started learning whatever he could about the disaster. A
seven-volume study of the earthquake published in 1976 by the
National Academy of Sciences had described it as "the best documented and most thoroughly studied earthquake in history,"
but much of that documentation had wound up scattered, piece-
meal, in arcane library collections or, like Genie's things, boxed
up in people's basements and forgotten. Mooallem was hunting
it down, and would ultimately collect, over the course of five
years, thousands of pages of letters, interviews, diaries, government reports, and scientific papers, and upward of thirty hours
of recordings of radio broadcasts in Anchorage. The resolution

at which so many people's lives had been captured was uncanny. The material he collected felt like a time capsule, scrupulously prepared but never revisited.

At times, there seemed to be too much. It was obvious there were far more stories than Mooallem could hope to write, and at some point, the excitement he felt at each new discovery became tinged with discouragement, or even guilt. One evening, he was finishing an interview with a former Anchorage resident, Nancy Yaw Davis, when she handed him, almost as an afterthought, her four-hundred-page anthropological dissertation documenting the experiences of people in Kaguyak and Old Harbor, two of the Native villages obliterated that weekend by tsunamis. The study, which Davis had never been able to publish, was so exhaustive and granular that it included hand-drawn maps of where in the village each individual had been that Good Friday before the quake, and what he or she had been doing: "Babysitting," "Duck hunting," "Playing Monopoly."

It was equally distressing for Mooallem not to know *everything*. He wasn't a historian; he was a reporter. Normally, he learned about people by talking to them and observing their lives for himself, often for days at a time. Now he was forced to cobble together a portrait of Genie, and a timeline of those first three days after the quake, from an array of discrete and disjointed perspectives, all preserved, statically, on paper. He had no way to ask those people questions, couldn't always flesh out the context connecting their stories or probe any inferences or contradictions that arose in their accounts. It left him uneasy, insecure: ultimately, he could do only so much to check his impressions of that Easter weekend—of what should be emphasized, and what could be glossed over—against the actual lived experience, because he hadn't been there in Anchorage himself, watching everyone live it. For him, the story of the disaster would always feel slightly set back from reality—a piece of theater, playing out behind some impenetrable fourth wall.

There were still some people around to talk to, of course. But Mooallem often worked to track down survivors of the earthquake only to wind up feeling defeated during their conversations. Early on, for example, he found Charlie Gray, KENI's head of engineering, now a ninety-five-year-old widower living with his son in rural Washington State. Gray recalled few specifics about the quake and, moreover, seemed baffled why anyone would care. His memories of his coworkers at KENI appeared to have compacted down to a single, salient attribute of each, like ancient pictographs or brushstrokes of minimalist calligraphy— Genie Chance: "Nice-looking lady." Ty Clark: "Good drinking man." Gray rattled them off with his arms folded, completely unbothered, as Mooallem sprayed esoteric follow-up questions at him, queries Gray couldn't possibly answer. Later that year, Mooallem visited Bill Davis in Sitka, Alaska. The intrepid mountaineer was eighty-eight years old and battling bladder cancer, among a raft of other difficulties, and sat in a wheelchair with a catheter bag in his lap while they spoke. His mind was sharp, though his memory was limited. Again and again, Mooallem naively double-checked some persnickety detail in one of the documents he'd brought with him and asked Davis questions like "So, you arrived at the Public Safety Building at around six on Saturday morning?" But Davis could only widen his eyes at the writer in what appeared to be bewilderment and pity.

Mooallem would experience this kind of peculiar vertigo repeatedly, all at once registering the perilous emptiness that stretched between him and those three days in 1964. Schoolkids he read about materialized as investment bankers or retired teachers. Bram's son, Al Bramstedt Jr.—fourteen years old at the time of the quake—had taken over KENI from his father in 1971 and was already long retired. On Mooallem's first trip to Anchorage, he found the Fourth Avenue Theatre shuttered and falling into mild disrepair as the incommunicative investment corporation that had purchased Cap Lathrop's masterpiece took its time deciding whether to tear the building down.

It felt like time travel to Mooallem—but he was only traveling forward, and mercilessly fast, flashing ahead to watch the story lines of that Easter weekend bend toward their ultimate endings. The knowledge of where everyone would wind up tinted that history with melancholy and awe. It wasn't a feeling you experienced in ordinary life, and Mooallem worried he'd never precisely describe it.

Then, he read *Our Town,* got to the Stage Manager's first omniscient aside in Act I—"Mrs. Gibbs died first"—and said to himself: *That's me.*

The boxes that Genie left behind in Jan's basement suggested she'd anticipated this problem and worked, compulsively, to guard against it. Genie had saved virtually everything, starting with a lock of her own baby hair. There was a photo of her posing in front of the KENI Kamper with Ty Clark shortly after she started at the station, when she was known as the "Kamper Kutie"; scripts she'd written for Bram's "News in Depth" commentaries; a reel-to-reel recording of KENI's coverage of the 1964 Fur Rendezvous sled-dog races; a copy of her daily crime report from the Public Safety Building that Good Friday morning; and the letter she'd been typing that evening, which cut off abruptly at the start of a new sentence on the top of page four: the moment her son Wins came in, asking for a ride to the bookstore downtown. There was an envelope of photos Genie took while scrambling around the collapsing exterior of the J. C. Penney building, minutes after the quake; and pages from her reporter's notebook from the three a.m. meeting in the Public Safety Building's basement—where, all alone, in the center of a fresh sheet, she'd written: "The worst is yet to come."

Mooallem found love letters from Winston, from the months before he and Genie married, stacked up and tied in lace, and a second cache of letters Winston had written twenty-four years later, pleading for Genie to take him back. After that came newspaper clippings she'd saved in the late 1970s and '80s: articles about facelifts, and columns empowering feminists to stand up to the misogynists in their lives. ("When I began to get successful in my career, that's when all hell broke loose," one woman explained.) And finally, there were Genie's diaries from the mid-1980s, a chronicle of the last fully cognizant and accessible years of her life.

At that point, Genie and Bill Boardman were spending their winters in Palm Springs. The entries started just before Boardman's heart attacks and strokes and went through the first phases of his decline. Genie's son Wins was sick. Her other son, Al, was in and out of a methadone clinic. She wondered, plaintively, what kind of mother she'd been, but told herself she'd done her best. She also vented about Boardman's escalating grouchiness as his quality of life declined: how infrequently he allowed her to host dinner parties or took her out to lunch. ("I thought he was a very social person when we married," she wrote.) Reading through box after box in Jan's basement, Mooallem had watched Genie come so far; now he found her bristling in a condominium in Palm Springs, resenting having to cook a curmudgeonly husband three meals a day.

Genie seemed equally confounded by the turn her life was taking. She was struggling with depression again—linked, she believed, to "the feeling of dependency upon Bill's uncertain future. When you get right down to it, none of us has a certain future. We must do with what we have available for the time being. So it's futile to put off living for fear something dreadful will happen. That has never been me."

In an entry from the fall of 1988, Genie described walking to the capitol building in Juneau one morning to lodge a complaint at the governor's office. She'd read about a proposed change to the state's ferry system, and had already phoned the governor's transportation czar to express her disapproval. No one called her back. When she showed up at the man's office, his assistant claimed he was in a meeting. Genie explained that she had served in the state legislature herself—three terms in the house, one in the senate. The woman at the desk absorbed this information, then told her, "Your name's not familiar."

"I must admit that hurt," Genie wrote. Intellectually, she understood that so much time had passed; staffers couldn't be expected to recognize every retired legislator's name. Still, she wrote, "emotionally, it's painful. You expect that when you're dead and gone your name is forgotten." But it was upsetting to watch her work be "relegated to the unimportant pile of deeds by anonymous persons" in real time.

As Mooallem moved through Genie's boxes, time itself

started to seem like a slow-moving natural disaster, imperceptibly shaking everything apart. Maybe nothing in our world is durable or stable. Maybe everything runs on pure chance.

He wondered how we are supposed to live on the surface of such unbearable randomness. What can we hold on to that's fixed?

SUNDAY

MARCH 29, 1964

16.

"LIFE BECOMES LIKE
MOLTEN METAL"

———

THE SOCIOLOGISTS TOUCH DOWN

THE FIRST TWO SOCIOLOGISTS TO ARRIVE—"THE ADVANCE team," their bosses called them—woke up in Anchorage on the Sunday morning after the quake, groping to make sense of where they'd landed late the night before.

The two young men were graduate students from the Disaster Research Center at Ohio State University, a new, first-of-its-kind institute devoted to studying how society functions in a crisis—or how it falls apart. The center aimed to dispatch teams of researchers to wherever disaster struck, as quickly as possible, to meticulously and dispassionately document people's behavior in the throes of that disarray—all while standing in the disarray themselves. If their work sounded preposterous, or futile, the sociologists were apparently too focused on doing it well to recognize that. They didn't know what they were going to find when they touched down in Anchorage—or that their findings would help rewrite centuries of pessimistic assumptions about human nature. They were just pointy-headed empiricists trying to analyze chaos.

This was the Disaster Research Center's first full-fledged field trip. The center had been founded the previous summer, in 1963, by three professors at Ohio State: Enrico Quarantelli, Russell Dynes, and Eugene Haas. Each had spent much of the preceding year casting about, somewhat aimlessly, for interesting research to do; Quarantelli was studying what he called "the professionalization process," interviewing dental students about how it felt to leave behind their training dummies and put their hands in the mouths of living human beings for the first time. Then, late that summer, the sociologists were suddenly beckoned to Washington to meet with the US Air Force and another arm of the military called the Office of Civil Defense. A few military officials had read a grant proposal, on which the three sociologists had once collaborated, outlining a study of how groups of people operate under stress. The proposal had been rejected by their university. Now the military was offering them a million dollars to conduct similar research—more than ten times the budget they'd originally requested—with hardly any strings attached.

The Cold War was escalating. It had been less than a year since the Cuban Missile Crisis, and Civil Defense was increasingly desperate to fulfill its mandate of preparing Americans for nuclear war with the Soviet Union. One of the agency's animating insights was that a bomb dropped on the United States wouldn't just cause physical destruction, but pandemonium. Civil Defense experts predicted "a mass outbreak of hysterical neurosis among the civilian population," as one historian would

put it. "Under this strain, many people would regress to an earlier level of needs and desires. They would behave like fright-
ened and unsatisfied children." Survivors would be panicked
and powerless, but also aggressive and cruel—liberated into violence, left to compete for limited resources and food. It was up to
Civil Defense to preemptively suppress that disorder, to guard
against this self-inflicted second wave of any Soviet attack.

Armageddon proved to be a hard thing to practice for,
however—or even to envision in detail. The government saw
natural disasters as realistic proxies. Each community hit by an
earthquake, hurricane, or flood was like a laboratory—a full-scale
simulation—in which to scrutinize the turmoil of nuclear war in
advance. A team of sociologists, parachuting into those disaster
areas, might glean truths about human behavior that could help
Civil Defense maintain control when the world's most fearsome
unnatural disaster struck. In Washington, the three sociologists
were taken aback by the military's interest in their work. (It was
a bizarre meeting, Quarantelli would remember—"mostly them
talking, rather than us.") But they accepted the government's
offer without hesitation and immediately got to work.

Back at Ohio State, the sociologists hired a few graduate students and set up their headquarters in a temporary building
across the train tracks from the rest of campus. They were starting virtually from scratch. Quarantelli felt they should first assemble a comprehensive library of disaster literature, of which
there was relatively little. Still, they hadn't even finished cata-
loguing their collection when, on Halloween, a large propane
tank exploded during a "Holidays on Ice" skating exhibition at a
fairgrounds in Indiana, about a three-hour drive away. The sociologists hadn't yet worked up a manual for the interviews they'd

conduct in their fieldwork, or protocols of any kind. But they dropped everything and scampered to Indiana anyway, seizing the opportunity to run a pilot study. (They drew up a list of questions in the car on the way.) In the months that followed, the Disaster Research Center would conduct half a dozen more practice trips—a nursing home fire near Sandusky, a dam break in Los Angeles, a flood in Cincinnati. They were working toward starting their larger-scale research, in earnest, sometime later that spring. Then the earth churned under Alaska and caught them off guard.

News of the earthquake had reached the Disaster Research Center in Ohio at around eight o'clock local time on Saturday morning. This was three a.m. in Anchorage, when communication from the city to the Outside was still scant, and rumors ricocheted wildly. The sociologists heard that downtown Anchorage was swallowed in a ball of fire. They heard three hundred people were dead. Or six hundred people. The details were shocking. The trauma and confusion would be horrific. Professionally speaking, it was too good to be true.

Quarantelli and his colleagues didn't feel totally ready to dispatch a field team. But they also sensed that if they wanted to conduct a comprehensive study of the quake, they'd need to get on the ground as soon as possible to observe the emergency at its height and to interview people before their memories shifted or became embellished. One foundational work in the center's little disaster library was the chronicle of a monstrous munitions explosion in Nova Scotia in 1917, which killed nearly two thousand people and injured nine thousand more. The author of the study, a Canadian priest and sociologist named Samuel Henry Prince, noted that "the word 'crisis' is of Greek origin, meaning a point of culmination and separation." The instant disaster strikes, "life becomes like molten metal," Prince wrote. "It enters a state of flux from which it must reset upon a principle, a creed, or purpose. It is shaken perhaps violently out of rut and routine. Old customs crumble, and instability rules."

If the sociologists at the Disaster Research Center wanted to see that instability for themselves, they needed to be in Alaska before that window closed. And so, early that Saturday morning, they scrambled two of their graduate assistants to Anchorage—an advance team—to check, first of all, if flying into the stricken city was even possible right now.

"They roused me out of bed and I threw on my duds," one of the grad students, Daniel Yutzy, explained. "And I was off to the airport in an hour and a half."

NEITHER YUTZY NOR BILL ANDERSON, his partner on the advance team, particularly looked like they belonged in Alaska, and side by side, the duo seemed almost comically mismatched.

Yutzy, the team's senior member, was a sturdy and gargantuan man—an ordained Mennonite minister who'd grown up Amish and, as one colleague put it, retained the physique of "someone who spent his days pulling a plow." Still, the colleague added, he was the opposite of intimidating: "You instantly trusted Dan," he said; imagine "the twinkle in the eye of a guy playing Santa Claus in a mall."

Anderson, meanwhile, was a baby-faced, somewhat bashful African American man with thick glasses. He was twenty-six years old, almost ten years younger than Yutzy, and came up to Yutzy's chest. Anderson had grown up in Akron, a working-class town of tire factories, and, before starting this kind of sociological fieldwork, had left Ohio only once in his life. Still, over time, Anderson would ascend to lead a disaster-related division of the National Science Foundation and work for the World Bank before dying in a bicycling accident on Kauai in 2013, while Yutzy would spend the bulk of his career in obscurity, teaching at a small Mennonite college in Indiana. Yutzy had retired from academia and was serving as the pastor of a church outside Buffalo when he was killed in a head-on car collision at age sixty-six.

The two men tromped off the plane at Elmendorf Air Force Base, north of downtown, at nine thirty on Saturday night. Yutzy got to work right away: observing, cogitating, probing. He had a portable tape recorder running, a state-of-the-art reel-to-reel apparatus that weighed thirty pounds and was worn over the shoulder in its own leather-bound briefcase, and was pointing its microphone at the unsuspecting Northwest Orient Airlines employee working the gate. The man was there to meet the flights being diverted to Elmendorf from the damaged airport in town. Presumably, the disaster was wreaking all kinds of havoc on the airline's normal operations, and Yutzy wanted to know, first off, who was making the decisions about how to issue and reissue tickets.

"There's nobody that makes them," the ticket agent told him, flatly. It had been only twenty-eight hours since the earthquake; apparently, everyone was making things up as they went.

"No?" Yutzy asked.

The man didn't know what to say.

"Therefore, *you*, the ticket agent, makes them?" Yutzy asked.

"Yeah," the ticket agent said. He was conceding the point,

which, in his mind, surely seemed academic. It *was* academic; the man asking was a doctoral student.

But Yutzy couldn't help himself. "Nobody coordinates these decisions, beyond what the ticket agent says?" he asked.

This time, the man didn't answer. Yutzy shut off his recorder.

Finding a place to stay in Anchorage that night was hopeless, but Yutzy and Anderson managed to secure two beds at Elmendorf's bachelor quarters. Early on Sunday morning, they were prepping their field kits at the base, hoping for a productive day one. They had their recorders and microphones, cameras, satchels of extra batteries and tapes, an austere-looking laminated letter identifying them as researchers affiliated with the US military, and a large, glaring placard to attach to the sun visor of a car, as soon as they obtained one, with the seal of their university alongside the words DISASTER RESEARCH CENTER. "Usually people at roadblocks are impressed by anything that is official," Quarantelli explained.

A radio was on at the base, tuned to a local station, and Anderson had just overheard something potentially significant. Yutzy switched on his tape recorder again and encouraged his partner to get this preliminary observation on the record. "Evidently," Anderson said into the microphone, "the radio station is serving as a disseminating center for news about evacuees, residents, and their friends and relatives." It was fascinating, he explained: the broadcasters were using the airwaves to connect the missing and displaced people in town.

Yutzy took back the microphone. "This last report at eight fifteen a.m. Alaska time, Sunday morning," he specified. "It seems apparent from our experience, even in these few short hours, that a portable transistor radio would be quite helpful in a disaster setting such as this, where many other means of communication are out." If the sociologists wanted to truly understand the experience of people in Anchorage, and to feel their way into the fabric of this emergency, they needed to be listening to the radio, like everyone else.

"I believe we should give some thought to this at headquarters," Yutzy said. Then he clicked off the recorder and went about finding them a ride into town.

17.

"THINGS ON THE EARTH"

———

ANCHORAGE BEGINS
RESURRECTING ITSELF

ANCHORAGE WOKE UP THAT SUNDAY MORNING DETERMINED to lurch back in the direction of normal. People lined up at the military's potable water tankers, holding buckets, jars, and coffee tins, and lingered over bowls of soup at the field kitchens set up in city parks, swapping stories with neighbors whom they hadn't seen since Friday.

The stockpile of heavy machinery donated to Disaster Control rolled out at first light: backhoes scattered to fix sewer lines, a fleet of seventy gravel trucks resumed filling in fissures and craters in the streets, and bulldozers ripped new, temporary roads through regions of Anchorage where the old maps had been wiped away. City leaders met to formulate a plan for reopening downtown and decided to let the business owners on Fourth Avenue past the barricade first. All afternoon, merchants would descend into their buried storefronts on wooden ladders and reemerge like worker ants, hauling any salvageable merchandise back to street level. Clusters of televisions, hi-fi cabinets, clothing, and office chairs would gradually accumulate up and down Fourth Avenue, like cargo collected from the tide after a shipwreck.

Cranes were already picking apart the ruptured facade of the J. C. Penney building; there was no doubt now that the department store would be a total loss. A few restaurants were readying to reopen, though they'd have to serve fried foods exclusively until the water came back on. And the staff of the *Anchorage Times* was reporting to work, picking up every tiny piece of movable type that had sprayed across the floor of their composing room, intent on once again putting out a newspaper.

It was Easter Sunday. Not everyone in Anchorage immediately remembered. Dainty wicker baskets still sat in one flower shop's shattered window downtown. Enormous stuffed bunnies lay where they'd listed forward on Good Friday evening, like blacked-out drunks, near a flyer for *Our Town*. The Salvation Army chose to broadcast its Easter service over the radio, given the bedraggled and uncertain condition of the city, but several churches went ahead with their morning worship as planned. At St. Mary's Episcopal, a significant share of the congregation lived in Turnagain and had lost their houses in the slide; at least twenty of the church's one hundred and fifty families had been rendered homeless and lost everything. Still, a woman named Tay Thomas remembered, at eight o'clock that morning, they "clumped down the aisles in borrowed boots and weird assortments of misfit clothing."

Tay had been watching television with her two small children at home in Turnagain when the shaking started. She immediately rushed the kids outside, only to find the ground disintegrating and cascading away from them. "I felt like we were on a Ferris wheel, going backwards," she explained. The landslide slung the three of them onto the tidal flat a hundred feet below. Then, Tay said, "everything stopped. There just wasn't a sound." She wasn't even sure how long they'd been stranded down there—without shoes, fighting back frostbite and trying and failing to hoist themselves up the craggy, sloppy cliff face—before a teenager, whom Tay didn't recognize and could never identify later, appeared overhead with a rope. At St. Mary's on Sunday morning, Tay's eight-year-old daughter, Anne, was still wearing the black wool coat that the anonymous teenager had wrapped around her to keep her warm. Tay had on a pair of men's corduroys that belonged to the minister. The hymns of thanks had never sounded so meaningful to her, and it was so cold inside the church that, when she looked around, she could see the parishioners' breaths billowing forward and rising like clouds.

After the service, Tay headed back to Turnagain, where an improbable salvage operation was getting under way at the wreckage of her home. The previous afternoon, Thomas's husband, an acclaimed travel writer named Lowell Thomas Jr., had gone down into the debris field and found a small company of mountaineers, led by Jim Scott, methodically tearing apart what was left of his next-door neighbor's house. Scott, the veterinarian, was still looking for the bodies of twelve-year-old Perry Mead Jr. and two-year-old Merrell Mead, the same brothers he'd hastily rappelled down to hunt for on Friday night; at the very least, he was now intent on giving the Mead family some closure. Lowell explained to Scott that he was looking for the many boxes of irreplaceable slides and films he'd shot on his travels around the world. Lowell was not optimistic. But Scott showed him all of the Meads' possessions that they'd managed to extract and set aside while searching and dismantling the structure: skis, a suite of photography equipment. Maybe Lowell would be surprised, Scott said. He offered to organize a team and come back the following morning to help.

And so, when Tay arrived on Easter Sunday, Scott was already down on the shoreline with fifteen young mountaineers, prying open the lopsided remains of the Thomases' home with crowbars. The men found Lowell's slides and films in short order, and unearthed much of the family's clothing, books, medicines, and some antique china as well. Tay watched the young men come out, one by one, cradling her life's memories and returning them to her. Every object felt simultaneously precious and gratuitous—something extra, given how narrowly she and her children had survived. She kept thinking of the epistle they'd read that morning in church: "Set your affection on things above, not on things on the Earth."

Soon the mountaineers set their sights on bigger, heavier items—chairs, dressers—and exhumed those as well, lashing everything to packboards, and hauling it all on their backs, like a brigade of human burros, up the steep and snowy escarpment, through a berserk wilderness of half-toppled spruces, until they reached the ridgeline above. The Thomases had an old ironwood chest that had been in Lowell's family for ages and weighed more than 250 pounds. One man carried it up by himself.

When they finished with the Thomases' place, they wanted to move on to other homes. Scott enlisted his Rotary Club for more manpower, but as he offered to help other acquaintances in Turnagain, he didn't initially find many takers. People's shock was wilting into fatalism. Few people in Anchorage had earth-quake insurance, and those in Turnagain seemed especially inclined to look down at their homes, shattered on the shore, and write off the entire spectacle as one abstract and nonnegotiable loss. It was a difficult idea to hold in one's mind: that this debris was still an assemblage of individual possessions; that the anarchic smear of material on the beach both was, and was no longer, your home. But Scott approached the situation pragmatically; he was only being frugal. He kept pointing out to the homeowners that anything he could recover was one less thing they'd have to pay to replace.

Ultimately, Scott's salvage operation would go on for five days. His workers would haul up mattresses, Danish Modern furniture, sinks, and entryway rugs. They'd take up their first washing machine, then their first piano. Once the heavy equipment arrived and the military got involved, the salvagers would start picking roofs clean off of houses with backhoes and reaching inside from above, even plucking cars from half-sunken garages.

In the end, more than three hundred volunteers worked to reclaim an estimated quarter of a million dollars' worth of property from more than thirty-eight different homes in Turnagain. That first Sunday, however, the homeowners remained skeptical. It took some convincing. Mostly, Scott would remember, people were shocked that anyone was so willing to help.

ONE HARROWING UNKNOWN STILL hung over the city on Sunday morning. On the radio, Anchorage officials were still confirming only twelve dead from the quake, but inside the Public

Safety Building, Mayor Sharrock was quietly stepping up the city's effort to get a definitive and more convincing count.

The mayor had walked away from the press conference the previous night feeling unnerved. He seemed to have difficulty shrugging off the Outside reporters' incredulousness over the low death toll because, deep down, he harbored similar skepticism. Sharrock had driven out to Turnagain on Saturday to get a look at the slide for himself. Turnagain was his neighborhood, and seeing familiar houses on the coastline below, mashed apart like fallen fruit, it seemed impossible that there weren't bodies down there that the city didn't yet know about. By nightfall, the area had been searched several times, by volunteers, firefighters, and the military, and the Mead boys appeared to be the only people still known to be missing for sure. But even if there weren't other fatalities sealed somewhere in that debris, Sharrock understood that the city would need a credible way to prove it, if only to convince the press. It amounted to proving a negative—which, as everyone knows, is impossible. Sharrock started thinking about how Anchorage might do the impossible.

By noon on Sunday, a strategy had surfaced—either Sharrock or his wife, Pauline, seemed to have come up with it. The way to definitively eliminate the specter of mass casualties, they realized, was to prove that everyone who *might* be dead in Turnagain was, in fact, alive and somewhere else. They would have to make a list of every neighborhood resident, pulling all conceivable data sets they could find: tax rolls, billing records from the utility companies, school registrations. They would go street by street, house by house, affixing names to every parcel on the map. Then, like teachers moving down a gargantuan attendance list, they would read those names over the radio and see, once and for all, who was present and who was absent.

The Sharrocks assembled a small team at the Public Safety Building to take on this project. The group became known as the Task Force, which suggests a crack squad of specialists. It was not; instead, it was a hastily assembled and seemingly arbitrary collection of volunteers and city workers who'd been floating around the building all weekend, entrenching themselves in one job and then, having helped bring that particular problem under control, finding another to solve—again and again. The Task Force included a midlevel bureaucrat in the city's planning department, a couple of secretaries, and an army soldier who washed up in the Public Safety Building shortly after the quake on Friday evening, proved himself useful, and never left. Pauline Sharrock joined in, too. She was forty-three years old, a bookkeeper at the Alaska Bank of Commerce, and would be memorably described in her obituary fifty-one years later as a "persistent action lady."

The Task Force claimed a room in the back of the building, adjacent to Bill Davis's "Central Search and Rescue Operations Center." The two teams would work closely together, with Davis and one of the Task Force leaders, Jim Parsons, shouting questions or encouragement through the propped-open door that connected their offices. Davis and Parsons happened to be colleagues and close friends. Parsons was the other half of Alaska Methodist University's two-man psychology faculty; Davis taught the theoretical stuff—Freud and Jung—while Parsons handled the clinical curriculum. Parsons had been the first practicing psychologist in Alaska when he arrived in the territory. He was suave-looking, with prominent eyebrows and a wide, invit-ing smile—a New York City native who, Davis and his wife would remember years later, always brought excellent wine to parties. Parsons was also gay, they added. No one in town talked about it, though no one seemed to care, really, either. Anchorage elected him to the state legislature twice.

Parsons's Task Force tacked a city map to the wall of their makeshift headquarters, just like Davis had done next door, and got to work. All day, the two operations would slog away in paral-lel like macabre mirror images: one scouring Anchorage for the dead, the other sounding its depths for the living.

18.

"THE WAY OF THE WIND"

GENIE STAYS BUSY IN
THE BACKGROUND

G ENIE CAUGHT ANOTHER BRIEF AND FITFUL NAP EARLY ON Sunday morning, around three a.m., and returned to work by six. She had started thinking of herself less as a KENI reporter than as an ad hoc press agent for the city government, relaying announcements and tending to the Outside media, who were now piling into Anchorage even faster than they had the day before.

It would prove difficult, later, to reconstruct what Genie did on Sunday with much specificity—for Mooallem, but also, it seemed, for Genie herself. Few of her memories of the disaster would map onto that particular day—perhaps because, as the weekend wore on, the nature of her role at the Public Safety Building changed. She worked another thirteen hours straight that Sunday, but the acute and constant shocks she'd been barraged with during the first phase of the emergency were receding. Her work settled into a more indiscriminate grind.

The public had a good grasp of the disaster by this point. Some working on the emergency response didn't feel it was helpful to still have KENI's reporters autonomously airing a rapid gush of news, often gleaned from what government employees disparaged as "unofficial" sources—that is, from ordinary people in town. The radio station had already broadcast a false evacuation order for an apartment complex, causing alarm. Eventually, a man arrived at the Public Safety Building on Sunday urging the city to restrict and better systematize the flow of information. He'd worked in broadcasting himself, as an announcer at one of KENI's rival stations, but also had a volunteer role in some of Anchorage's local Civil Defense planning. At some point that weekend, he'd even started wearing his old Civil Defense hard hat around town. In the past, he'd felt insecure about wearing the hard hat, but now he was amazed by the delicious power it granted him: how freely people let him through roadblocks or into their offices—wherever he wanted to go. "It was fantastic," the man would later marvel, "the respect this thing created." Gradually, he took strict control over how the media operated at the Public Safety Building, issuing endless press releases and rules. His name was Merrill Mael. He was the same man who'd chased Genie out of her first radio job in Anchorage.

KENI still had its hands full, however, relaying telegrams and calls from people around Alaska and the Lower 48, hoping to make contact with family in Anchorage. The station was swamped, and the requests were piling up in the radio booth at KFQD, too, where a smaller stable of announcers struggled to stay on top of them from within a thickening plume of cigarette smoke. There were new kinds of announcements flooding in as well: requests for extra clothing or supplies; *offers* of extra clothing and supplies; and people opening up their homes to anyone needing a place to sleep. All weekend, Frank Brink had been listening to these messages rise out of the damaged city and onto its airwaves. Tuned to KFQD that Sunday morning at home, he not only felt compelled to offer up space in his own house, but was so moved by the exhaustion in the announcers' voices that he eventually went down to the station and offered to take a shift behind the microphone himself.

Brink read for hours: "Frank Dipietro has space available for a couple with one or two children near Abbott Loop School," and so on. At one point, he was handed the latest Associated Press dispatch from Anchorage and performed what amounted to a dramatic reading of the article, infusing it with solemnity and pathos, as though it were a Shakespearean monologue. "'Alaska's biggest city looked today as if it had been shaken and clawed by monster hands,'" Brink began. "'Many buildings and private homes lay in dismal ruin, some in holes where there'd been no holes before. Others heaved up onto ridges where there'd been no ridges before.'" He would stay at the station for much of Sunday afternoon, then return periodically over the next several days to do it again. Brink found the rawness and humanity of the personal messages he was reading to be deeply affecting—also, exhilarating: dramaturgically speaking, it was unbelievably good material. He recognized that each plea for help, or offer to help, that flashed past him in the radio booth told a different story— and collectively, they told an epic story about their town: "a story of patience in deprivation," as Brink later described it, "and selflessness in a moment of great need." He started recording the broadcasts, preserving them all.

As a sideline to his theater productions, Brink occasionally produced oral history records for a series of documentary LPs he called *Sounds of Alaska*. It became clear to him that he would be scrapping his next planned volume and producing a record about the Good Friday Earthquake instead. Within a few days, he had enlisted Genie as a partner.

Genie had experienced the disaster unfolding from essentially the same panoramic perspective that Brink glimpsed that Sunday in the radio booth. She also had hours of her own recordings to contribute; she'd made sure Big Winston and the kids were taping KENI off their transistor radio at home. In the weeks that followed, she would record another hundred hours of interviews, collecting stories of the earthquake from shoppers who'd been stuck inside Penney's, business owners on Fourth Avenue, dockworkers in Seward and fishermen in Valdez, ham radio operators, and military and government officials. A week after the quake, she and Brink would visit a Quonset hut outside Anchorage together to interview those who'd been evacuated from two of the decimated Aleut villages on Kodiak Island. Several women recounted their community's scramble up a hillside while, behind them, tsunamis crashed over their homes and pulled their husbands and other family members out to sea. One older man, Peter Alexanderoff, noted that this was the first time he'd been away from the village of Old Harbor in his life.

Brink had high hopes for their record. He had contacts at Capitol Records and suspected that a deal for the finished documentary might pull in upward of three thousand dollars each for him and Genie. He even hired a local singer and a classical guitarist to perform a new, operatic folk song, called "The Way of the Wind," that he'd written to give the record a concluding musical flourish. The theme of the lyrics was the unpredictability of life on earth—or, as Brink preferred to frame it, how "only man's love of life, his remarkable courage and his generous human spirit will outshine the unfathomable forces of nature that, through the ages, have brought him to his knees."

But no deal with Capitol Records materialized. Genie and Brink paid to press a small number of copies of the record themselves, then mailed them around to acquaintances and friends. A half century later, Mooallem would find one in Jan's basement and feel as though the text printed on the back of the album had been written explicitly to him: "In the future, if such questions as 'What happened?,' 'What did people think and do?,' and 'How did people feel?' are asked by strangers to the quake, it is hoped that this album may furnish some of the most significant answers."

19.

"FACTS ABOUT FALLOUT"

---

*DR. QUARANTELLI TAKES A
GOOD LOOK AROUND*

THE THREE FOUNDERS OF THE DISASTER RESEARCH CENTER reached Anchorage, from Ohio, at nine thirty on Sunday morning, twelve hours after their advance team had landed and sent back an all clear. By late morning, they were stepping into the Public Safety Building, trying to get a bead on which discrete pockets of the overall spectacle they should scrutinize first.

The space was rich with disorganization: a sprawl of bodies, in which civilians weren't necessarily distinguishable from authorities. The building looked nothing like a typical police station on a typical day. Uniformed soldiers walked through the offices carrying rifles and fixed bayonets. Runners skittered by with messages. All the male workers were unshaven and their shirt collars were open; the women weren't wearing heels—telltale signs that the "emergency period," as Enrico Quarantelli and his colleagues would label it, was still in full swing.

Quarantelli was thirty-nine years old, small, bald, and known to his associates as Henry, or simply "Q." He was warm and jovial to a point, then exceedingly private. He virtually never spoke about his personal life, never married, and addressed every aspect of existence with an unbending pragmatism that seemed both entertaining and subtly alienating to those who worked alongside him. One student would later remember, for instance, that back in Ohio, Quarantelli drove a black car—not because he liked the color black, but because he'd deduced that black would retain the highest proportion of heat from the sun and melt the snow off his vehicle marginally faster.

Quarantelli grew up in New York City, the son of Italian immigrants, and found refuge at the New York Public Library at an early age. He read ravenously and indiscriminately: Roman history, cowboy novels, entire shelves of plays. He couldn't often afford baseball tickets, but discovered that the ushers at the Polo Grounds would let people into Giants games for free after the seventh inning. He was recognizing a hidden truth about how society worked: there were rules, but also unofficial rules, which quietly undermined them. Similarly, while serving as an army radio operator in Europe during World War II, he fixated on the hidden organizational peculiarities of military life. Years later, it would be hard for Quarantelli to reflect on how seeing combat had affected him, but he would remember very clearly a more esoteric epiphany, gleaned from a particular clerical error in November 1945. Six hundred and fifty men from Quarantelli's unit had been temporarily assigned elsewhere that Thanksgiving, but Quarantelli found it was simpler to erroneously report in his paperwork that they were all still present, rather than figure out how to squeeze a convoluted explanation for their absence into the standardized forms. Consequently, his unit was sent a glut of extra food for the holiday; the cooks were ecstatic. Official records, Quarantelli realized, were "social constructions": authoritative fictions that didn't always match the reality they claimed to preserve.

By the time Quarantelli finished his doctorate in 1959, he had learned to distrust documents and official narratives of any kind. They possessed a kind of problematic gravity, pulling at people's memories of an experience and distorting them. After a dramatic event, it didn't take long for people to begin revising their stories of it, if only subconsciously, to conform to their expectations of how it was *supposed* to have gone: in retrospect, decisions were always said to have been made methodically and by the appropriate people; smart decisions made by women during an emergency were frequently attributed to men. To piece together the real story, Quarantelli was learning, you had to talk to as many different people as you could, or be there to scrutinize the situation for yourself. At the time of the quake, five years into his career as a sociologist, Quarantelli's compulsion to notice everything and passively accept nothing already appeared to define him—not just as a social scientist, but as a human being. Years later, near the end of his life, he would begin an oral history interview for the Disaster Research Center by saying, "I was born on November 10, 1924"—and when he added, "For some reason, I remember nothing about the first five years of my life," he was clearly joking, but also sounded genuinely aggrieved by this lapse in his observational record.

At the Public Safety Building, Quarantelli and his colleagues decided to split up, to cover more ground. Quarantelli went to find Anchorage's local Office of Civil Defense, a small agency of the city government, which, like others set up around the country, adhered to the same basic philosophy and playbook as the federal agency in Washington that was backing the Disaster Research Center. Presumably, Anchorage's Civil Defense bureau would be acting as a kind of mission control for the emergency response. But walking in, Quarantelli discovered an atmosphere of almost antic ineffectualness. He tucked himself out of the way and started taking notes: "Considerable amount of confusion," his observations began.

Ordinarily, the city's Office of Civil Defense was headquartered in the basement of the Public Safety Building. But the quake had shattered the fluorescent lights in that room and buckled the door, jamming it shut, so they'd set up in the fire department instead. Quarantelli looked around the space they'd commandeered and took an inventory. He counted seven people working in the office, all of them apparently volunteers. Two were children: Explorer Scouts, tasked with running messages to other parts of the building. A third was a teenage girl, answering the phones. Beyond the two telephones, there was minimal equipment of any kind. Later, someone would bring in a mimeograph machine, though Quarantelli noted that nobody in the office seemed to know how to work it.

Quarantelli watched a gale of people whoosh in and out of the office all morning and afternoon. Many came in with questions for Civil Defense or information to report, and though some of these questions and updates sounded rather serious to Quarantelli—like the pastor who worried that his church building was structurally unsound, or the man who reported that some people were apparently having a "violent reaction" to the typhoid shots the city health department was issuing—rarely did he hear anyone give these people satisfying answers, or offer any substantive help.

QUARANTELLI WOULD EVENTUALLY LEARN THAT, prior to the disaster, Anchorage's Civil Defense agency had been in dismal decline. As was happening nationwide, the public was growing disillusioned with the agency's mission. Whether it was fatalism or just common sense, people looked at the many pamphlets and instructional films the American Civil Defense apparatus was producing—"Alert Today, Alive Tomorrow"; "Facts About Fallout"—and still felt utterly helpless in the face of a nuclear bomb. Anchorage's agency had only two full-time employees, a director and a secretary, but even so, a few city council members had started singling out Civil Defense as a flagrantly wasteful line item in the municipal budget. The director, a retired army colonel named Douglas Clure, realized his operation was shriveling up and elected to resign. He wanted to spend more time on his fish-processing business, he said. Clure had quit on March 15, twelve days before the earthquake.

Mayor Sharrock had run into Clure, by chance, late in the confusion on Friday night, and rehired him on the spot. He then introduced Clure at the big three a.m. meeting in the basement of the Public Safety Building, explaining that, from that point on, Civil Defense would coordinate the recovery; whatever equipment or support those at the meeting needed to do their jobs, Clure would get it for them. But once the sun came up on Saturday, many of those working in the building found it was faster, and less frustrating, to bypass Clure and ask a colonel from one

of the military bases instead, or just to solve the problem themselves. They complained that Clure's people moved too slowly,
or in circles. Clure seemed hamstrung by finicky questions of
protocol. "Who's going to give me this authority?" one Disaster
Control worker remembered him asking continually, whenever
some unconventional emergency action was proposed.

The entire mind-set of Civil Defense seemed inapplicable to
the situation. Anchorage needed people to pitch in construc-
tively and solve problems together, not evacuate, or hide out in
bomb shelters, until those problems passed. Genie had always
bought into Civil Defense's mission before the quake. She studied their literature and stocked her family's basement with food
and water, sleeping bags, and lanterns. Now, though, she realized
she'd never stopped to think about what Civil Defense was supposed to do during an actual emergency—and it seemed to her
like Civil Defense may not have contemplated that, either. Not
long after sunrise on Saturday, several people appeared at the
police counter, asking Genie for help. They'd found shelter
overnight at the Greek Orthodox Church, they said, and needed
transportation to get everyone still there to one of the field kitchens to eat. Genie walked the group back to Clure's office; she
had taken the mayor at his word during the three a.m. meeting
and was intent on following the new chain of command. But, she
later explained, when she asked what could be done, Clure told
her, "I don't know." The people from the church pleaded with
Clure directly: They were hungry. There were babies at the
church without any milk. Clure still wasn't sure. Genie would
endure several episodes like this with Civil Defense. Whatever
problem Genie presented Clure with, it seemed, he could only

tell her, "I don't know." Ultimately, she interpreted the man's paralysis as shock: "All Saturday," she said, "he was walking around in a haze."

In other words, the agency officially responsible for keeping Anchorage from falling apart in a crisis appeared to have unraveled under that stress itself. The longer Quarantelli sat around at Civil Defense on Sunday, the more fascinated he seemed by the foibles unfolding in front of him. At one o'clock, he watched an exasperated fireman enter the office and bark at the teenager sitting by the telephones: "Why are you people not answering the calls that are coming for you? Don't you people pay attention to that little buzzer?"

Apparently, no one in the room understood how to properly work the phone—even now, almost forty-eight hours after the quake. "Ah," the young woman said finally. "*That's* what that little noise is."

Quarantelli put it down in his notes.

20.

"EVERYBODY DOING A LITTLE BIT OF EVERYTHING FOR EVERYBODY"

———

THE DISASTER RESEARCHERS DIG IN

THE SOCIOLOGISTS WERE FANNING OUT, SWITCHING ON. Even catching a ride into the Public Safety Building at one point, Daniel Yutzy, the Disaster Research Center's towering and single-minded Mennonite graduate student, would get his tape recorder whirring and start spraying questions at his driver.

"You were in the downtown area when it hit?"

"Yes," the driver explained. In fact, he'd watched Blanche Clark's station wagon get flattened outside Penney's with his own eyes. "I could see her when that wall fell on her," he said. He had immediately joined the group of people working to extract her from the car. "The steering wheel was bent down on her legs," he explained to Yutzy. "Both legs were broke." Ultimately, they had to wrap a chain around the wheel and all heave at once to free her. The woman's injuries looked terrible, he said, but they had lifted her out alive.

"Were a lot of people around?" Yutzy asked.

"Everybody was trying to help," the driver explained. "Nobody's left hand knew what his right hand was doing." As soon as the ambulance took Clark away, someone shouted that there was another person alive in another car, buried under a pile of broken concrete, so the group started digging out that vehicle, too. The engine of this second car was still running, the man explained; they could hear it popping and its hoses exploding, while they worked. Despite these hazards, they kept digging for at least forty-five minutes. That was how long it took them to discover there wasn't anyone inside the car, after all. At that point, the group of rescuers disbanded as spontaneously as it had formed. Yutzy's driver had headed for Fourth Avenue, he explained, and helped other people there.

"Everybody tried to help," he repeated. "Clerks, bookkeepers. Everybody jumped right in. Everybody was trying to do a little bit of everything for everybody."

The man seemed grateful that someone wanted to hear his story, and the disaster researchers were good and patient listeners. Quarantelli had trained them to be personable and outgoing, but never in the way. ("Once you have made an introduction, then simply blend into the background and observe," he would say.) And Yutzy, in particular, was a natural. On Monday afternoon, Quarantelli happened by the KENI Kamper, still in operation outside the Public Safety Building. Inside, Ty Clark and several other announcers were live on the air, digging into a fresh round of coffee and snacks from the Salvation Army, which had just come through on one of its runs. And there among the broadcasters, Quarantelli spotted Yutzy, his microphone out and tape machine rolling. Yutzy had even helped himself to a package of oatmeal cookies.

The KENI staff was explaining how they'd first gotten the station back on the air on Friday night. "Who decided what you would broadcast?" Yutzy asked them

"Uh," one of the announcers said, searching for an answer, "we were just talking."

THE SOCIOLOGISTS WERE FOREVER asking questions like this: Who instructed you to do that? Why was one particular decision made instead of another? It was as though they were groping to fill in some imaginary flowchart or decision tree, attempting to map the contours of an experience that, for those who'd lived it, felt like a blur. The punctilious specificity of their questions frequently left people flummoxed. When, for example, Yutzy asked a worker at a Salvation Army shelter how many sandwiches his volunteers had just finished making, the man could only tell him that it was "a lot of food. They weren't petit fours, either. They were man-sized sandwiches." When you're making sandwiches after an earthquake, he added, "you don't get too statistical-minded."

The sociologists would spend a week in Anchorage after the quake, then make five subsequent trips to Alaska over the next eighteen months. They conducted nearly five hundred interviews, assembling a meticulous chronology of the immediate aftermath of the quake and reconstructing many of the same stories from Friday night and Saturday that you've already read in this book. Little of that action, they discovered, had unfolded methodically at all; it was all imprecise and instinctual.

Virtually none of the panic, violence, or other antisocial behavior the sociologists had arrived ready to document seemed to
be materializing, either. Yutzy soon learned that some of the volunteers Dick Taylor recruited to guard the vulnerable storefronts
downtown after the quake, and whom he'd outfitted with armbands and offered firearms, were transients who'd scampered
into the Public Safety Building from the bars on Fourth Avenue:
"denizens of the Skid Row section," as one of the sociologists'
reports would label them. Some even had criminal records. Still,
the report concluded, there had been "very little looting and pil-
fering in a situation where many stores and offices were wide
open so that anyone passing by could enter." One of the few
credible cases of looting the sociologists were told about in their
interviews appeared to have been perpetrated by a police officer.

Instead, the stories people recounted illustrated a staggering
amount of collaboration and compassion. Yutzy pieced together
the impromptu evacuation of Anchorage's Presbyterian Hospital, for example. Twenty-two of the hospital's fifty beds had been
occupied by immobilized patients when the building started filling with gas after the quake, and more people, injured in a landslide nearby on L Street, were already arriving. Right away, the
hospital's chaplain rushed outside and started flagging down
vehicles, amassing an armada of taxis, police cars, and ordinary
citizens driving by. Soon, everyone was loading stretchers into
the backs of station wagons. Boy Scouts who'd been distributing
phone books in the neighborhood walked patients down three
or four flights of stairs. Bob Fleming, the KENI announcer who
had been picking up his wife, Dolly, from her nursing shift at
Presbyterian, wound up with three patients in his back seat, including one woman in labor, plus a nurse to help hold their IV

bags high. In the end, all of Presbyterian's patients were transplanted safely to Providence Hospital, on the opposite side of Anchorage, in under two hours.

"It's there in front of you, so you do it," Dolly Fleming would later explain; she could find no more substantive theory to account for all the cooperation she'd witnessed. She herself had been leaving the hospital when the quake struck, and spotted the young son of one of her coworkers outside—all alone on the thrashing front staircase. She tucked the child under her arm and strained to hold them both steady against the railing as it shook. "It was as if I was an observer," Fleming said. "You lose all sense of time. You lose all sense of reality. What's happening is almost beyond what you can absorb." Decades later, at age ninety-two, the one cogent thought she could remember having through the four and a half minutes of the earthquake was this: "I'm thankful I'm here. I'm thankful I'm here so I can hold on to this little guy."

SO MUCH OF WHAT the researchers learned in their interviews that week was only an elaboration of what Yutzy's driver had told him shortly after he touched down: everybody in Anchorage had done a little bit of everything for everybody. It was startling, and cut against conventional wisdom's predictions of savagery and hysteria. Yet for Enrico Quarantelli, it seemed only to be concrete confirmation of a wild idea he'd discovered years earlier.

Quarantelli was unique among the three founders of the Disaster Research Center in that he'd actually done research in disaster zones before. As a graduate student, he had worked at a government institute at the University of Chicago called the National Opinion Research Council, under the mentorship of a scholar named Charles Fritz. Fritz and several colleagues were broadening the council's mission to examine human behavior in emergencies and disasters when Quarantelli came on board. Two years later, in 1952, they dispatched him on a field trip to White County, Arkansas, after the region was stampeded by a series of large tornados. Two hundred and thirty-one people died, and another eighteen hundred were injured. Quarantelli expected to find mayhem—a breakdown of society. "But the more I interviewed people," he later explained, "the more I said, 'Boy, these people handled the situation very well!'" After that, Quarantelli struggled to write his master's thesis. It was supposed to be about panic, but he was having trouble finding any instances of it.

Eventually, Fritz tried to synthesize what his team was learning from their fieldwork in an essay he called "Disasters and Mental Health." "Disasters," he wrote, "are, of course, occasions for profound human misery." But they didn't appear to create the chaos people feared. "The notions that disaster survivors inevitably or typically engage in panic, looting, and scapegoating, or become helpless, hysterical, and neurotic simply do not stand the test of critical research scrutiny." In fact, Fritz claimed, the people in those ruined communities seemed pretty happy. There might even be "therapeutic effects" to disasters, he argued—and from there, his speculations grew even more radical: "As social animals," he wrote, "people perhaps come closer to fulfilling their basic human needs in the aftermath of disaster than at any other time."

Fritz was arguing that disasters may bring out the best in human beings, rather than liberating some essential darkness in their nature. But at the time of the Good Friday Earthquake, Quarantelli was one of only a few people, even within the field of sociology, who would have been aware of that possibility. Fritz had written "Disasters and Mental Health" three years before the quake, as a chapter for an upcoming textbook. The book's editors rejected it. The essay would not be published for another thirty-five years.

21.

"A SPECIAL MYSTIQUE"

BILL DAVIS PROPOSES A THEORY

THE CITY HELD ITS SECOND PRESS CONFERENCE OF THE weekend on Sunday at four o'clock. Overall, conditions in Anchorage were continuing to stabilize and improve. Moreover, Mayor Sharrock stepped forward to explain, "I think that I should say that the people of Anchorage have been admirable in this thing. We have seen no indication of any panic whatsoever. Their spirits have been wonderful."

The city manager reported that the number of dead in the city stood at twelve. But the mayor interrupted: "I'd like to correct that," Sharrock said. "The latest figures we have indicate *five* persons dead." The mayor didn't mention the Task Force he'd set up to scrutinize that number—only that some initial reports of victims had turned out to be duplicates. That is, not only had searchers failed to uncover any new bodies since yesterday, but the quake had killed fewer people than they thought.

To the press, this new information didn't make sense. The possibility that only five people had died felt outlandish; a body count of twelve had already seemed implausibly low when city officials first announced it the night before. Now, some twenty hours later, that death toll had actually *decreased*? At first the journalists in the room acted as though they hadn't heard the number five leave the mayor's lips. Several called out for the same information again, one asked—phrasing their queries slightly differently each time, hoping a fresh attempt might draw out a different answer. It was hard to accept: instead of finding the dead, Anchorage appeared to be resurrecting them.

Bill Davis, the mountaineering psychologist who'd stumbled into the position of "Coordinator of Search and Rescue Operations," had reported the body count at the press conference the night before, but insisted on sitting out this second briefing. He had no desire to step into the spotlight again; it wasn't in his nature. But truthfully, it was also likely helpful, right now, not to remind the skeptical press corps that this work was being overseen by a civilian volunteer. It was always a jarring discovery—and maybe most of all for Quarantelli and his colleagues from the Disaster Research Center, who, expecting to find the head of some elite military unit directing Anchorage's search-and-rescue effort, instead discovered that the job had fallen to a self-deprecating and cerebral professor of the social sciences, just like them.

QUARANTELLI AND DAVIS WOUND UP chatting after the press conference and appeared to hit it off. Eventually, Quarantelli caught Davis with some downtime in his makeshift office in the fire department and set up his tape recorder to conduct a formal interview. Davis talked for close to an hour, with Quarantelli interjecting only sparingly. As consumed by the search and rescue operation as Davis had been all weekend, it was clear that part of him remained detached. He was a perspicacious and inquisitive observer, just like Quarantelli, and was studying the emergency while he lived it. "What I found when I came on the scene early Saturday morning was essentially a leadership void," he told Quarantelli, describing the initial breakdown at the fire department with regard to search and rescue. "Or if not a leadership void," he quickly qualified, "a decision-making void."

Quarantelli seemed fascinated by Davis and eager to understand how, exactly, he and his civilian mountaineers had managed to get so integrally involved. While some authority structures, like Civil Defense, appeared to have floundered after the quake, here was a totally informal group that had stepped in, organically, to pick up the slack. There were also brand-new ad hoc organizations like Disaster Control that had formed on the fly. The effectiveness of these improvised collectives was sharpening into focus for Quarantelli; it would be one of his primary takeaways from his time in Alaska. He would eventually label them "emergent groups," and he and other sociologists would witness them rising, spontaneously, after countless other natural disasters around the world. Two decades after the earthquake in Alaska, for example, when a devastating quake struck Mexico City, self-organizing teams of civilians calling themselves *topos,* or "moles," would search the city's wreckage for survivors. Two decades after that, in New Orleans, a makeshift flotilla of four hundred civilian boat owners, eventually known as the Cajun Navy, would rescue ten thousand people from the floods after

Hurricane Katrina. Then, in the fall of 2017, after another quake in Mexico City, volunteer *topos* would spontaneously dig in the rubble again, and a new Cajun Navy would rush into Houston after Hurricane Harvey.

Suddenly, a buzzer on Davis's desk went off and a siren blared, and he and Quarantelli paused their interview momentarily to watch a stampede of firefighters rush past the office, clamber onto one engine, then another, and drive off to attend to some minor blaze or secondary building collapse. By now, it was hardly a remarkable sight.

"Yes, all right. Anyhow," Davis continued. He was laying out a theory for the sociologist, speculating as to why Anchorage was handling the earthquake with such aplomb. He suspected it had to do with something fundamental about the community's character, or its idiosyncratic history as a boomtown, which he felt encouraged different kinds of people to live alongside one another in relative peace. Anchorage's population was less than 10 percent black, for example, and its neighborhoods were largely segregated by redlining, yet a national magazine called *Negro Digest* had recently visited the city and judged it to be as inclusive and comfortable a community for black people as currently existed in America. Overt racism in Anchorage seemed reserved, instead, for Alaska Natives; Davis set them aside as a shameful exception to the picture he was painting. Likewise, there were a few exceptionally wealthy folks at the top of Anchorage society, too. But everyone else was more or less the same: all coming to Alaska to effectively start again, or propelled out of the Lower 48 by some mounting, ineffable angst with conventional life that Davis found hard to pin down. ("I'd call it 'American Disenchantment Syndrome,'" he said.) They were all here, sloshing around in one equitable middle class, none of them feeling particularly superior or inferior to anyone else.

Davis believed this "excessive egalitarianism," as he put it, served Anchorage during the emergency: encouraging camaraderie, discouraging violence. Moreover, he explained to Quarantelli, this was a city where people still considered themselves pioneers and were accustomed to roughing it. The power in town goes out regularly, Davis said, the water pipes freeze a dozen times every winter, and everyone is expected to pitch in and overcome those complications collectively. And so, Davis ventured, this might explain why Anchorage had been less fazed by the disaster than, say, New Yorkers would have been; why the community was not fracturing, or succumbing to hysteria. This was all just one man's rambling hypothesis, he told Quarantelli, but he suspected "there's something fierce about the egalitarian attitudes of the people in Alaska that allowed them to work together in the disaster . . . And this idea that you're grappling with hardship all the time—it minimized the panic."

Quarantelli and his colleagues would hear this theory frequently in Anchorage. The Alaskans were essentially arguing that the conventional wisdom about disasters was correct: they *did* bring out the worst in people—just not in Alaska, where people were simply kinder, tougher, and better prepared. As Genie would write, "Alaskans have always been an independent breed of people. They have to be. They live in this land at the top of the world knowing the great distances to the continental United States—knowing the proximity to possible dangers from the Soviet Union—knowing that, at any moment, they may find it necessary to fend for themselves and learn to live with the elements of nature—a nature that is always unpredictable and sometimes violent."

The singular resilience of Alaskans came up often enough that Daniel Yutzy would be compelled to evaluate it in his final report on the earthquake, completed five years later. "These 'frontier' attitudes and analogies," Yutzy wrote, "were constantly expressed to imply there was a special mystique of emotional resources which Anchorage had that would be absent in other American communities faced with similar problems." And yet, Yutzy argued, most of what unfolded in Anchorage appeared to be merely typical human behavior, as already observed in other disasters, and as would continue to be documented around the world.

Much of the sociologists' work in Alaska would be incorporated into a landmark report on the disaster, commissioned by President Lyndon B. Johnson. Their studies of the earthquake would legitimize both the Disaster Research Center and the very idea of examining the social science of natural disasters. Gradually, an entire field—disaster studies—would blossom around Quarantelli and his colleagues and, as it grew, it would be stunning to recognize how much of what the sociologists had seen in Anchorage turned out to be characteristic of all disasters everywhere: People tended to act rationally, and even selflessly, rushing in to help like the crowds at the Public Safety Building. Mass hysteria was largely mythical, even though some entirely reasonable and effective responses to danger—like running, en masse, as fast as possible from a collapsing building—were easily mistaken for it. Looting was an exceedingly rare phenomenon after disasters, though paranoia about looting was always irrationally high. (In some cases, authorities are so overcome with worry about mass panic and looting that they preemptively clamp down on the public, even turning violently on innocent citizens who themselves aren't actually panicked at all. Disaster scholars refer to this phenomenon as "elite panic.") In short, our ugliest assumptions about human behavior would be almost uniformly rebuked by the ways actual humans behaved—again and again and again.

After Quarantelli died, in 2017—at age ninety-two, a colossus of the field—a former student would remember hopping a flight to an earthquake-stricken region of Nicaragua and listening to Quarantelli lay out what he should expect to find once he got on the ground. The student was confused; Quarantelli spoke with a kind of offhanded authority, like he'd already been to Nicaragua and witnessed the scene for himself. He hadn't, of course—the quake had only just occurred. But for Quarantelli, these kinds of random disasters had become some of the least surprising things on earth.

In fact, even Bill Davis's assumption that Anchorage was atypical would turn out to be typical. Eventually, it would be possible to look back on disaster after disaster and recognize that so many communities tended to interpret their own levelheaded and altruistic conduct as exceptional—New Orleanians being New Orleanians, or Puerto Ricans being Puerto Ricans—instead of wholly consistent with a half century of rigorous social science. It would be hard to accept that our goodness is ordinary.

"If the frontier spirit means self-reliance and an aggressive independence," Yutzy concluded in his report on the quake, "it was no more visible in Anchorage than in other disaster-stricken communities. This again should not be regarded as criticism," he was careful to add, "just a notation that Alaskans are normal human beings, motivated by wants and aspirations similar to most Americans. Their behavior during the height of the emergency period was similar to what can be found in other American communities."

That is, Anchorage was just like everywhere else in America. It was a demoralizing conclusion. It was, also, exactly the recognition the young city had always craved.

22.

"SOME MENTAL EFFECTS OF THE EARTHQUAKE"

———

A WINDOW CLOSES

MANY OF KENI'S EMPLOYEES HAD BEEN LIVING IN THE Fourth Avenue Theatre all weekend. They were sleeping on couches or on the plush carpet of the station's offices and taking shifts, along with several of their wives, to run the radio broadcast and field the dismayed phone calls from around Alaska and the Lower 48. Every evening, the Salvation Army pulled into the alley behind the theater and unloaded a hot meal for the staff, and every morning and afternoon, volunteers came through the studio offering coffee and a bemusing selection of sandwiches: turkey on raisin bread, or tuna on cinnamon bread—whatever ingredients they had to work with.

The building still had no heat and only minimal electricity; everything was running off an auxiliary generator downstairs. But at five o'clock on Sunday evening, power from the city grid was suddenly restored, and the building burst back to life. Right away, Charlie Gray and his engineers wondered if they could put KENI-TV on the air again.

Gray headed to the basement and started tinkering in the television studio, testing the equipment. It looked promising, he reported back. The police had imposed a curfew; they'd seal off the downtown area at six. So, at 5:25, KENI put a call over the radio for the station's young projectionist to hustle into work. He had thirty minutes to get there, they said, and should come prepared to spend the night.

There was an aftershock—a sizable one—but the engineers carried on working. By six o'clock, Gray was convinced they could make it happen: the gear in the studio was now operational; the antenna on the roof was tuned. The crew put a test pattern on the air and scrambled to throw together a quick, barebones newscast. Soon, Gray was hollering for a movie, too—something lighthearted, he said, to relieve the city's nerves. Before long, they were live. As the sun set on Easter, televisions around Anchorage were once again humming and bright.

A few hours later, shortly after ten, Mayor Sharrock's Task Force sent over an announcement for KENI to broadcast. Since its formation that afternoon, the Task Force had been working diligently in the Public Safety Building, probing every conceivable city record to draw up a master list of Turnagain residents and ascertain, once and for all, if anyone else had vanished in the slide. They'd also been working with the Salvation Army, which was operating its own clearinghouse to reunite separated families. Gradually, they had collected the names of 330 people—all still potentially unaccounted for. Now, on the radio, they were asking anyone who lived in Turnagain to simply call in, hoping to scratch off whomever they could.

The response was tremendous; the station's phone lines sparked right away. People called in, reporting themselves safe or confirming the safety of others whom they'd taken into their homes. Four hours later, the Task Force sent its updated list to KENI: a hundred names remained. Each name was read over the air, then read again at daybreak. And again, the number of potential casualties shrank rapidly as voices around Anchorage rose up, reached out, checked in. By Monday afternoon, the number of names on the Task Force's list had dropped to fifty. By Monday evening, there were only sixteen names left. Ninety minutes after those names were broadcast, the list had been cut in half again.

But gradually, some of the hopefulness seemed to drain from the project. Everyone understood that, at some point, the calls from the public would level off, and without the broadcasters even realizing it, this winnowing roster of names they were reading on the radio would no longer be a list of those who were potentially missing but a list of those who were definitively dead. And so, before going through the last names again on Monday night, a KENI announcer chose to do something unusual, to flip that dynamic around. "Now I would like to go over that *first* list, and give you the names of the people who've been *heard* from," he said. "In other words, they are safe and are not in trouble."

He recited the names slowly and stoically. "Joe E. Clauson, Robert D. Clarkson, Peter M. Clack—all these people are all right," he said. "Ralph W. DeLaRonde: all right. Opal M. Everett: all right. Donald C. Hartman: all right. Clarence A. Hirschbeck: all right. Donald Crow, also all right." The recitation took on the steadying cadence of a prayer. The announcer's "all rights" became tick marks with which to take a reassuring measure of how much they'd accomplished, working together, and how many souls they had found.

The Task Force would stop clearing names off its list the following morning. Ultimately, one hundred and fifteen deaths were confirmed around the state of Alaska, the vast majority of them in the small communities that had been struck by tsunamis. But the final death toll in Anchorage was only nine. Among the dead were the two Mead brothers from Turnagain, whose bodies were never found. A story surfaced that the older boy, Perry Jr., had died running back into the house to rescue his baby brother. But on the fiftieth anniversary of the earthquake, in 2014, the boys' sister would explain to a reporter in Anchorage that the media must have invented that detail, to make the tragedy more palatable. The truth was, she had watched the earth swallow her brother Perry with her own eyes. Seconds later, determined to protect her two younger brothers, she'd lifted the first to safety on the roof of the family's car but, when she turned back to grab two-year-old Merrell, she found he had vanished, too. "A crevasse opened up and took him, sand peeling from its sides," she explained. She saw it seal shut around him.

"It is unbelievable," Genie explained on the air, once the final death toll had been confirmed, "that such mass destruction could take place with so little loss of life." Anchorage had been lucky: when the quake struck, most people were home for the start of the holiday weekend—safe, in small and durable wooden structures. The city's larger buildings and roads hadn't been crowded; its schools had been empty. The tsunami that was projected never arrived. There were no major fires.

There was another reason, too, why the city's search-and-rescue workers hadn't kept finding more victims all weekend, like everyone had expected they would. As Genie interviewed more people in Anchorage, it became clear to her that the frenzied rescuers she'd seen digging in the rubble at Penney's and peeling that woman out of her flattened car weren't an anomaly. All over town, she wrote, "organized groups consisting of teachers, bankers, lawyers, laborers, bookkeepers—from all occupations and all walks of life—first methodically searched the ruins for survivors and fatalities." There was the airline employee she'd interviewed on the radio that first night, who described running toward the wreckage of the control tower. On Fourth Avenue, store owners had climbed out of the trenches into which their buildings had fallen, then immediately scurried back in to search for anyone who'd been trapped. People in Turnagain described hauling neighbors out of the debris field with ropes, loading the injured into their cars and driving them to Providence Hospital—effectively picking the area clean hours before Jim Scott descended into the slide for the first time with his mountaineering buddies to hunt for survivors, in the middle of the night. In the end, this diffuse wave of unofficial first responders had reclaimed almost all of the city's injured and dead before nightfall on Friday night—and most within the first hour after the quake. Everywhere in Anchorage, clusters of ordinary people had gone to work immediately, spontaneously, teaming up and switching on like a kind of civic immune response.

The individual stories went on and on; it would take months to compile them all. On Monday morning, as some of the stress of the weekend seemed to slacken, Genie would sit at her typewriter and start getting them down. At the top of the page, she put a title: HEROISM IN ANCHORAGE.

AN OUTSIDE PSYCHOLOGIST WHO'D been visiting Alaska that Easter weekend later wrote an article describing how uncannily his experience of the disaster mirrored the description of another earthquake, written a half century earlier by the psychologist and philosopher William James. James was a New Englander who—similarly by chance—had been visiting California when the great San Francisco earthquake struck in April 1906. James astutely chronicled its aftermath in an essay he called "On Some Mental Effects of the Earthquake."

Wandering around the city, James was left with two major impressions: "Both are reassuring as to human nature," he wrote. "The first of these was the rapidity of the improvisation of order out of chaos." James saw no panic, only purposefulness—people, "whether amateurs or officials, came to the front immediately" and got to work. "It was indeed a strange sight to see an entire population in the streets," he explained, "busy as ants in an uncovered ant-hill scurrying to save their eggs and larvae."

His second observation was less concrete, more spiritual. Even amid all that devastation, people seemed happy—even gleeful. Somehow, James wrote, the shattered city was overtaken by "universal equanimity." He described people sleeping outside for several nights afterward, partly to keep safe from aftershocks, "but also to work off their emotion, and get the full unusualness out of the experience." People felt a connection to one another, a kinship that's often lacking in ordinary life, and this togetherness seemed to make their problems more bearable.

"Surely the cutting edge of all our usual misfortunates comes from their character of loneliness," James wrote. In regular life, we suffer alone. But in San Francisco, each person's "private miseries were merged in the vast general sum of privation." As a result, to James, the victims didn't seem like victims; they seemed empowered. He did not hear "a single whine or plaintive word," even among those who'd suffered the starkest losses. There was only "cheerfulness."

This was also true in Anchorage. Many Alaskans discovered a peculiar joy in the immediate aftermath of the disaster, as they fed and sheltered neighbors, or huddled around a shared radio. There was camaraderie and altruism flowering everywhere. When, for example, the Alcantra family, who ran Alaska's largest egg farm, on the outskirts of the city, discovered that the earthquake had spooked their hens out of laying, they invited the whole town to come and take home six or eight chickens apiece—meat with which to keep themselves fed through the emergency. The family claimed to have thirty thousand chickens when they started. "And a week later," Patricia Alcantra would later explain, "the chickens are gone."

It was as though daily life had suddenly separated from history. The fallibility and arbitrariness of absolutely everything was exposed, and other, more generous ways of being seemed possible. "I think people's values have changed considerably," one man said. There was no such thing as "prestige" anymore, he explained: "A home has no value. The car has no value. If you have your wife and your family, you're rich." That simplicity, and the spirit of possibility and togetherness it fostered, reminded many residents of the Alaska they'd first moved to, a decade earlier or more. Everyone in town trusted each other again, another man said: "Just like it used to be up here."

Maybe these sentiments sound cliché. But for a time, they didn't—and that's the point: a special window had been cleaved open by the quake, during which such feelings were experienced as meaningful and real, untainted by irony or self-consciousness. A ticket agent at Northern Consolidated Airlines remembered that magic taking hold right away, before the earth had even stopped moving. He'd found himself standing face-to-face with the ticket agent from Pacific Northern Airlines, both of them fighting to stay upright as they watched the airport's control tower crash to the ground. "We both had our arms on each other's shoulders, supporting one another," he said. "Somehow, at the time, he wasn't a competitor."

After Sunday night, that heightened quality of the atmosphere in Anchorage began to dwindle. The disaster hadn't ended; the city still had a slew of fearsome problems ahead of it—How would Anchorage pay for its reconstruction? How much help would the federal government provide? Was the ground even safe to rebuild on?—but those challenges were of a different magnitude, and far less straightforward, than the ones the community had been scrappily surmounting so far. Finding solutions to them—if solutions even existed—would take months, if not years, and involve towers of paperwork, recondite financial calculations, studies by Outside geologists and soil scientists, and protracted squabbling with aloof bureaucracies in Washington. The work would be embittering and exhausting, convoluted and boring; as time wore on, the story of Anchorage's recovery would sprawl far beyond the satisfying outlines of the drama that had unfolded in the city over the last three days. Before long, Genie would vent about "chasing around at the heels of federal officials that have been traipsing in and out of Anchorage. Each one would have the same type of syrupy, say-nothing public statement to make at planeside when he arrived, then have his picture taken standing in front of the rubble, then talk to some groups and repeat the first statements he'd made to the press, then have a press conference prior to departure and say the same thing."

But that fuss was in the future. In retrospect, that Sunday night would feel like a turning point, a hazy transition between one chapter of the disaster and the next. As the Task Force's list of missing persons was recited over KENI and the responses streamed in over the phone, Anchorage appeared to be finishing off the last of its *first* kind of problems—the immediate and obvious ones that everyone in the community had been hacking through, collectively, since the moment the shaking started on Friday night. They were resolving the last, big question they were equipped to answer for themselves: Who in their town was living, and who was dead? Once they figured that out, the emergency would be over. The long catastrophe would come into view.

THE SIGNS WERE EVERYWHERE that Sunday night: life was de-pressurizing, resetting. The heat was back on at the Chance home, and Genie was in her own bed, lying next to a husband who both comforted and terrorized her, getting her first real night of sleep in three days. Meanwhile, on an airplane overhead, KENI's cheerful and arthritic patriarch, Bram, was returning home, too, descending out of a brilliant scrim of stars toward the city he loved, after what felt like a head-spinning intercontinental fever dream.

Bram's trip to Tokyo had been brief. He and his cohort of Alaskan business leaders were just settling into their hotel on Saturday morning when they first got word of the quake. One of the men received an emergency phone call from Fairbanks; there'd been an accident at one of his coal mines, killing an old friend. But then the voice on the other end said, "Wait a minute, we're having an earthquake here," and the connection cut off.

The men didn't think much of it initially; in Alaska, earthquakes happened all the time. They went and had lunch. But after a preliminary report about the disaster aired on Japanese radio, the group scrambled for more information. What Bram heard, he later explained, "made my hair stand on end."

The Alaskans started making arrangements to fly home, through whatever circuitous connections were available, coordinating with the American embassy, then with a kindly lieutenant general of the armed forces in Japan—all while trying to reach their wives and children back in Anchorage by phone. Many of the businessmen lived in Turnagain, including Bram. They had heard about the slide.

The delegation departed Tokyo about twenty-four hours after it arrived, first thing Sunday morning. The flight back was long and somber. The men braced for the worst. "We traveled a total of 12,000 miles over the weekend," Bram would explain, "and we had two Easter Sundays. I can't say they were the happiest."

When their plane finally landed at Anchorage International late on Sunday night, the airport had just reopened, but barely. The runway lights were out. The terminal was shut down. There were no airline employees to assist them. Taxis and wives drove straight up to the aircraft on the tarmac, as Bram and the other passengers trundled down the stairs. A worker unloaded their bags directly onto the ground. The disordered carcass of the control tower still sat where it had fallen, in a thirty-foot pile, silhouetted beyond them like a jagged mountain range in the dark.

Bram surveyed the sprawl of luggage. It was hard to see; you just had to do your best to figure out which suitcases were yours. Then, there among the businessmen waiting on the tarmac, Bram noticed an unfamiliar face: "a typical urbane tourist type," he said, who had somehow wound up on the last leg of their flight—slipping in like an apparition from the ordinary world. The man was complaining, obliviously and loudly enough for everyone around him to hear. He was griping about the lack of service.

Bram couldn't believe it. He watched the man flail, confronting the unimaginable: this upended, amenity-free reality into which he'd suddenly been dropped. Whatever was happening right now, Bram heard the man insisting, was the most outrageous thing he'd ever experienced in his life.

ONE WEEK AFTER

FRIDAY, APRIL 3, 1964

23.

"WHAT IS SAFETY, ANYWAY?"

———

ORDINARY TIME RESUMES

Early the following Friday morning, one week after Good Friday, Genie was flying with Governor Egan to Juneau where, returning to the capital for the first time since the disaster, he would address a special joint session of Alaska's legislature. The traveling party had assembled in Anchorage at three a.m. and lifted off at four. The weather was frigid and foggy, and they were forced to fly low, through a single, ceaseless cloudbank; for four and a half hours, it was like they were tunneling through the interior of a pillow.

There were twelve other people on the flight, most of them packed awkwardly into a renovated house trailer that had been installed in the hull of the military cargo plane, in lieu of a proper cabin. Genie looked around, took out her portable tape recorder, and tested some material for the story she'd be broadcasting about the trip. "If you think politics makes strange bedfellows," she whispered, "you should see what disaster and fatigue does to the politicians as they're bedded down on this Alaska National Guard C-123, and sleeping under most cramped conditions."

All the men looked wrecked. Genie, wide-awake, amused herself by taking stock of the strange positions each had wound up in. A few had curled up on cushions they'd stripped from the benches and laid side by side on the floor. Others were crimped into medical stretchers like unwieldy infants in bassinets. On the opposite end of the aircraft, Genie had watched the adjutant general of the National Guard sit directly on the floor, cross his legs, fold his arms, and tuck his head, touching his chin to his chest, then—pinched together this way like a contorted Buddha— somehow pass resolutely into sleep. More incredibly, he would seem wholly reinvigorated when he woke up later. This was Thomas Carroll: the self-possessed major general whom Genie had interviewed in the Public Safety Building on Good Friday night, and who would die on a National Guard airplane just like this one—likely this exact plane, in fact—when it plunged into Prince William Sound twenty-three days from now.

Genie was sitting next to Governor Egan. The governor seemed to have taken a liking to her in the preceding week as Genie shadowed him, reporting on the state's relief efforts and the many federal officials swishing through Anchorage to meet with him. When President Johnson's secretary of state, Dean Rusk, arrived for a tour of downtown, Egan made a point of introducing him to Genie—"the voice of Alaska to the outside world," he called her. (Rusk thanked Egan for the introduction, Genie later wrote, but also noted that one privilege of being secretary of state was that "you can talk to pretty ladies without being introduced.") After takeoff, as everyone aboard hunkered down and fell asleep, Genie watched Egan take out a pen and begin reworking his speech. But eventually, his eyes drooped and his head slumped forward, coming to rest on his script.

The future of Alaska was riding, in part, on how Egan's address would be received. The quake had dealt a profound and potentially irreversible blow to the state's economy and infrastructure. It seemed like it would still be months before any definitive damage estimate could be reached, though one federal official had already projected that the reconstruction could cost half a billion dollars—far more than Alaska could afford, particularly with some untold share of its future tax revenue now obliterated. In truth, Alaska had never reached a point of full, financial self-sufficiency to begin with; nearly half of Anchorage still collected its paychecks from the federal government. As one newspaper put it that Friday, "Uncle Sam shares Alaska's problem whether he wants to or not. He will have to decide whether he wants to rebuild his stepchild."

In two days, Egan would be flying to Washington to ask President Johnson for federal assistance. But he first wanted to show the administration that Alaskans were willing to help themselves. And so, in Juneau that afternoon, he planned to ask the legislature to pass an emergency, $50 million bond measure. For Alaskans, this was a startling proposition—"far, far larger than anything we have before attempted as a state or territory," Egan would concede. He was essentially groveling. He felt he had to—here, among his fellow Alaskans—before he went groveling to the president of the United States.

Egan's address was scheduled for early that afternoon. As soon as Genie entered the capitol building, a state senator recognized her and enthusiastically introduced her around. One after another, lawmakers kept thanking her. "They would shake hands or hug me, each with tears in their eyes," she remembered. An unfamiliar energy seemed to be crackling in the air around her: the same prestige that would estrange her from her colleagues at KENI in the following months, then eventually get her elected to a seat in this very chamber. One lawmaker invited her to sit with him. And then, with all of Alaska listening, on a statewide radio hookup that Genie herself had organized for the speech, Alaska's Speaker of the House called the session to order and surprised Genie by formally introducing her and asking her to stand. She was struck dumb—thrown into "complete stupefaction," she said—when everyone in the chamber suddenly stood up, too, and started applauding.

The governor did not speak long. "In all of our history," he said, "there has never been a natural disaster equal to the one Alaska suffered almost at this very hour exactly one week ago." Those four and a half minutes, and the entire week that had followed, Egan said, would be hard for Outsiders to comprehend. "What is it like to have your world turned upside down?" he asked. "To lose relatives and friends? To lose homes? To watch buildings crumble and familiar landmarks erased from the earth in an instant? And then, to bounce back, pick up the pieces and look to the future? That is what the majority of Alaskans have done since Friday." Any despondency people felt would be understandable: their state was still new; they'd only just built what the quake had rent apart. But Egan believed that "a united and determined people has been welded together from the heat and shock of disaster," he said. "We are a young state. We are a young people, but we are mature."

When the speech was over, Genie mingled through the hall, recording interviews for KENI's coverage. Soon, she felt someone tugging on her sleeve. He leaned in to whisper some news: another earthquake had just hammered Anchorage.

THE AFTERSHOCK HIT AT 12:41, Anchorage time. "We could feel it coming," one woman said. The rattling was mild at first, and everyone had become so desensitized to the tremors reverberating through the city by then that their first instinct was to wait out the inconvenience.

People stopped on the streets downtown and stared tentatively at each other. Around a table at the Alaska Methodist University cafeteria, forks and spoons froze halfway to people's mouths. At city hall, the city manager, Robert Oldland, stood near his secretary's desk, receiving two visitors from out of town. The secretary was the first to feel the motion and, looking down, saw her hand vibrating on the surface of her desk. "That wasn't an earthquake, was it?" she asked. Then the bucking started in earnest, and everyone ran out the back door.

Genie would later report the aftershock's magnitude as 6.7 on the Richter scale; it was a quake that demanded attention. People scrambled for the door of a bank downtown and clogged it. Policemen fled the Public Safety Building. At the public library, an aging librarian vaulted over the reference desk like a gazelle. The tremor lasted only several seconds, but the experience registered less like riding out yet another aftershock than as living through a second big one: after a solid week of exhausted, little pushes, the earth now seemed to birth a breached and screaming twin.

The damage to Anchorage was minor. The real, lasting wreckage was emotional. The first quake had already left people traumatized, trampling their sense of security. For days after escaping J. C. Penney on Good Friday, a young jeweler had refused to take off his clothes before bed, in case he needed to evacuate again. Then, he did start undressing, but would leave his clothes strewn in a trail between his bed and the door, roughly in the order he'd want to snatch them up and throw them on if he had to make a run for it. This second quake was too much. It tore people down.

"Many spur of the moment decisions were made to leave Alaska" that Friday afternoon, two researchers would find. All at once, the aftershock set off an exodus for the Lower 48 that would continue, just as heavily, the following day. Regular flight schedules had only just resumed from Anchorage International Airport. One airline had sold only thirty seats on its night flight out of Anchorage before the aftershock, but that afternoon, the flight sold out. By nightfall, the airport was jammed; the scene was viscerally tense. Children were crying. Many of those fleeing were mothers, taking their kids back to wherever they'd moved from initially, while their husbands remained to weather the rawness that would characterize life in Anchorage until the city could be rebuilt. That is, the city was being drained of its families in precisely the opposite way it had been settled in the boomtown days, when men from the Lower 48, like Winston, came up first on their own.

Time seemed to be rewinding, heading toward history. An estimated four thousand people would leave the city that spring. As the first full flights lifted off, it was easy to worry that Anchorage was losing its status as a "city of permanence," as a local paper had put it on the opening night of Cap Lathrop's Fourth

Avenue Theatre all those years ago—a "city in which families live, work, play and die."

The fragility of the city's future seemed even more dire from afar. Genie's mother, Den, had spent the week since the earthquake in Texas vibrating with anxiety. Unlike many Outsiders with children in Alaska, Den had been lucky enough to hear her daughter's voice on the radio right away; she knew the Chance family was all right. Yet she'd been subject to the same barrage of catastrophic misinformation since then, and seemed especially susceptible to it. Den's mind kept generating exaggerated chains of worst-case scenarios. The Chance family might be all right, she reasoned, but their home had undoubtedly collapsed, leaving them out in the cold. If Genie was up all night broadcasting, she'd get pneumonia, and without proper medical care, in the burned-out ruins of Anchorage, she'd never get healthy again. And even if Genie did kick the pneumonia, she'd be irrevocably scarred emotionally. "She'll break up after the stress is over," Den predicted. "She's that much like her mother. Through crisis, she puts down all fear, anxiety, and lets it serve as a dynamo for her apparent poise. Then, in the end, she'll go to pieces."

Den had no outlet for her dread. She'd heard on the radio that families should refrain from phoning Anchorage, to keep the lines clear, and her friends told her not to bother sending mail. "My thought," Den explained, "was to grit my teeth and sit it out." But she'd continued to read about, or simply imagine, her daughter's city as a buckled and charred dystopia, where ruptured sewage lines would inevitably lead to epidemics of communicable disease.

Finally, the Wednesday after the earthquake, Den wrote to

her daughter. "Emma Gene," she began sternly. "I am so concerned about health hazards in that area of impurities. Why don't you get those children out of there!! The entire family should get out, at least until sewage is corrected all over the area. Come home and stay until conditions are not so conducive to pestilence. And if you don't come yourselves, please send those children!" The kids' well-being was paramount, Den insisted; Genie shouldn't take any more chances with their safety. "Please do something," she wrote.

Genie was inclined to dismiss her mother's worry, but couldn't—just as she couldn't fault those families in Anchorage who were drawing similar conclusions and decamping for the Lower 48. In fact, writing her mother back, Genie confessed:

I must admit that during that first dark, cold night, as I began to understand the tremendous scope of the problems that would be facing us in the months and years to come, I toyed with the idea of sending the children out on a plane to stay with you until everything settled down. Working there in the headquarters, where the reports were coming in from the survey teams throughout the city, I realized that there could possibly be a real health hazard for some time to come. I realized that the schools might not be able to resume for an indefinite period of time. It looked for a few hours as if the damage had been so extensive to all utilities and streets that even a semblance of normal life could not be resumed for weeks or months. If this were to be, I knew that Winston and I would stay here and do what we could to help—

but this might mean that the children would be neglected.

But this was just a fleeting thought in a weary mind. I would have been ashamed of myself had it not been for the next thought that came so swiftly: We must be together. They must not be a great distance away and wonder and fear about the safety of their parents. That night I saw strain, heavy hearts, and fear in people separated from their loved ones by the sudden disaster. I could not make my children live through that. And Winston and I could not leave. As long as we are together, we are confident of the future . . .

That Good Friday night I knew that we had survived miraculously. And for this reason, there must be a purpose to our lives. Apparently the children must sense this, too. For they have remained calm. They have been fully aware of the emergency, but they have not feared. We are proud that they are such dependable, responsible youngsters. I would not undermine their confidence in the future—in themselves—by sending them away for safety.

What is safety, anyway? How can you predict where or when tragedy will occur? You can only learn to live with it and make the best of it when it happens. These children have learned this—and they are all the better for it. They were in the midst of devastation. And they feel that they are a part of the tremendous task ahead in rebuilding this land we love . . .

The children are not afraid. Their father and I are not afraid. Please, don't you fear for us.

What is safety, anyway? Genie seemed to be conceding how randomly our lives are jostled and spun around, that nothing is fixed, that even the ground we stand on is in motion. Underneath us, there is only instability. Beyond us, there's only chance.

But she'd also recognized a way of surviving such a world. It was what Genie had created in Anchorage that weekend by talking on the radio, and what she planned to stay focused on now: not an antidote to that unpredictability, exactly, but at least a strategy for withstanding it, for wringing meaning from a life we know to be unsteady and provisional. The best she and her family could do was to hold on to one another.

Our force for counteracting chaos is connection.

24.

"THE SPECIAL PRIVILEGE
OF PROVIDING A LINK"

TIME COLLAPSES

OUR TOWN REOPENED AT ALASKA METHODIST UNIVERSITY the following Monday, three days after the aftershock and Governor Egan's speech. It was 25 degrees in Anchorage and had been snowing heavily. The mood was dour. "Tension," Genie explained on the KENI newscast, "is showing on the faces of a proud people. The realization that the Good Friday Earthquake will have long-range repercussions on the entire state is beginning to strike at their hearts."

For days, Frank Brink had been running new ads for the play in the local paper—"Take Time to RELAX," they said—but his cast arrived at the Grant Hall theater that evening worried that no one in Anchorage was ready to relax yet, and skeptical that anyone would come. As curtain time approached, however, one of Brink's actors peered into the house apprehensively and watched as, slowly, all two hundred of its seats filled.

"This play is called *Our Town*," the Stage Manager began. He was played by a reedy and bespectacled older man named Jim Tracy, who'd just moved to Anchorage from the Los Angeles area after a divorce to be near his grandchildren. Tracy was the rare actor in town who'd actually done some professional work before, on the stage and in television back in California. Years later, talking to the writer Jon Mooallem, one *Our Town* cast member would remember Tracy as the only actor who'd arrived at their first rehearsal that winter with all his lines memorized. "He was a marvel," the man would explain. Then, looking off, squinting as though he could still see Tracy pacing the proscenium, he added, "God, people like that should be allowed to live forever."

Tracy instantly settled the audience. The room was with him from the start of his first expository monologue. The action started on the scenery-less stage behind him: the two mothers fixed breakfast in their neighboring houses, the doctor staggered home from his overnight house call, and the paperboy appeared, played by the son of one of Brink's colleagues on the university faculty. Suddenly, the Stage Manager flashed forward omnisciently, explaining to the audience how that little kid delivering papers would eventually get a scholarship to MIT and leave the town of Grover's Corners behind. He was going to be a brilliant engineer. "But the war broke out and he died in France. All that education for nothing," the Stage Manager lamented. Then he quickly changed the subject. "Here comes Howie Newsome," he said, "deliverin' the milk."

In walked a buoyant and powerfully built African American man, delivering milk. The actor, Brady Jackson, was a fixture of Anchorage's community theater scene—he'd recently directed his own production of *A Streetcar Named Desire*—and a charismatic presence around town. Jackson and his wife, Gary, regularly cleared the dance floor at nightclubs with routines they worked up at home. He was also a painter and a poet, taught kids to box at the local Boys Club, and had recently held Alaska's Light Heavyweight Champion title himself; when people passed Jackson on the sidewalk, they called him "Champ." Two years later, in 1966, he would fight Sonny Liston when a promoter brought Liston to Anchorage and staged an exhibition bout. Three years after that, Jackson would be working on the roof of his house and fall, then spend the rest of his life in a wheelchair as a paraplegic. His son would tell Mooallem, "I'm sure Dad must have had internal battles, but he didn't show it." In fact, Jackson would become an early and energetic advocate for disability rights in Alaska. Now he strolled across the stage, handing out milk bottles and collecting empties from Mrs. Webb—a young middle school English teacher who would die of complications from heart surgery forty-seven years later, in Denver.

The play progressed. A church choir rehearsed, under the erratic direction of Grover's Corners' alcoholic preacher, played by one of Brink's most loyal young protégés, Robert Pond. "I don't think I was much of an actor, but I could do a drunk," Pond would confess a half century later, when Mooallem visited him at his home in Anchorage. Pond had gone on to serve as the artistic director of the city's largest theater for more than twenty years, effectively filling his old mentor's niche. He was eighty years old and a recent widower—Mooallem would notice his wife's automatic chair lift still installed in the front stairway—but nevertheless had one of the sharpest memories of anyone Mooallem encountered in his interviews about the quake. Still, as they talked that morning, Pond would occasionally seem stunned, and even oddly embarrassed, whenever some ancient, trivial detail escaped him, such as whether a particular actor in that *Our Town* production had been a member of Anchorage's plumbers and fitters union. "Ha!" Pond would say, leaning back, mystified, as though that missing bit of information had been lodged securely in his mind only moments ago and he'd taken for granted that he would know it forever. Several months later, Mooallem would reach out to another of Brink's acolytes in the *Our Town* cast, Bob Deloach—the young gay man with the coke-bottle glasses, who, in 2014, became one half of the first same-sex couple to legally marry in Alaska. When Deloach picked up the phone, Mooallem mentioned, by way of introduction, that he had already met with Deloach's old friend Robert Pond. Deloach explained that Pond had just passed away.

Act I ended. Act II began. Before long, it was George and Emily's wedding day, and the scene between Emily and her father that had blown up in rehearsals a few weeks earlier when the play's prim and insecure lead, the beauty queen Susan Koslosky, fell apart in Brink's office, worried she had no authentic self. Brink would continue to look out for Koslosky after the quake, finessing a grant application to qualify her for student housing, getting her out of her volatile mother's house and into the university dorms. Eventually, Brink would encourage Koslosky to transfer to a small college in Michigan and escape Anchorage altogether; if she didn't leave now, he told her, she would never create a life of her own. By the time Mooallem would track down Koslosky, she had changed her name to Michale Gabriel and, at age seventy-two, was living in Costa Rica, returning frequently to the United States to run storytelling workshops for corporate executives—helping them, she explained, "express themselves authentically." After a pause, she added, "I haven't actually connected it back to Frank and *Our Town* until now."

Brink would leave Anchorage himself in 1976, when Alaska Methodist University's dream of creating a Harvard of the North collapsed and the school shut down. Brink and his wife, Jo, settled in Shreveport, Louisiana, where he was hired to revitalize a community theater. There, he would continue to do his one-man *Christmas Carol* every holiday season, and throw himself into yet another reworking of his Alaskan epic, *Cry of the Wild Ram*— still rolling that dramatic boulder uphill. In 2002, the Brinks would move into a nursing home in rural Arkansas; by then, Frank had developed a debilitating case of Lyme disease, and Jo was showing signs of Parkinson's. Each also suffered with Alzheimer's-like symptoms, though Jo's grew far fiercer than Frank's. Near the end, she'd hear babies crying, or see men walking toward her with guns.

Jo died first. When Frank finally passed, in 2009, at the age of ninety-three, the *Anchorage Daily News* would run a short obituary, but no one in the city would think to hold a memorial service. A young woman on the crew of *Our Town* that Easter weekend, Robin Niemann, had become like family to the Brinks and had stepped in to oversee their care as they declined. She would explain to Mooallem that Frank never unraveled mentally to the extent that Jo had. Even near the end, when Niemann visited the Brinks in Arkansas, she said, she and Frank would sit together in the garden, reminiscing at length about Alaska and their triumphs in the theater. His memory seemed solid, Niemann insisted; he was keeping up. Then again, she added, he was such a talented actor—who knows.

The excruciating climax of *Our Town* came toward the end of Act III. It was now nine years after the wedding, the Stage Manager told the audience. At the town cemetery, a funeral was getting under way. It was Emily's funeral—she had died in childbirth.

Koslosky walked onstage in a white dress and sat wordlessly in a chair alongside several other actors. These were the dead of Grover's Corners—their souls—invisible to the living characters but not to the audience. Emily was joining them to watch her own burial. But as the scene unfolded, she discovered she had the option of ineffably going back, somehow, and reliving moments from her life. The other souls pleaded with her not to; it's too painful, they said. Finally, the Stage Manager explained why: "You not only live it," he told her, "but you watch yourself living it. And as you watch it, you see the thing that they—down there—never know. You see the future. You know what's going to happen afterwards."

Emily couldn't possibly understand these warnings. She wanted to go back. She chose an ordinary Tuesday morning fourteen years earlier, and suddenly, on Brink's stage, the same timeless daily routine unfolded again: the mothers fixing breakfast in their neighboring houses, the milkman, the paperboy. Except this time, as Emily watched from one side of the stage and the audience watched through her eyes, the routine did not feel mundane at all, but precious and fleeting. The people living that life had no idea how fragile it was.

Koslosky stood frozen among the dead, overcome, slowly phasing from wonder into grief. It pained her to watch her mother scurry around their kitchen distractedly, nagging Emily's younger self to chew her bacon and get to school. "Oh Mama," Koslosky pleaded. "Just look at me one minute as though you really saw me. Mama, fourteen years have gone by. I'm dead." But her mother couldn't hear her. And the longer the scene played, the more wrenching her obliviousness became. "I can't!" Koslosky finally told the Stage Manager, surrendering. "It goes so fast. We don't have time to look at one another."

In the darkness of the theater, Koslosky heard someone sobbing. She could feel a wave of vulnerability surge through the room. It felt to her as though the earthquake had broken everybody's hearts open, and now this play—her lines—was pouring straight in. In retrospect, the parallel was clear: the disaster had shaken Anchorage out of its ordinary existence and into some shapeless, adjacent realm where, just like Emily, everyone could look back on their lives and appreciate the beauty and interconnectedness they hadn't recognized before. But unlike Emily, the people in Anchorage had the privilege of returning to that life and trying again.

Years later, Enrico Quarantelli would coauthor an article speculating about why the Disaster Research Center was documenting so little conflict in its studies of disaster-stricken communities around the world. In the paper, he compared a town coping with disaster to an audience watching a play. Like good theater, Quarantelli wrote, "disasters do not involve mundane matters but often the very issue of human life itself." These themes, usually dormant in daily life, suddenly spill out in public for all to see. An unrelenting immediacy sets in: "Worries about the past and future are unrealistic when judged against the realities of the moment." And distinctions between people fall away, leaving only "human beings responding to one another as human beings . . . As a consequence, all those who share in the experience are brought together in a very powerful psychological sense, by their common participation in such a dramatic event. To victims, the disaster is 'our' disaster."

Now, ten days after Anchorage's disaster, *Our Town* appeared to be serendipitously bookending the experience, making some of those same epiphanies available to the community. A town that worried it was temporary had learned that it *was* temporary. But it was recognizing something permanent about itself, too.

Genie was not in the theater that night—not as far as Mooallem could tell, at least. There was no mention of *Our Town* in any of the documents Mooallem found in her daughter's basement. The only item bearing that day's date was a stray typewritten page—a kind of diary entry, it seemed, written after Genie had returned from Juneau with the governor and finally taken her first full day off since the quake. For nine days, she had pushed the stress and brutal imagery of the previous weekend out of her mind: that piece of a woman in the snow; the people downtown in every conceivable variety of shock: screaming or wailing, or staring absently forward in silence. But climbing into bed at the end of her day off, the hurt overtook her. She burst out weeping and cried uncontrollably into her pillow for hours, she wrote— breaking down, just like her mother had predicted she would. Then, just as suddenly, she stopped. "I slept like a lamb," Genie explained in a subsequent letter, "and have been a new person ever since."

Mooallem was moving through Genie's boxes less enthusiastically by then, unsealing each new one with vaguely demoralizing unease—a feeling that reminded him of what the mountaineers had described, entering the ruined homes of Turnagain. He found it unnerving that anyone's life could be compacted into boxes, and he'd learned enough about the earthquake to under-stand that—just like Genie herself had always insisted—hers was only one story of the disaster worth telling. It had no special claim to being the most important one, either.

When Mooallem first phoned Genie's daughter, he was thirty-six years old. By the time he finished writing about the earthquake, he would be almost forty-two, and presume to be entering the second half of his life. Then again, maybe a cancer was already clotting inside him, or he would drive over black ice; he instructed his publisher, once the time came, to fill in the de-tails here. He started picturing his own boxes. He imagined how many other boxes were already out there, in other people's base-ments, and how many people hadn't left boxes at all. Still, he clung to Genie's story, as small as it ultimately might be, because it brought that profusion of other lives into focus, and because it suggested the unpredictable connections branching between them, or even reaching forward, unknowably, through time.

At the bottom of one of Genie's last boxes, from the years just before her dementia took hold, Mooallem found a blue three-ring binder with "Genie Chance" stamped neatly on the cover. On the first pages were vignettes she had written about her child-hood in Texas—memories of her parents; the story of her first day of school, when she'd gotten so intimidated that she turned tail and ran straight home. Behind those, Mooallem found an article Genie had clipped from the Rotary Club magazine titled "How to Write Your Own Life Story."

"The important thing," the article explained, "is not to let any of your memories get away before you are ready to write about them . . . You have the special privilege of providing a link to your heritage for coming generations. You can put the words on paper which will prevent your life and the lives of other members of your family from slipping into oblivion."

But that was it. The binder Mooallem was holding was full of paper—thicker, even, than the book in your hands—but the rest of those pages were blank.

ACKNOWLEDGMENTS

———

WRITING THIS BOOK RELIED ON THE TRUST, GOODWILL, AND cooperation of so many people, but of one person especially: Jan Blankenship opened her home and her mother's boxes to me without restrictions or conditions—but not, understandably, without apprehension. I'm thankful for her kindness, openness, and patience and hope this book delivers on that tremendous leap of faith. I had a lot of fun getting to know her and Chuck and am glad to have met their kids, Jeremiah and Verity, as well.

I very quickly gained staggering and overdue appreciation for archivists and the work they do. Thank you to Pat Young and Valerie Marlowe at the Disaster Research Center's E. L. Quarantelli Resource Collection, as well as to the center's directors, Tricia Wachtendorf and James Kendra, for welcoming me into their world. I'm equally grateful to Arlene Schmuland, Gwen Sieja, and Veronica Denison at the University of Alaska Anchorage Archives and Special Collections for their extensive assistance and guidance and for sharing my fascination with Genie.

It was a total privilege to hear the stories of so many residents of Anchorage, past and present, all of whom are acknowledged in the source notes. Their affection for that time and place always moved me; I hope that comes through. I'm especially grateful to Al Bramstedt Jr., Barbara Brinkerhoff, Nancy Yaw Davis, Michael Janecek, and Robin

Niemann for their help and patience over the years, and to Bill Davis and Robert Pond, who sadly aren't around to see what all my nitpicky questions finally amounted to. Thanks also to Tom Drabek, whose memories of the early days of the Disaster Research Center were invaluable.

Jin Auh at the Wylie Agency knew—far more confidently than I did initially—that I should write this book. I'm grateful to her for reminding me that the decision was entirely mine and for empowering me to make it. Andy Ward is as skillful and sensitive an editor and collaborator as everyone says he is. It's hard to imagine having two sharper or more exceptionally supportive people in my corner—it just feels so good.

Thank you to everyone at Random House who has played a part in the creation and promotion of this book: Craig Adams, Jess Bonet, Maria Braeckel, Barbara Fillon, Susan Kamil, London King, Matthew Martin, Tom Perry, and Chayenne Skeete. Thanks to Bruce Merrell, who helped with research in Anchorage at the very beginning and end of this project, but also generously read the manuscript and offered the kind of meaningful feedback and approval that only a genuine Alaskan could; Sonner Kehrt, who brought her impressive journalistic talents to the job of fact-checking the manuscript, shoring up its accuracy and my emotional well-being; Jason Richman at UTA for his advocacy and hard work on my behalf; the exemplary editors and fact-checkers at *The New York Times Magazine,* particularly Sheila Glaser, Jake Silverstein, Jessica Lustig, Bill Wasik, Rob Liguori, and Lia Miller, who've continually made me a better reporter and writer in thousands of obvious and imperceptible ways; and all the brilliant friends to whom I continually turned for advice, favors, comfort, and criticism as I went along: Laurel Braitman, Alexis Coe, Jack Hitt, Starlee Kine, Jamie Lowe, Claire Cain Miller, Caroline Paul, Meghann Riepenhoff, Rebecca Skloot, Amy Standen, and especially Wendy MacNaughton and Chris Colin. Also: Evan Ratliff and I had a standing phone call every other Thursday for two years to chat about the books we were writing. Anyone writing a book should make sure to have an Evan Ratliff.

This Is Chance! started as a collaboration with the musicians Jenny Conlee-Drizos, Chris Funk, John Moen, Jon Neufeld, and Nate Query for a live show produced by Radiotopia and the podcast *99% Invisible*. Thank you to Roman Mars for his extraordinary trust in us and the chance to first dig into the story, and to Avery Trufelman, who played Genie in the original production. Thanks to my musical collaborators— the Brink Players—for making it a totally joyous experience and helping to set the tone.

This book is for Rose, who would have preferred I wrote a book about bees but isn't holding it against me. It is also for Isla. It is also for Wandee. Everything is.

NOTES ON SOURCES

————

THIS BOOK IS NONFICTION, BASED EXTENSIVELY ON PRIMARY AND unpublished materials. Anything in quotation marks comes directly from a radio broadcast, letter, interview transcript, or other document. Quotations are not someone's memory of what another person said, except in small cases noted below—e.g., Genie quoting her son yelling "Come quick! Penney's building is falling down!" in a letter written shortly after the quake.

As I mention in the book, drawing out a cohesive, readable narrative from a trove of disjointed and static documents was often an unnerving challenge; as a journalist, I'm accustomed to asking people lots and lots of follow-up questions. The possibility that, given these limitations, I may have unknowingly misreported small details of this story still makes me uncomfortable, though I'm convinced—and feel like I should assure you, the reader—that I worked with a deep commitment to getting everything right. For example: I lost sleep—literally lost sleep one night—over the question of whether Genie took that phone call from the Omaha radio station while she was standing at the police counter, or if she carried the phone some distance away from the counter and talked to the caller there. (She described it happening both ways, in two different documents.) Ultimately, I chose to play it safe and not specify where she took the call. Maybe that sounds ridiculous. It definitely *felt* ridiculous at times. Still, that was my approach.

An explanation of some key resources:

GENIE'S BOXES (GB): These are the boxes in Jan's basement: an exhaustive collection of letters, photographs, diaries, KENI scripts, unpublished memoir fragments, audio recordings, mementos, and so on—as described in the book. Unless otherwise specified, letters in these notes cited "GB" were written by Genie to her parents and/or sisters in the Lower 48. Typically, she addressed her letters to "Folks at All Points" and sent one copy to each of their households.

THE GENIE CHANCE PAPERS AT THE UNIVERSITY OF ALASKA ANCHORAGE ARCHIVES AND SPECIAL COLLECTIONS (UAA) AND THE "CHRONOLOGY OF PHYSICAL EVENTS" (CPE): Genie sent some of her professional papers to the university before her death. Most cover her legislative career, but series 1 contains earthquake-related documents, including a report, titled "Chronology of Physical Events of the Alaska Earthquake" (CPE), that Genie completed in 1966 with a grant from the National Science Foundation, assembling hundreds of eyewitness accounts of the quake from around the state. The report is also available online in the university's Alaska Digital Archives.

Series 2 contains audio recordings—mostly reel-to-reel recordings, which I paid to have digitized. Some of these turned out to be duplicates of recordings in GB, which had its own collection of reels. In addition, Genie annotated transcripts of many of these recordings, mainly covering Friday night and Saturday, providing context for what was happening on the air. (These annotations were in the Disaster Research Center archive—see next page). In short, any time someone in the book is speaking on the radio, I am quoting from these recordings or transcripts. Almost all of the available recordings from the weekend of the earthquake are at

UAA. I tried to confirm the spellings of the many names spoken over the air, but couldn't nail them all down.

The abbreviation UAA refers to Genie's papers; the other collections I used at the UAA archives are specified.

INTERVIEWS WITH THE DISASTER RESEARCH CENTER (DRC): I'm told that I am the first journalist (or non-academic researcher) to be granted access to the DRC's "raw data": that is, the field notes, supplementary materials, and transcripts of the hundreds of interviews that the sociologists conducted in Alaska. Virtually all the interviews I'm citing were conducted within a few days of the earthquake; a notable exception is the center's interview with Genie, which was conducted during their second trip to Anchorage, on May 5. Confidentiality requirements and agreements made between the center and its interview subjects at the time keep me from naming certain individuals and citing some documents as transparently as I'd like. I gratefully acknowledge the DRC for access to the E. L. Quarantelli Resource Collection. While some material in this document was derived from the DRC's material, I assume full responsibility for the content of this document.

COMMITTEE ON THE ALASKA EARTHQUAKE "HUMAN ECOLOGY" VOLUME (HE): As mentioned in the book, some of the DRC's work was folded into a seven-volume study of the disaster requested by President Johnson, titled *The Great Alaska Earthquake of 1964*, by the Committee on the Alaska Earthquake, under the auspices of the National Academy of Sciences. I drew extensively from the committee's "Human Ecology" volume, published in 1970. Unless otherwise noted, "HE" refers to section IV of the volume, which covers Anchorage and is based on the DRC's interviews and other fieldwork there.

ONE MONTH BEFORE

Chapter 1

George W. Rogers described Anchorage's "essential spirit" in *The Future of Alaska: Economic Consequences of Statehood* (Baltimore: Johns Hopkins Press, 1962), pp. 9–10. Other key sources on Anchorage and Alaska history: Charles Wohlforth, *From the Shores of Ship Creek: Stories of Anchorage's First 100 Years* (Anchorage: Todd Communications, 2014); James Barnett and Ian Hartman, eds., *Imagining Anchorage* (Anchorage: University of Alaska Press, 2018); Claus-M. Naske and Herman E. Slotnick, *Alaska: A History* (Norman: University of Oklahoma Press, 2011); Jack Roderick, *Crude Dreams: A Personal History of Oil & Politics in Alaska* (Kenmore, WA: Epicenter Press, 1997); Elizabeth Tower, *Anchorage: From Its Humble Origins as a Railroad Construction Camp* (Kenmore, WA: Epicenter Press, 1999); Evangeline Atwood, *Anchorage: All-America City* (Hillsboro, OR: Binfords & Mort, 1957); Victor Fischer, *To Russia with Love: An Alaskan's Journey* (College, AK: University of Alaska Press, 2012); and John McPhee, *Coming into the Country* (New York: Noonday Press, 1967). Also, the blog *Growing Up Anchorage,* which is now defunct.

Willard Stump compared the quake to "a dog shaking an animal" in CPE, p. 105, and Charles Clark estimated the ground waves were four feet high on p. 38. The *LIFE* quote comes from "What Causes Earthquakes, Hopes for Predicting Them," April 10, 1964.

Details of the 1964 Fur Rendezvous come from the records of the Greater Anchorage, Inc., Fur Rendezvous at UAA. The file included a copy of the February 1964 edition of *Winter Amusements* magazine, which called the carnival a "Mardi Gras of the North." I also read coverage in the *Anchorage Daily Times.* (In the book, I refer to this newspaper as the *Anchorage Times,* which is how it was always known locally, even before it officially dropped the "Daily" from its name in 1976.) A complete recording of KENI's broadcast that Sunday was in a Ziploc bag in GB.

My understanding of KENI and Anchorage broadcasting in 1964, and of Bram personally, was rooted in my many conversations with Bram's son, Al Bramstedt Jr.; Robin A. Chlupach, *Airwaves over Alaska: The Story of Pioneer Broadcaster Augie Hiebert* (Sammamish, WA: Sammamish Press, 1992); Heather E. Hudson, *Connecting Alaskans: Telecommunications in Alaska from Telegraph to Broadband* (College, AK: University of Alaska Press, 2015); and oral history interviews in the Hilary Hilscher Alaska Telecommunications History Project records at UAA. Population figures come from the US Census. Anchorage was called the "fastest growing city" in "Guard Patrolling Anchorage; City Lacks Water," *The New York Times,* March 29, 1964.

An undated recording of Bram's "News in Depth" about mushers was in GB. I learned about Ty Clark from interviews with Al Bramstedt Jr., Dolly Fleming, and John Davis, who worked with Clark at KSRM on the Kenai Peninsula. It was Fleming who remembered Clark singing "Tiny Bubbles," apparently at some point after the quake, since the song was released in 1966. Clark is quoted in "Terminal Cancer Fails to Silence Radio Host," *Sitka Sentinel,* February 24, 1993.

See the notes for chapter 13 for sources on Frank Brink and *Our Town.*

Genie described her Fur Rendezvous assignment in a letter the following week (GB). Her pleading to keep kids off the trail was on the recording of KENI's coverage. She explained her motivations for moving to Alaska—"the great land of plenty and opportunity"—in "Mrs. Chance Kept the World Posted," *The Washington Post,* May 17, 1965. This same story described her doing a "man-sized job." She called herself insatiably curious in a September 17, 1964, letter to William Benson of the National Science Foundation (GB). Details of her career come from various letters and nominations for awards (GB) and "Genie Has Some Spirit!," *New York Daily News,* November 11, 1965. A *McCall's Magazine* press release about her Golden Mic award (GB) noted she was the first female newscaster in Alaska. B. G. Randlett, whom I interviewed in Anchorage, felt she was "kind of obnoxious."

Genie's daughter, Jan Blankenship, saved a press release from the governor's office, requesting flags be flown at half-staff. Jack Roderick told me, "Everything moves."

FRIDAY

Chapter 2

GB included the unfinished letter Genie was writing that evening; a July 31 letter about murders and "Alaskan divorce"; her notes from the Public Safety Building that morning; many letters describing her day-to-day juggling of career and family life; an April 30, 1964, letter to NBC in which Genie describes herself as "accustomed to being in the middle of everything"; and the "News in Depth" script on which Bram scrawled his message. (I confirmed it was Bram's handwriting with his son.) Genie relayed the scene of Bram returning from Seattle in a March 14, 1964, letter (GB).

My characterization of Winston is based on conversations with his daughter, Jan, and Joy Dresie, the Chances' friend and neighbor at the time, who called him a "big, good guy." Genie recounts the smokejumper anecdote in a July 14, 1962, letter, then quotes Winston when she tells it again in a letter in 1965 (both GB).

Genie exhaustively chronicled her own experience—from the moment Wins interrupted her through roughly the first hour of the quake—in multiple places with astonishing consistency. These sources include a long April 2, 1964, letter to family in the Lower 48 (GB, copy at UAA); an audio diary she recorded on April 6 (UAA); CPE, pp. 146–57; an interview with the DRC; and a documentary for radio station KFAR (GB, drafts of script at UAA). In many of these documents, Genie quotes herself and her children, recording their dialogue ("I'll finish my letter when we get back . . ." and so on). This quoted dialogue remains virtually identical in each version.

The story of Genie's dental surgery was in a letter dated August 14, 1963; the "time of my life" letter was dated February 28, 1964 (both GB). The latter also includes Jan bragging about Genie to the neighbor and to Winston over breakfast.

To get a feel for the era, I read Jon Margolis's *The Last Innocent Year: America in 1964* (New York: Perennial, 2000). Stephanie Coontz used the word "seismic" in an adaptation of that book for PBS's *American Experience*.

Genie's breathlessness and her colleague's response were on the recording of the broadcast (GB).

Chapter 3

Sources for Genie's experience just before the quake, and through the first hour after, are listed in the notes for chapter 2. (I also retraced her path, on foot, when I was in Anchorage to get a better lay of the land.)

The Salvation Army service is described in "That Fearful Fortnight," an essay by Mrs. Forrest Mosely (UAA). Coloring Easter eggs is mentioned in *Bad Friday: The Great and Terrible 1964 Alaska Earthquake* by Lew Freedman (Kenmore, WA: Epicenter Press, 2013). Robert Pond told me about tidying up the costume closet. The "savage, grinding roll" is in HE, p. 253.

Big Winston's ersatz heart attack: CPE, p. 167. Woman with moose stew: *Bad Friday,* p. 42. Discovering the road wouldn't stay still: CPE, p. 111. The mayor's raven: Henry Fountain, *The Great Quake: How the Biggest Earthquake in North America Changed Our Understanding of the Planet* (New York: Crown, 2017), p. 120. The high school track star is Michael Janecek, who walked me around downtown, telling me what he saw. The kid in the elevator: CPE, p. 132, and audio interview with Logan Wakefield (UAA).

Dale Teel walked on a barrel, Lt. Col. Robert M. Raines was "completely defenseless," and Perry Johnson was the gas company employee in the parking lot: all CPE, pp. 166, 106, 108. Michael Janecek saw the woman yelling to repent. Sue Hamilton described evergreen trees waving on the now defunct *Growing Up Anchorage* blog. *Bad Friday* describes muddy water burbling. "Fearsomely" and "gargantuan hand": Betsy M. Woodman, "Savage Seven Minutes," *Kalamazoo Gazette,* April 2, 1964. (Woodman also sometimes spelled her name "Betzi.") The remaining descriptions in these paragraphs come from CPE (pp. 110, 101, 121–22, 125), except the disappearing car, which was in Wohlforth's *From the Shores of Ship Creek,* p. 77, and the quake's "slithery sound," which was described by Robert Atwood on the LP of Genie and Frank Brink's *Sounds of Alaska: The Good Friday Earthquake* (GB, UAA).

Damage to communities outside Anchorage, and scientific details about the quake and its causes, are detailed throughout HE, and in "Alaska's Good Friday Earthquake: A Preliminary Geologic Evaluation" by Arthur Grantz, George Plafker, and Reuben Kachadoorian (US Geological Survey Circular 491). Tossing boats in a bathtub: "Earthquake in Alaska," *LIFE,* April 10, 1964. "A huge tide of fire": "Horror Strikes on Good Friday," *National Geographic,* July 1964.

The experiences of the Alaska Native villagers are chronicled most reliably in "The Role of the Russian Orthodox Church in Five Pacific Eskimo Villages as Revealed by the Earthquake," a chapter by Nancy Yaw Davis in HE, and Nancy's 1971 University of Washington dissertation, "The Effects of the 1964 Alaska Earthquake, Tsunami, and Resettlement on Two Koniag Eskimo Villages." The red snapper detail is in Grantz et al., "Alaska's Good Friday Earthquake: A Preliminary Geologic Evaluation," p. 16.

Scientists at Caltech said the earth rang like a bell in "Earth Rang Like a Bell, Caltech Scientists Say," *Los Angeles Times,* March 29, 1964. Shaking water in wells is detailed in the preface to HE, and the Baton Rouge swimming pool is mentioned in "United States Earthquakes, 1964" by Carl A. Von Hake and William K. Cloud (US Geological Survey).

Charles Richter described his evening in "The Alaskan Earthquake," *Engineering and Science* 27, no. 7 (April 1964), pp. 7–11. Susan Elizabeth Hough described Richter in *Richter's Scale: Measure of an Earthquake, Measure of a Man* (Princeton, NJ: Princeton University Press, 2007).

Chapter 4

This portion of Genie's story is, again, recounted in the many sources cited earlier. Genie's photos of the damage to the department store were in GB; there are many, many more in the Alaska Digital Archives.

Genie described witnessing "enough horror to last two lifetimes" in a draft script for a KFAR documentary (UAA). Albert and Jan tell their stories in their own entries of CPE, as does Richard Dresie. I also interviewed Jan, Joy Dresie, and Richard Dresie. Genie quotes Albert and Jan in her audio diary (UAA).

Franklin Barber and Golda Mae Caston describe the scene inside Penney's in CPE, on the *Sounds of Alaska* LP, and in longer, recorded versions of those interviews at UAA. The scene is also detailed in a March 27, 1989, *Anchorage Daily News* story by Sheila Toomey, "'64 Quake: Ordinary People, a Fateful Day Some Survived, Some Didn't." (There's some disagreement as to how dark it was inside, and for how long.) "Earthquake!" in the July 1964 *National Geographic* quotes Carol Tucker, who tore ligaments in her leg. Caston was wearing the cocktail dress. The twins are mentioned in *Bad Friday,* p. 67. Details about Blanche Clark come, in part, from the Toomey article, one of many accounts of her ordeal. Clark herself appears in a Civil Defense film about the quake, *Though the Earth Be Moved,* which is on YouTube.

There are various claims about how far the storefronts on Fourth Avenue dropped but this one, in HE (p. 253), seemed most credible. Descriptions of the wreckage are from Genie's accounts and photographs in UAA's Alaska Digital Archives.

Genie talks about "sights my mind could not have stood under other circumstances" in a piece of writing that begins "Last night I wept," and about everyone living through their own hell in an April 6 letter to Jim Quigley at NBC (both GB, copies at UAA). She discusses the governor's Cuban Missile Crisis address in a letter from the time (GB).

KFQD is covered in HE, interviews with KFQD staffers (DRC), and a report Bram wrote, "Civilian Communications During Alaska Earthquake" (UAA). Both the HE timeline in appendix A and Bram's

"Civilian Communications" report say KENI started broadcasting again at 6:40. Genie puts it slightly earlier in CPE.

Genie quotes Winston asking her to stay in her DRC interview. Clark and Genie appear to have re-created their first broadcasts, after KENI got back on the air, for the *Sounds of Alaska* record—I'm quoting that. Data on aftershocks is on p. 9 of the Geological Survey study by Grantz et al. Genie said she "talked constantly" in her April 2 letter.

Chapter 5

The interior of the Public Safety Building is shown in the Civil Defense film *Though the Earth Be Moved*, which initially seemed (improbably) to include footage from the night of the quake—until I discovered Genie's May 21, 1964, letter (GB) describing the making of the film: Civil Defense asked everyone to come back, dressed in the same clothes they'd worn on Good Friday evening, to film a reenactment. Other details about the scene in the lobby come from Genie's accounts, HE, and interviews with many city workers (DRC), including a city planning official who described the efficacy of shouting for people and waving.

Genie covers this portion of the evening, from her perspective, in CPE, her audio diary (UAA), and her DRC interview. She called George Burns an "old goat" and relayed his retirement plans in a letter after his death (GB). Burns was interviewed by the DRC before he died, and the work of the fire department is covered there, in HE, and in several other DRC publications. I spotted his memorial plaque in the background of *Though the Earth Be Moved*.

The small fires and broken gas main are mentioned in HE (p. 264), Genie's notes from the three a.m. meeting (GB, copy at UAA), and on the radio on Friday night. The fuel tank rupture: HE, p. 263. The missile battery: *Though the Earth Be Moved* and Fountain's *Great Quake*, which reported that the missiles were nuclear.

Genie relays her conversation with Flanigan in several places, but quotes herself talking to him in her DRC interview. Flanigan explained his concerns about the public in his own DRC interview.

Dolly Fleming told me about losing her "connection to everything." Her husband, Bob, told the story about seeing blood at Presbyterian on the air on Friday night. Robert Atwood said, "Maybe you're the last man" in CPE, p. 114. Merrill Mael told his DRC interviewer that he'd initially assumed no other part of Anchorage could be ruined as badly as his neighborhood. Joy Dresie told me, "Information is a *form* of comfort." The concluding quote comes from my interview with Victor Fischer, who also wrote about Genie's broadcasts in *To Russia with Love*.

My sketch of Robert Oldland draws from his DRC transcripts; information and photographs in Anchorage's 1964 Annual Report (GB); and a recording of a long interview he did with Genie (UAA). The "old-timer" is quoted by Genie in her report "Year of Decision and Inaction," in "The Alaska Earthquake, March 27, 1964: Field Investigations and Reconstruction Effort" (US Geological Survey Professional Paper 541).

Dick Taylor's contributions were covered in many places, including HE; David S. Adams, *Emergency Actions and Disaster Reactions: An Analysis of the Anchorage Public Works Department in the 1964 Alaskan Earthquake,* Disaster Research Center Monograph Series, no. 5; and Daniel Yutzy, *Community Priorities in the Anchorage, Alaska Earthquake, 1964,* Disaster Research Center Monograph Series, no. 4. I'm quoting from his DRC interview. Another anonymized DRC interviewee called him a "honcho," free of "mental agony."

Clarence Myers's story comes from CPE (p. 135) and "Young Soldier Tells of Woman Trapped in Quake," *Fairbanks Daily News Miner*, April 7, 1964. Myers compared the earthquake to war in an undated audio clip from Armed Forces Radio (GB). "Mass confusion" was described in an anonymized DRC interview.

Chapter 6

The descriptions and history of the Fourth Avenue Theatre, and biographical information about Cap Lathrop, come from a National Register of Historic Places nomination submitted in 1982. (It quotes, for example, the "culmination of the Art Deco" praise, and the *Anchorage*

Daily Times "city of permanence" editorial.) Additional details come from photos Genie took around the KENI studios (GB), Hudson's *Connecting Alaskans,* Chlupach's *Airwaves over Alaska,* and the websites of the Cook Inlet Historical Society and Friends of the 4th Avenue Theatre. Jack Roderick told me, "You had the feeling that everything was temporary."

Photos and film footage of Eisenhower's and Glenn's visits and the statehood celebration are in the Alaska Museum and UAA archives. KENI's work during the statehood party is chronicled in "The Day They Made Alaska a State" in the October 1958 *Broadcast News,* a trade magazine published by RCA. That's where the igloo quote appears.

Al Bramstedt Jr. told me about Lathrop's ghost one afternoon, over coffee at a Barnes & Noble in Anchorage. The full story is amazing. I think I believe him.

The *Sword in the Stone* matinee is covered in HE (p. 253), among other sources. The sequence of events that starts in KENI's basement studio, continues at the transmitter building, and concludes at the Public Safety Building, when Genie gets set up inside, is pulled together from DRC interviews with Ty Clark and a second, anonymized KENI employee; Genie's recorded interviews with Charles Gray and engineer Don Porter (UAA); my interviews with Gray, B. G. Randlett, and Michael Janecek; and Bram's "Civilian Communications During Alaska Earthquake" (UAA). KENI broadcaster Otto Miller—who wrote "Earthquake" on the broadcast log and skedaddled—and Darrell Comstock told the story about the two salesmen in the floating studio on the air.

Ty Clark told the DRC about "corks bobbing." Gray told Genie he imagined the television antenna slicing through the building in their recorded interview (UAA). Gray told me about the chimney landing on the car.

The section on Gray and his engineering escapades draw from Genie's interviews with Gray and Porter (UAA) and my interviews with Gray, Bramstedt Jr., Dolly Fleming, and Janecek. Janecek described Gray firing at the sandbag; Gray kind of shrugged and told me he didn't remember that.

So many Alaskans I interviewed had something nostalgic to say about the Mukluk Telegraph. Caroline Toloff writes about sitting still as a child in *Going Home* (iUniverse, 2015).

Ty Clark and the anonymized KENI employee talked about playing down the death toll (DRC). I found photos of Nat Brook (GB) and exchanged emails with his daughter, Merry-Rae Dunn. Genie describes working alongside Brook, and mentions his dose of scotch wearing off, in her broadcast annotations (DRC).

Chapter 7

Other fragments of Genie's broadcasts from this stretch of the night, beyond what's on the recordings, were transcribed at UAA. She discussed her experiences inside the building primarily in her DRC interview and her annotations (DRC), as well as in the documents that covered the previous hour, in chapter 2. She wrote about "mass hysteria" in her April 6 letter to Jim Quigley at NBC (GB) and the "Last night I wept" fragment (GB, copies in UAA).

Genie wrote about her coverage of the Northwest Orient Airlines crash in letters from that June (GB), though more directly discussed the sexism involved years later, in an undated sheaf of papers that appeared to be a mix of memoirs and speeches for civic and women's groups (GB). The scene of Carroll's arrival is covered in Genie's interview and broadcast annotations (DRC). The military's involvement is chronicled in HE and a number of military publications (GB). Other details about Carroll are drawn from newspaper stories, including "General Carroll Renamed AG for Alaska," *Fairbanks Daily News Miner,* September 24, 1959; and "General of Alaska Guard Is Missing in Plane Crash," *The New York Times,* April 26, 1964.

The military population in Anchorage is given in HE, p. 20. Genie's trip to the backcountry is covered in a memoir fragment (GB). She saved a clipping about Wins firing his rocket from the *Anchorage Daily Times,* April 6, 1963 (GB).

The nuclear war simulation by ham radio operators is detailed in

HE, pp. 269–70, and in an unidentified radio story about the group (GB). Genie recorded an interview with Walt Sauerbier and saved his QSL card (UAA). I read about the so-called Eskimo Scouts in "Special Eskimo Unit Guards America's Frigid Frontier on Soviet Border," *The Washington Post*, March 27, 1988. *The New York Times* covered the death of Carroll's son on November 13, 1992, in "8, Including General, Killed in Plane Crash."

The tsunami warnings are covered in HE and Genie's broadcast annotations (DRC). The tsunamis are detailed in the chapters covering each affected community in HE, as is the chain reaction that moved down the coast; I also read various newspaper accounts from each region. Fountain provides the detail about Antarctica in *Great Quake*, p. 151. In addition to the recording of Chris von Imhof's on-air interview, I consulted his portion of CPE, pp. 103–4.

Chapter 8

Genie wrote about the "topsy-turvy" world in an April 5, 1964, letter to KOIL (UAA)—one of many letters, both at UAA and in GB, which show her doggedly piecing together where in the world her broadcasts reached, and how. She similarly reached out to ham radio operators across Alaska and the Lower 48.

The rumors in San Francisco and Vancouver were mentioned on KENI on Friday night. Gray talks about their visit to Government Hill in his interview with Genie (UAA), and the anonymized colleague who was with him told the same story to the DRC. The role of ACS is covered in HE (p. 282); a booklet published by the Associated Press, *Earthquake in Alaska* (GB); and an ACS press release (UAA).

I found a reel of Genie's interview with Addison, a KOIL documentary describing how it came about (GB), and letters about the call later exchanged between Genie and Addison (UAA). Genie also described it to the DRC (this is where she quotes Addison asking her for a "news story") and in a letter to *McCall's Magazine* (GB). The police officer could be heard on the air, asking Genie to come talk to London. Genie describes that phone call in her DRC interview.

I learned about Bob Fleming's life from his widow, Dolly Fleming, who lives, it turns out, about an hour from my house, and found Bob's obituary in the September 20, 2011, *Kitsap Sun*. Fleming recounted his experience in the hospital basement on the air and in an interview with Genie (UAA).

Genie told the DRC that those coming to her counter were "heartbreaking." Bram's "four thousand messages" claim is from his "Civilian Communications" report (UAA). Sauerbier made his "Grand Central Station" crack in his interview with Genie at UAA. The ham who relayed six hundred messages was interviewed by the DRC. HE describes the five hams whose homes were destroyed (p. 270). I read about Harris Hug in a letter to the American Radio Relay League nominating Hug for a commendation—Genie had a copy (GB). The "beacon of light" and Clam Gulch letters were in GB. I shamelessly pilfered the phrase "affirming flames" from W. H. Auden's "September 1, 1939." Jo Butler's letter wound up at UAA.

Mayor Sharrock describes the communication problems on Friday night and the genesis of the three a.m. meeting in his DRC interview. Yutzy estimates three thousand displaced people in *Community Priorities*. Details about where they settled in for the night are strewn throughout the HE volume (pp. 274–75, 406, 277). I'm quoting again from Woodman's "Savage Seven Minutes." Bob Fleming described the city as a "wounded thing" in his interview with Genie (UAA). The KENI broadcasters could be heard, on the air, realizing that the tidal wave never hit.

SATURDAY

Chapter 9

The scene in Bonham is recorded in an effusive, almost manic eleven-page letter from Den to Genie dated March 30, 1964 (GB). I gathered details about the Broadfoots from numerous GB letters and newspaper clippings, including "Judge Broadfoot's Wife Is Native of Hopkins County," *Hopkins County Echo* (Sulphur Springs, TX), August 20, 1954. Jan Blankenship elaborated on what I read in those documents, telling me about Den's "genealogy trips" and covert house-moving scheme. Genie described Den's attempt to drive to Anchorage solo in a memoir fragment, "Mom, Dad" (GB).

Genie relays her family's "mandate" in the same sheaf of speeches and memoirs noted earlier (GB). Her collegiate activities come from copies of the *Yucca*, North Texas State College's yearbook. Genie's letters with Winston, in the summer of 1947, were still tied in lace (GB). Win's hobo party was written up in "Winston Chance Jr., Six Years Old," *Bonham Daily Favorite*, May 9, 1956, and the Mother's Day portrait ran in the same paper four days later. Jan remembered Genie always saying "We're not poor . . . ," and, based on conversations with her mother as an adult, was able to elaborate on Genie's trepidation about the move to Alaska beyond what Genie revealed in letters from the time. Genie wrote about schoolteachers "alone in huge, dreary homes" and her reticence to move in a memoir fragment titled "Texas to Anchorage." Her parents' disappointment was discussed in letters before and after the move (GB), and at particular length in one dated September 24, 1959. "Texas to Anchorage" contains the thirteen steps detail.

Genie chronicled their journey and arrival in Alaska in a fourteen-page letter to her parents, which, she says, she started writing the day they touched down (GB). She tells the story again, with more emphasis on her disillusionment, in "Texas to Anchorage" and "Mom, Dad," claiming she "felt heartsick" and "sat there in deep despair." These memoirs were likely written more than twenty years after the fact: while it's possible the move felt more dispiriting in retrospect—or at least made for a better story, now that she'd divorced Winston and managed to thrive in Alaska without him—it's also almost certain that Genie would have played down her unhappiness at the time, especially in a letter to her anxious and disapproving parents. I bore these credibility issues in mind even if, in the end, I wasn't really sure what to do with them.

The section that describes Genie settling into Anchorage is derived, largely, from a series of seventeen long letters written in Genie's first ten weeks in Alaska (GB). These included the nights out at the Idle Hour and the Hofbrau. She talked about a "new world being built" in "Genie Has Some Spirit," *New York Daily News,* November 11, 1965. I was skeptical that Genie and Winston would have been able to see the northern lights in August, but a piece in the September 27, 2016, *Anchorage Daily News* titled "Viewing Northern Lights in the Bright Alaska Summer: Is It Possible?" assured me that—spoiler alert—it *is* possible.

Genie's foray into the Anchorage workforce—including details about Winston's struggles at the dealership, the day care arrangement with Dottie Snodgrass, and Genie's problems with Mael—is chronicled in many contemporaneous letters home and then elaborated on, often with a sharper perspective, in the memoir fragments "Texas to Anchorage" and "KBYR" (all GB). Jim French claimed, "The world needs millions of Merrill Maels," in "Radio's Lost One of Its Most Golden Voices," *Daily Herald* (Everett, WA), November 2, 2000.

Genie saved a tremendous amount of material from her time at KBYR (GB). She quotes Winston telling her to quit and to get off her "fat fanny" in the memoir fragment "Changes" (GB). This is also where Genie writes, "It seemed that everything I did was wrong . . ."

Chapter 10

Specifics about the damage in Anchorage are reported in countless sources, often with many disparities. One comprehensive and reliably credible source—while also concise enough to be user-friendly—was *Earthquake Hazard Mitigation: Planning and Policy Implementation, The Alaska Case,* a report published in 1984 and the product of a UAA symposium convened ahead of the quake's twentieth anniversary. I wouldn't have known about this invaluable resource, except that my neighbor Steve Johnson happened to have worked on the report. Thanks, Steve!

Other sources include HE; Wallace R. Hansen "Effects of the Earthquake of March 27, 1964 at Anchorage, Alaska" (US Geological Survey Professional Paper 542-A), which, among other things, describes the failure of Turnagain's Bootlegger Cove Clay; and E. E. Thoms, *1964 Great Alaska Earthquake: A Photographic Tour of Anchorage Alaska* (US Geological Survey, 2014). I also benefited from the enormous cache of images in UAA's Alaska Digital Archives and maps prepared by the Engineering Geology Evaluation Group (GB).

I inadvertently plagiarized the gorgeous and evocative phrase "shapes with no names" from one of our family's favorite picture books, *Triangle,* by Mac Barnett and Jon Klassen (Somerville, MA: Candlewick, 2017). Once I realized this, I emailed Mac; he says it's OK.

The observation that the "devil ground his heel" into downtown appeared in the papers of Associated Press reporter Ward Sims at UAA. Sims saved the actual reams of paper from the AP Teletype machine, as reporters around the world tried to make contact with Anchorage and got answers back; it was impossible for me to identify who in that long scrum of messages wrote this particular line.

Comstock claimed there was "absolutely no pattern" and Bram lamented damage to "the proudest of our buildings" on an audio reel of an undated KENI-TV newscast, which I believe to be from Monday, March 30. The recording of Comstock's flight over Turnagain was at UAA. The second KENI broadcaster in an airplane was Jim Dodson; his wife, Jessie Dodson, was also an experienced pilot and seems to have done some of the flying that day.

Robert Atwood was interviewed at length by Genie for CPE, pp. 112–17, and other parts of the same interview appear on the *Sounds of Alaska* LP. Atwood described hanging on to his trumpet in "Eyewitnesses Tell of Quake in Anchorage," *Chicago Tribune,* March 29, 1964. On Atwood's wealth, influence, and championing of statehood, see Naske and Slotnick's *Alaska: A History* and Claus-M.

Naske, "Alaska Becomes the 49th State," *The New York Times*, January 4, 1959.

Chapter 11

A typewritten script of Genie's report on the three a.m. meeting was in GB, with a copy at UAA. I assume she typed it up afterward, for posterity, and therefore chose to quote this version sparingly. A crack in the basement stairwell was still visible in the Civil Defense reenactment. Douglas Clure acknowledged that everyone was "thinking the worst" (DRC). Woodman wrote about fatigue carving lines in faces in "Seven Savage Minutes." The meeting was chronicled in Genie's report, DRC interviews with attendees, HE, and, most intimately, Genie's audio diary at UAA.

Taylor's request for more volunteers, and the crowds in the lobby, are covered in Genie's DRC interview. The formation of "Manpower Control" is described in HE and in interviews with Taylor and the two volunteers (DRC). Their names were Bill Horsfell (the HE volume spells it "Horsefall," but I believe that's incorrect) and Red Mayo. "Red Mayo" is not a typo; it is simply a wonderful name.

Ty Clark's beleaguered call for cigarettes was part of the broadcast. Genie listed the hours she worked, and the sleep she managed to get, on a page of the notebook she was using (GB) and in a memo dated "1st Wednesday after quake" (UAA). The shift change with Theda is described in Genie's DRC interview, where she provides the dialogue I'm quoting, and in her annotations (DRC). Genie's opinion of Theda prior to the earthquake is articulated pretty amusingly in a February 28, 1964, letter (GB). Al Bramstedt Jr., who worked as a cameraman on Theda's show as a teenager before working his way up to run KENI, was the source for the Mexican food anecdote and the description of the mammogram episode of *The Woman's Touch*.

Genie told the DRC about the police's handling of foot traffic and how "none of the departments knew what the other was calling for."

Theda's obituary ran in the *Anchorage Daily News* on February 1, 1998.

Chapter 12

Bill Davis's story is drawn from his DRC interview and HE, as well as my interview with him in September 2017, about a year before his death. Though, as mentioned later in the book, Bill's memory had lost hold of many details in the intervening fifty-three years, both he and his wife, Nancy Yaw Davis, were exceptionally helpful in contextualizing what was in the documents I'd read. (Bill's quote about the "ethos of the frontier" comes from that interview.) They also loaned me a copy of the 1964 *Amulet,* AMU's yearbook. Joe Lawton called Davis "a nutty professor" when I interviewed him in Palmer.

A separate timeline detailing the search-and-rescue operation appears in HE (p. 403), and Yutzy's *Community Priorities* analyzes the lack of action before Davis's arrival. Yutzy describes search and rescue unfolding "more by accident than by plan" and theorizes that it took so long because there was no analog for that work in ordinary life.

The morticians are covered in DRC interviews with Genie and city officials, and in "Reports from Anchorage" by mortuary manager R. D. Rome in the May 1964 edition of *Mid Continent Mortician Magazine,* which has a delightful cover photo of two (living) children fishing in a stream. Davis called himself "the great impostor" in his DRC interview and a "factotum" when we met. The body at Penney's is covered in HE.

Davis told the DRC about assembling and dispatching his searchers and confessed his concern that "there wouldn't be enough people" based on his experience in Wyoming.

Biographical information about Jim Scott comes from an obituary and other posts on the website of Bird TLC, the organization Scott eventually started. Scott's colleague is quoted in the February 1, 2017, KTUU Web story "Founder of Bird TLC Remembered for Dedication to Alaska Wildlife." Scott's search-and-rescue efforts are chronicled in his DRC interview, HE, and a transcript of an interview he and another searcher, Alan Combs, gave to Merrill Mael, likely for the Civil Defense film (DRC). Betsy M. Woodman's "Picking Up the Pieces," in the June 1964 issue of *The Rotarian,* also covers Scott's work; it includes the haunting anecdote about the dog photo and the detail about Brink's *Our Town* banner falling on Scott's car. HE explains that the army specialists were on the ridgeline "at the same time . . . or shortly after" Scott and his crew were below, and notes that Genie broadcast the names of the dead.

Chapter 13

Writing about Frank Brink would not have been possible without the help of Robin Niemann, who was close to Frank and Jo for four decades and kept many of Frank's letters, playbills, CVs, photographs, and writings. Robin was also the stage manager on the crew of *Our Town* that weekend, and recalled seeing the mushers from the window during Fur Rendezvous (in chapter 1). Also invaluable: the cooperation of the late Robert Pond, who had his own collection of materials and wrote a thesis for Portland State University in 1980 titled "The History of Community Theatre in Anchorage, Alaska, 1946–1976." (The description of Brink as "our Moses of the stage" in chapter 1 comes from one of my interviews with Pond.) I read Catherine J. Stadem's *The History of Theater in Anchorage, Alaska 1915–2005: From a Wilderness Tent to a Multi-Million Dollar Stage* (Lewiston, NY: Edwin Mellen Press, 2009) and correspondence and notes for that book in Stadem's papers at UAA. I also interviewed Joe Lawton, Bob Deloach, and Michale Gabriel, who acted for Brink regularly.

Bill Davis called Brink "the very avatar of a creative person." Pond described him "always staging." Niemann built the house with Brink and shared photos of it. Brink's epic sentence is from the *Sounds of Alaska* record. His description of *Our Town* as "the greatest play" is from the 1964 *Amulet,* AMU's yearbook, which also included photos of the play and rehearsals. Brink reminisced about his childhood in an undated letter to a "Mr. Bloom" in Niemann's collection. He discussed hitchhiking to see an opera and leaving home in an *Anchorage Daily Times* profile, "Plays, Films, Fill Up Frank Brink's Spare Time." (A clipping was in Stadem's papers at UAA, but did not include the date and I have not been able to track it down.) Niemann knew about Brink's tropical disease. Brink discussed his "desire . . . to experience the adventure of Alaska" in an interview for Pond's thesis. Both Stadem and Pond write about *Ladies in Retirement;* Stadem seems to believe the Heston story is apocryphal. Pond described Brink's first *Our Town* as "a religious experience" in our interview, and provided a copy of the original playbill, which lists all the pre-show happenings. Pond also wrote about that 1946 production in the playbill for his own production of *Our Town* at the Anchorage Community Theatre in 2001.

Brink called the theater "as necessary as food" and "a place . . . to recognize oneself and others" in an essay in his *Cry of the Wild Ram* playbill from July 1960. He used the phrase "community-wide playmaking" in the playbill for *The Rainmaker* in January of the following year. He called himself a "Community Leader" on a CV from the mid-1970s.

Nancy Sellin claims "There was no faking it with Frank," and Bob Deloach calls Brink "a tyrant" in Stadem's book (pp. 16, 19). Pond told me that *The Miracle Worker* "touched the face of God." The Boris Karloff story is mentioned in Stadem, but spun out wonderfully in Gordon B. Shriver's *Boris Karloff: The Man Remembered* (Frederick, MD: Publish America, 2004), which includes Brink's letter about Karloff's "solicitude." Holly Horn, in Ohio, told me she found the shoe.

Cry of the Wild Ram was covered by *The New York Times* ("Alaskan Drama Bows," July 16, 1960). The musical version was titled *The Good Land.* Stadem describes Brink humming and whistling, as well as the production of more than two hundred costumes and a harpsichord. John Villesvik told Stadem it was "so damn long."

I checked Pond's description of Baranov against Kenneth N. Owens's *Empire Maker: Aleksandr Baranov and Russian Colonial Expansion into Alaska and Northern California* (Seattle: University of

Washington Press, 2015). Stadem quotes Bruce Marcus on Brink in New York: "the most sophisticated primitive . . ." My understanding of Brink's potential regrets, and his motivations for taking the job at AMU, is rooted in conversations with Robin Niemann, who said Brink's untested potential in New York "weighed on him."

The decline of Anchorage theater prior to 1964 is evident from Pond's thesis, and spelled out in a December 21, 1963, *Anchorage Daily News* story by Bill Edwards, which Stadem transcribed in her notes at UAA. The Grant Hall theater is described in "Bringing Down the House," *Anchorage Daily News,* February 5, 2001.

When quoting from *Our Town,* I'm using the 1957 edition of the script published by Harper & Row. The play's debut and spread through the United States is detailed in an afterword, written by Tappan Wilder, to a reissued Harper Perennial edition from 2003. My interpretation and appreciation of *Our Town* owes a lot to both that afterword and to the same edition's foreword, by Donald Margulies. (Until starting this project, my main reference point for the play was an episode of *Growing Pains* in which Kirk Cameron plays the Stage Manager.) *New York Times* critic Mel Gussow called the play "misunderstood and misinterpreted" in "Stage View; A Theatrical Vision Endures," December 20, 1987. Eleanor Roosevelt called it depressing in her "My Day" newspaper column on March 2, 1938. Donald C. Haberman writes of "confronting overwhelming disaster" in *Our Town: An American Play* (Boston: Twayne, 1989), p. 15. Wilder's preface about Roman ruins and "Night Bell" plaques is reprinted in the Harper Perennial edition.

Robert Pond shared a playbill from the 1964 production, then proceeded to tell me every detail he knew about each cast member listed, as did Robin Niemann, who explained Brink's gift for "seeing the hurt in people." The navy veteran is Joe Lawton, who told me he wanted to meet girls. Michale Gabriel (formerly Susan Koslosky) shared her story with me in several phone interviews and emails. I'm quoting Brink shouting "I don't believe you!" based solely on her memory. (Maybe I should have just put it in italics or something? I don't know.)

Brink describes his experience of the quake, and his immediate concern for Alaskans, in an interview with Genie (UAA).

Chapter 14

Jan told me about Big Winston taking her to the Public Safety Building. The two quotes from arriving reporters come from "Earthquake!" in the July 1964 issue of *National Geographic* and "The Alaska Quake" in *Newsweek,* April 6, 1964.

The general condition of the city on Saturday night is covered in HE and in press releases issued by the city (DRC). The Saturday press conference is mentioned in numerous places, but its actual substance seems to be preserved only in a set of limited notes taken by Nancy Yaw Davis, who was there taking notes for no particular reason other than her general interest as an anthropologist. Later, she contracted with the DRC; I was lucky to find her notes in their supplementary materials. The notes quote Oldland, Egan, and Bill Davis, and include the observation that no one was yawning. Nancy told me about the man's whiskers.

I learned about Governor Egan from Roderick's *Crude Dreams* and Egan's obituary in *The New York Times,* May 7, 1984. His arrival in Anchorage that day is detailed in HE and "Anchorage Still Reels from Blow, Begins Restoring Vital Utilities," *The Washington Post,* March 30, 1964.

Tension with the media, including the passes to downtown, is evident in interviews with many city officials (DRC) and in Quarantelli's field notes. It's also discussed in Yutzy's *Community Priorities,* which notes the additional wrinkle that some Eskimo Scouts had difficulty reading the passes. The quote about the "youngster bawling her head off" was in Ward Sims's Teletype papers at UAA. The "aggravated reporter" is quoted from a transcript of a press conference on Sunday, recorded by Yutzy (DRC). An anonymized DRC interviewee relayed the mayor and reporter's argument about marshal law.

I'm quoting the Norwegian editor "flooded by calls from anxious people" from Sims's Teletype papers. Davis concedes that bodies may have been swept out to sea in a transcript of a press conference on Monday (DRC). The discovery of Styer's body is covered in HE, p. 265, and Mary Lochner reported about Styer's life in "When the Earth Came in Waves," *Alaska Press,* March 27, 2014.

The scene with Clure and the European reporters is reconstructed from Genie's DRC interview. As mentioned earlier, many GB letters show Genie working hard to retrace where and how her voice traveled beyond Anchorage. She even procured a few recordings from those Outside stations, including this one from Seattle.

The 1964 Great Alaska Earthquake and Tsunamis—A Modern Perspective and Enduring Legacies, published in 2014 by the US Geological Survey, notes that the Space Needle swayed. KFQD's Jay Perry called Genie "instrumental in avoiding panic" when he nominated her for the Golden Mic award (GB). A KOIL press release and radio documentary later detailed the spread of Genie's interview around the world (GB). Den describes hearing Genie's voice and hanging up on people in her March 30, 1964, letter (GB). Genie talks about the reporters stranded in Seattle and the "weird feeling" of being embraced in her April 2 letter (GB, copy at UAA). Bram recounts hearing Genie in Tokyo in an undated "News in Depth" shortly after he returned (GB).

Chapter 15

Genie's day on Good Friday 1965 is chronicled in a letter dated April 18, 1965 (GB). Note that this was Good Friday, but not March 27: as Genie put it, March 27 "was just a day"; but Good Friday, regardless of which date it fell on, would always feel like the anniversary of the quake.

"Few Alaskans will ever forget" Genie is from an untitled clipping in GB from the August 1965 issue of *Alaska Sportsman* magazine. The nomination package for the Golden Mic award, mentioned in the notes for chapter 14, included the subsequent superlatives, as well as the letters from Governor Egan; Creath A. Tooley, an official at the Office of

Emergency Planning in Washington who talked about "the weaker sex"; and Alfred H. George, of the University of Alaska, who liked Genie's "well-modulated, calm voice." "The Genie Chance" dance letter was at UAA. Genie expressed discomfort with her fame in letters to her mother that summer, an undated script for the NBC radio show *Monitor,* and a letter to London's *News of the World* (GB). She tells the story of leaving KENI in other letters, and in the undated sheaf of speeches and memoirs referred to earlier (GB).

GB contained a great big burst of letters and newspaper clippings chronicling Genie's entrepreneurship and travels in the year after she left KENI. Her enlistment by the chamber of commerce to tout reindeer steaks was mentioned in "Genie Goes to New York!," *Anchorage Daily News,* May 6, 1965. She was invited to, but did not, appear on *To Tell the Truth.* The fashion show was covered in "Genie Has Some Spirit!," *New York Daily News,* November 11, 1965.

Barbara Brinkerhoff, Genie's right-hand woman through most of her legislative career, was an invaluable oral historian of this period, and also helped me understand Genie's actions and persona in the context of her time. Both Brinkerhoff and Jan Blankenship spoke openly about Winston's abuse. The journal entry about women who love "the very vibrations of life" was in GB. The "family member" I'm quoting is Jan's husband, Chuck. The letters from Winston following the violent episode in Juneau were in GB. Winston's arrival at the house in Anchorage, and his confrontation with Boardman, were detailed in a deposition Boardman gave, seemingly as part of Genie's divorce proceedings (GB). Boardman quotes Winston threatening to kill him.

Genie's assessment of her male colleagues in the legislature is drawn from the speeches file mentioned earlier (GB). Bill Parker told me Genie "was not a glass of warm milk" when I interviewed him in Anchorage. My synopsis of her legislative initiatives comes from conversations with Brinkerhoff and Jan, from leafing through her legislative papers at UAA, and from coverage in the Alaska press. Genie talks about the Equal Rights Amendment in "Equal Rights: 'We've Come a

Long Way,'" *Anchorage Daily News,* March 25, 1972. Brinkerhoff described Genie's style—the wig, the boots—with admiration. Genie's anecdote about the grumpy old man criticizing her wardrobe was in the speeches file (GB).

The end of Genie's political career and her concurrent family troubles are documented in letters from that time (GB). Jan also filled in details about Den's dementia. Criticism of Bill Sumner and his campaign tactics abound—in GB, but also, for example, in "Ad Campaigns Draw Charge of Smear," *Anchorage Daily News,* August 20, 1974. Fischer also writes about Sumner in *To Russia with Love.* The former legislator who called Sumner's hair "ridiculous" preferred not to be named. Genie's pleading letter to her mother is dated January 22, 1977 (GB).

Boardman's health, Al's struggles with addiction, and Wins's illness are covered in a diary Genie kept during these years (GB). I also spoke at length with Jan about this period, and relied on interviews with her to recount Genie's dementia and death. I had the pleasure of meeting the parrot, Misty Grey, in person.

The report of Genie's that, early on, led me to Jan was the CPE. The National Academy of Sciences described the quake as "thoroughly studied" in the preface to HE. Nancy Yaw Davis handed me her 1971 University of Washington dissertation, "The Effects of the 1964 Alaska Earthquake, Tsunami, and Resettlement on Two Koniag Eskimo Villages." The current saga of the Fourth Avenue Theatre has been covered by KTVU and the *Anchorage Daily News.*

Genie relayed her painfully thwarted attempt to talk to the governor's transportation czar in a diary entry dated September 10, 1988 (GB).

SUNDAY

Chapter 16

The origins of the DRC, and its decision to go to Anchorage, are covered in Thomas E. Drabek, "Launching the DRC: Historical Context and Future Directions," in *Disaster Research and the Second Environmental Crisis: Assessing the Challenges Ahead,* ed. James Kendra, Scott G. Knowles, and Tricia Wachtendorf (New York: Springer, 2019); E. L. Quarantelli, "The Early History of the Disaster Research Center," published on the DRC's website; an interview with William A. Anderson from *Connections: EERI Oral History Series* (Earthquake Engineering Research Institute, 2011); a twelve-part oral history interview with Quarantelli (DRC); and William A. Anderson, "The Great Alaska Earthquake and the Dawn of U.S. Social Science Earthquake Research," *Proceedings of the 10th National Conference on Earthquake Engineering* (Anchorage, 2014). I also spoke at length with Thomas Drabek, who was hired along with Yutzy and Anderson as the center's first graduate students. Scott Gabriel Knowles also chronicles the rise of the DRC and the field more broadly in his excellent book *The Disaster Experts: Mastering Risk in Modern America* (Philadelphia: University of Pennsylvania Press, 2011). And I owe a tremendous debt to *A Paradise Built in Hell: The Extraordinary Communities That Arise in Disaster* by Rebecca Solnit (New York: Viking, 2009), an astonishing and beautifully crafted book that first introduced me to this field of research and the many truths about humankind it has documented.

Drabek described Quarantelli's dentistry research, the location of the first DRC headquarters, and the assembly of the literature library in our interview. Solnit quotes M. Titmuss summarizing concerns of "hysterical neurosis" in *A Paradise Built in Hell,* p. 99.

Quarantelli remembers the military mostly talking ("rather than us") in his oral history interview (DRC). Haas, Dynes, and Quarantelli describe first learning about the quake in "Some Preliminary Observation on the Responses of Community Organizations Involved in the Emergency Period of the Alaskan Earthquake" (working paper no. 2, Disaster Research Center, 1964). Yutzy adds details about the damage reports they heard while interviewing an anonymized journalist in Anchorage (DRC). This was also where Yutzy talks about throwing on his "duds." Samuel Henry Prince's foundational study on Halifax is "Catastrophe and Social Change: Based upon a Sociological Study of the Halifax Disaster" (Columbia University, 1920). Drabek confirmed that it was in the center's original library.

Yutzy's son, Phil Yutzy, filled in biographical details about his father's youth and later years. Drabek is the colleague who compares Yutzy to a mall Santa Claus. Anderson talks about his childhood in the EERI oral history interview. *The Washington Post* published an obituary for Anderson on January 18, 2014. The *Buffalo News* ran an obituary for Yutzy on September 19, 1995.

Anderson describes their recording equipment in the EERI interview. The recordings of Yutzy's discussions with the ticket agent upon arrival and with Anderson the following morning were transcribed in his field notes (DRC). Quarantelli lists the contents of their field kits and notes how "impressed" people get by "anything that is official" in *Problems of Field Research: Techniques and Procedures of the Disaster Research Center in the 1960s* (working paper no. 11, Disaster Research Center Historical and Comparative Disaster Series, 1998).

Chapter 17

Scenes of people gathering on Sunday morning are drawn from "Alaska Quake Toll May Top Total of 100," *The Wilmington News Journal,* March 30, 1964; and "Shaken As If by a Monster," *Fairbanks Daily News Miner*/Associated Press, March 30, 1964. An anonymized worker with Disaster Control relayed the repairs happening (DRC). The Fourth Avenue activity is recorded in HE, p. 421; Yutzy's *Community Priorities,* pp. 141–42; and in many photos in UAA's Alaska Digital Archives. KENI broadcasters announced restaurants were reopening and that the *Times* staff was getting back to work. Civil Defense shot footage of the toppled bunnies and other damage on Fourth Avenue for the film *Though the Earth Be Moved.*

Tay Thomas told her story in "An Alaskan Family's Night of Terror," *National Geographic,* July 1964; the article includes her descriptions of her and her children at church. In addition, Genie interviewed Thomas at length on April 15, 1964; excerpts from that interview

were included on the *Sounds of Alaska* record and in CPE, but I tried
to rely on the raw tape of the interview (at UAA) when possible, since
there were minor edits in the other two documents. Thomas's *National Geographic* piece includes the genesis of the salvage operation.
Jim Scott told this story as well—including first encountering Lowell
Thomas on the shoreline—in his DRC interview and in Woodman's
"Picking Up the Pieces." *Though the Earth Be Moved* showed the
mountaineers working. The workers were also featured in "The Quake
Story," an *Anchorage Daily Times* supplement published April 14,
1964.

The story of the Task Force (occasionally referred to as the "Task
Team") is drawn from DRC interviews with Mayor Sharrock and
three anonymized team members, and from HE, pp. 404–5. Additionally, Jim Parsons prepared a memo for the DRC. The Pauline Sharrock obituary ran in the *Anchorage Daily News* on July 21, 2015. I
gathered biographical information about Parsons from conversations
with Bill and Nancy Yaw Davis as well as from their copies of the AMU
Amulet and other promotional publications from the university's
founding.

Chapter 18

Genie listed the hours she worked, and the sleep she managed to get,
on a page of the notebook she was using (GB) and in a memo dated
"1st Wednesday after quake" (UAA). The city's attempt to tamp down
KENI's independent reporting on Sunday is discussed in DRC interviews with Douglas Clure, Bram, and Merrill Mael (this is where Mael
brags about his fantastic hard hat); in a report on the quake produced
by the City Manager's Office (DRC); and in Yutzy's *Community Priorities*.

Recordings of KFQD on Sunday morning, including some of
Brink's stint in the booth, are at UAA. Robin Niemann, who was with
Brink and his wife for much of the weekend, and later helped him and
Genie produce the *Sounds of Alaska* record, described Brink's motiva-

tions. The AP story that Brink read is "Shaken As If by a Monster," cited earlier. Brink refers to "selflessness in a moment of great need" on the *Sounds of Alaska* record.

Genie mentions that her family recorded her broadcasts in the CPE introduction. I am summarizing audio of her interviews with Alexanderoff and the others (GB). Genie relays Brink's connections at Capitol Records, and his hopes for a big payout, in an April 9, 1964, letter (GB). Brink rhapsodizes about "man's love of life" when he introduces the song on the record.

Chapter 19

The arrival of the three DRC founders is covered in the "Preliminary Observation" DRC working paper, and in field notes recorded at the time by Haas and Quarantelli.

I learned about Quarantelli's early life and outlook largely from his twelve-part oral history interview (DRC), and from interviews with several colleagues: Tom Drabek, Kathleen Tierney, Tricia Wachtendorf, and Pat Young. (Drabek discussed the black car; Quarantelli tells the Thanksgiving paperwork story on the oral history recording.) Quarantelli stresses the importance of direct observation in the "Problems of Field Research" DRC working paper. His observations at the Civil Defense office were transcribed (DRC).

The decline of Civil Defense in Anchorage is discussed in HE, p. 272; interviews with Clure and Mael (DRC); and the sociologists' field notes (DRC). Knowles's *The Disaster Experts* covers the decline of Civil Defense nationally. Clure's resignation is discussed in Anchorage's March 1964 municipal bulletin (DRC). Many of those working alongside Clure told the DRC about his ineffectiveness on Friday and Saturday, though the sociologists seem to have underplayed that in their publications about the disaster—possibly because Clure eventually righted his operation; by the end of the day on Monday, Civil Defense had clearly taken charge and assumed a far more productive role in the recovery. Dick Taylor quoted Clure asking, "Who's going to give me this authority?" (DRC). Genie conveyed her frustrating experiences with Clure to the DRC.

Chapter 20

The conversation between Yutzy and his unnamed driver appeared in a long transcript of Yutzy's sporadically recorded field notes (DRC). It's not totally clear when this conversation took place; I suspect it was early Monday morning, but it could have been late on Sunday. Quarantelli talks about "blending into the background" in "Problems of Field Research." The scene of Yutzy eating oatmeal cookies in the Kamper, and so forth, was preserved in the transcript of the interview Yutzy was conducting.

The back-and-forth about "man-sized sandwiches" was also in the field notes transcript. Anderson includes a list of the sociologists' trips to Alaska in his 1966 Ohio State University dissertation, "Disaster and Organizational Change: A Study of Some of the Long-Term Consequences of the March 27, 1964 Alaska Earthquake," p. 28. The total number of DRC interviews appears in HE, p. 245. Disaster Control's use of "denizens of the Skid Row section" is discussed in the DRC's "Preliminary Observation" report and Yutzy's *Community Priorities,* and was pieced together from interviews with several Disaster Control workers and city police officers (DRC). Mayor Sharrock told Quarantelli about a police officer looting at a warehouse (DRC), though I found no record of whether this was ever investigated or debunked.

Yutzy detailed the evacuation of Presbyterian Hospital in *Community Priorities.* Additional information appears in HE, a Presbyterian Hospital newsletter (GB), and in Bob Fleming's interview with Genie (UAA). Dolly Fleming's account is taken from our interview.

Quarantelli discusses his early career, under Charles Fritz, in his oral history interview (DRC) and in an interview he did with Rebecca Solnit in August 2007. (Rebecca kindly shared the transcript with me.) The DRC published Fritz's *Disasters and Mental Health: Thera-*

peutic Principles Drawn from Disaster Studies in 1996 as no. 10 in its Historical and Comparative Disaster Series; a foreword by Quarantelli reveals the piece's origin and ultimate rejection from the textbook. Drabek helped me understand the relative obscurity of these ideas at the time of the quake.

Chapter 21

Yutzy recorded the Sunday press conference (transcript at DRC). Davis told me about his reticence to participate, and he and Drabek recounted the researchers being surprised to discover that Davis was a psychologist.

I am quoting from the transcript of Quarantelli's interview with Davis (DRC). Anderson notes that Quarantelli came away from Alaska focused on "emergent groups" in his "Great Alaska Earthquake" paper. Kathleen Tierney and Tricia Wachtendorf spoke to me about Quarantelli's continued focus on these groups, and pointed me to the examples of the *topos* and Cajun Navy.

Ian Hartman, associate professor of history at UAA, taught me about the city's African American population at the time; "A Bonanza for Blacks?," Hartman's chapter in *Imagining Anchorage,* the book he coedited, also provided context for Davis's comments here. The *Negro Digest* article "Prices Are High, Prejudice Is Low . . . So Far" was written by Julia Gaines Mighty and published in November 1963.

Genie calls Alaskans "an independent breed of people" in an untitled piece—possibly a "News in Depth" script—which, though undated, describes the earthquake as happening "four weeks ago" (GB, copy at UAA). I am quoting, again, from Yutzy's *Community Priorities.*

My summary of the eventual findings of disaster studies is drawn from conversations with Wachtendorf and Tierney, chronicled in Solnit's *A Paradise Built in Hell,* and crisply summarized in "When Disaster Strikes (It Isn't Much Like What You've Heard and Read

About)," a piece Quarantelli and Dynes published in *Psychology Today* in February 1972. I'm also cribbing from "Enrico L. Quarantelli: He Proved That Disasters Bring Out the Best in Us," a short piece I wrote on Quarantelli for the December 28, 2017, issue of *The New York Times Magazine.*

Ian Davis told the story of Quarantelli sending him off to Nicaragua in the comments of an "In Memoriam" page published on the DRC's website on April 3, 2017. Yutzy discussed the "frontier spirit" and affirmed that Alaskans are "normal human beings" in *Community Priorities,* p. 160.

Chapter 22

B. G. Randlett, Michael Janacek, and Dolly Fleming described living in the KENI offices in our interviews; these particular, haphazardly assembled sandwiches are the examples Dolly remembered. Gray and Don Porter described the process of returning KENI-TV to the air in their interview with Genie (UAA), as did Randlett, the station's projectionist, in my interview with him.

The Task Force's broadcasts are chronicled in Yutzy's *Community Priorities,* Jim Parsons's memo for the DRC, and an interview with another anonymized Task Force member (DRC). The KENI announcer reading the "all right" names on the air was Jim Dodson (UAA). Penny "Mossy" Mead revealed the true story of her brothers' deaths to reporter Julia O'Malley in "March 27, 1964: The Day the Earth Fell to Pieces for One Family," *Anchorage Daily News,* March 22, 2014.

Genie wrote of the "unbelievable" low death toll and the rescuers from "all walks of life" in a March 31, 1964, radio script (UAA). The specific examples that follow are drawn from that document and from Genie's "Heroism in Anchorage" manuscript, dated March 30, 1964 (GB, UAA). Yutzy also describes this phenomenon, and reports that Turnagain residents immediately helped their neighbors, in *Community Priorities,* pp. 60–61.

The Outside psychologist who wrote about William James was Robert M. Arvidson; his piece, also called "On Some Mental Effects of Earthquakes," was published in *American Psychologist* 24, no. 6 (1969). I'm quoting James's essay from *William James: Writings 1902–1910* (New York: Library of America, 1987), and am channeling Solnit's discussion of James in *A Paradise Built in Hell.*

The owner of the egg farm, John Alcantra—also an assistant to Governor Egan—relayed this anecdote in his DRC interview; Alcantra's wife, Patricia, and son, John Jr., elaborated on the story in our interview. The two anonymous men describing the new mood in Anchorage were interviewed by Merrill Mael, likely for a Civil Defense film; a fragment of the transcript is at DRC. The Northern Consolidated ticket agent is quoted in "The 1964 Great Alaskan Earthquake: Reactions and Observations," an unpublished manuscript by Lyman Woodman in the Betzi and Lyman Woodman papers at UAA.

My characterization of Anchorage's longer-term reconstruction process is based, in part, on "A Year of Decision and Inaction" and Genie's many letters from that time; the letter in which she vents about "syrupy, say-nothing public statements" is dated May 13, 1965 (GB). Bram tells the story of his time in Tokyo and arrival at Anchorage International Airport in a "News in Depth" commentary (GB), and HE provides additional details about the condition of the airport (p. 418).

ONE WEEK AFTER

Chapter 23

Genie's notes from the trip to Juneau, including a detailed account of the flight, were at UAA, as was a copy of an April 2, 1964, letter, describing it. I also found the recording she made on the airplane (GB). The Dean Rusk story is drawn from Genie's April 14, 1964, letter (GB). The estimate of half a billion dollars and the quote about Uncle Sam's "stepchild" are from "A Week After the Earthquake," *Anchorage*

Daily Times, April 3, 1964. Forty percent of civilians in Anchorage were employed by the government, according to tables in HE (pp. 428, 447).

Egan's speech, and Alaska's predicament in general, were covered in the *Anchorage Daily Times* and other papers around the country, including "Egan Seeking $50 Million Bond Issue to Aid Alaska," *The New York Times,* April 3, 1964. Genie relays her experience in the chamber before and after the address in her April 2 letter (GB). The DRC archive had a copy of the speech.

Robin Niemann told me everyone could "feel [the aftershock] coming" and watched people's utensils freeze midway to their mouths in the AMU cafeteria. Oldland's secretary, Alice Roessner, told this story to the DRC. I found only two sources that gave the magnitude of the aftershock: an April 14 letter from Genie (UAA), and *The Prince William Sound, Alaska, Earthquake of 1964 and Aftershocks,* vol. 1 (U.S. Coast and Geodetic Survey, 1966), p. 68. I'd normally consider the latter, which put it at 6.0, to be the more credible source, but that table also had the time of the quake wrong and seemed to contain other small errors. So I ultimately went with Genie's report. Honestly, I'm still not sure if that was the right decision. "Anchorage Jolted by Aftershock," an April 4 United Press International story, described people stopping and staring and the other details from downtown. Pond told me about the leaping librarian.

The plight of jeweler Larry Gage is relayed in "'64 Quake: Ordinary People, a Fateful Day Some Survived, Some Didn't," *Anchorage Daily News,* March 27, 1989. Rodman Wilson, MD, and William Rader, MD, wrote of "many spur of the moment decisions" and chronicled the scene at the airport in a February 19, 1965, talk at the Pacific Northwest Meeting of the American College of Physicians, a copy of which was at DRC. (The talk appears to have been later adapted into "Interstate Travel and School Enrollment After Alaska Good Friday Earthquake," *Alaska Medicine,* 1968.) Den's letters were in GB, as was Genie's letter asking "What is safety, anyway?"

Chapter 24

Weather data for that Monday comes from the website Weather Underground. Genie described the "tension" on "the faces of a proud people" in a radio script (GB). The "Time to RELAX" ad ran in several editions of the *Anchorage Daily Times* in the preceding days. My reconstruction of the reopening of *Our Town* relies on interviews with Robin Niemann, Robert Pond (who wished Jim Tracy could "live forever"), Joe Lawton, and Michale Gabriel, whose memory of being onstage during the final scene, saying those lines aloud, appeared to be indelible. Jim Tracy Jr. told me about his father, Jim Tracy Sr. Brady Jackson III told me about his father, Brady Jackson II. The elder Jackson was also featured in the *Negro Digest* article and "Sonny Liston Says He Will Regain World Boxing Title," *Fairbanks Daily News-Miner,* April 4, 1966. An obituary for Silver Stanfill, who played Mrs. Webb, ran on November 17, 2011, in the *Montrose Daily Press* (Colorado).

I read about Brink's exit from Alaska in Stadem's book. His work in Louisiana was regularly covered in the *Shreveport Times.* It was only with the help of Niemann—who, as mentioned, remained in close touch with the Brinks until the end—that I could fill in this last chapter of Frank and Jo's story.

Quarantelli was a total theater nut; according to those who worked with him, he frequently spent his vacation time in New York or London, seeing as many productions as he could. He and Russell Dynes compared disasters to theater in "Community Conflict: Its Absence and Its Presence in Natural Disasters" (working paper no. 34, Disaster Research Center, 1971).

Genie describes the trauma of the quake finally hitting her in the "Last night I wept" fragment (GB, copy at UAA). She claimed to have "slept like a lamb" in an April 9 letter (GB). "How to Write Your Own Life Story," by Lois Daniel, appeared in the September 1981 issue of *The Rotarian.*

PHOTO CREDITS

———

JON MOOALLEM is a longtime writer at large for *The New York Times Magazine* and a contributor to numerous radio shows and other magazines, including *This American Life* and *Wired*. His first book, *Wild Ones,* was chosen as a notable book of the year by *The New York Times Book Review, The New Yorker,* NPR's *Science Friday,* and Canada's *National Post,* among others. He lives on Bainbridge Island, outside Seattle, with his family.

jonmooallem.com

Twitter: @jmooallem

ABOUT THE TYPE

This book was set in Bulmer, a typeface designed in the late eighteenth century by the London type cutter William Martin (1757–1830). The typeface was created especially for the Shakespeare Press, directed by William Bulmer (1757–1830)—hence the font's name. Bulmer is considered to be a transitional typeface, containing characteristics of old-style and modern designs. It is recognized for its elegantly proportioned letters, with their long ascenders and descenders.